AN INTRODUCTION TO DOING BUSINESS IN MEXICO

William E. Mooz, Jr.

Transnational Juris Publications, Inc., Irvington, NY

Library of Congress Cataloging-in-Publication Data

Mooz, William E.
Introduction to doing business in Mexico / by William E. Mooz, Jr.
p. cm.
ISBN 1-56425-037-7
1. Business law --Mexico. 2. Foreign trade regulation--Mexico.
3. Investments, Foreign--Law and legislation--Mexico.
4. Corporations, American--Law and legislation--Mexico. I. Title.
KGF333.B86M66 1994
346.72'07--dc20
[347.2067] 94-7487
CIP

Manufactured in the United States of America

Contents

Introduction

For many years, the United States economy operated in virtual isolation, content with its rapid internal expansion and seemingly limitless domestic resources. The emergence of other competing economic powers and the gradual exhaustion of our domestic resources has forced the country to look outward. This shift toward a more international vision has been accelerated by the recent revolution in communications technology that makes any country a mere telephone call or fax away, and by the ardent fervor with which the world's emerging economies have opened their markets to foreign investment. Businesses in the United States are well aware of this trend, and trade with all corners of the world increases daily.

Nowhere has the nation's new emphasis on foreign trade been more pronounced that with Mexico. Mexico's geographic proximity, tremendous resources, and cultural affinity have finally succeeded in breaking down years of negative stereotypes and protectionist attitudes on both sides of the border. With the advent of the North American Free Trade Agreement, the countries have taken the formal step of ratifying what has been occurring already: the integration of the United States, Canadian, and Mexican economies.

This integration undoubtedly will be a gradual and constantly-expanding process. Laws, standards, ways of doing business, and attitudes do not change overnight, and there is little doubt that the United States and Mexico will continue to adhere to their own unique cultures and languages. Thus, it is essential that businesses in each country have an understanding of the cultural and legal pillars that undergird the ways in which the United States and Mexico each manage international trade and investment.

The purpose of this book is to provide readers in the United States with a basic understanding of the primary laws that will govern their conduct as they do business with Mexico. The approach taken is one of identifying the most important issues that companies from the United States are likely to confront when doing business in Mexico, and to provide an overview of the law that will control the resolution of those issues.

I am confident that companies doing business in Mexico will have a long-term rewarding experience as they develop the attendant economic and personal relationships. To the extent that this book unlocks the door to participation in this process, or provides the knowledge necessary to reduce the inevitable frustrations that are part of dealing with another country, it will have achieved its goal.

CHAPTER 1

Overview of Mexico's Economic System*

Jose Luis Gutierrez
American Chamber of Commerce of Mexico

The opportunities that exist for doing business with Mexico depend in large part on the economic policies that Mexico pursues. The current economic system relies heavily on free-market principles and places a heavy emphasis on encouraging foreign trade and investment. This system, however, represents a significant change from past policies. One cannot accurately assess the longterm benefits that doing business with Mexico can offer, or the risks that it can present, without a basic understanding of Mexico's economic system, and how it has developed.

I. Historic Sources of Economic Development

Mexico's modern economic history begins with President Cardenas's expropriation and nationalization of the petroleum industry in 1938. This event, which is still celebrated as a national holiday, marked the end of an era of violence and instability rooted in the revolution of 1910. At the same time that oil was being nationalized, the United States' need for a strategic partner in World War II protected Mexico from draconian retaliation, and even provided Mexico with an opportunity to end its dependence on a rural economy and to quickly enter the industrial age.

* This chapter was edited and supplemented by William E. Mooz, Jr.

Between 1940 and 1947, certain markets in the United States were opened to Mexico. Mexico was able to establish and profit from a variety of industrial alliances and alliances of business enterprises. Financing for these initiatives came predominantly from Mexico's internal savings, with a lesser amount coming from abroad.

In the following six-year presidency (1947–1952), Mexico experienced a dynamic period of basic industrialization. This industrialization was financed through growing rates of internal savings, and the first big entrance of foreign investment since the beginning of the century.

From 1953 to 1970, the country entered into a period known as "stabilized growth." During this stage, the country focused on domestic consumer demand, with a high rate of industrialization being spurred by a policy of protecting domestic industry from imported goods. The resulting economic growth was financed primarily by the extraordinary increase in the rate of internal savings, in the form of unprecedented bank deposits and financial deposits, and a high level of retained earnings by companies.

The period of "stabilized growth" yielded impressive economic results. Between 1946 and 1970, Mexico's gross national product quadrupled while its population merely doubled. Inflation averaged scarcely 5 percent annually. At the end of the 1960s, the Mexican economy was growing robustly, but the fruits of that growth in no way approached being distributed in an equitable manner.

By the late 1960s, dissatisfaction over the inequitable distribution (and indeed, substantial concentration) of the benefits of Mexico's economic growth reached acute levels. This dissatisfaction was particularly strong among the new generation of highly-capable, middle-class Mexicans who found the doors of political power being closed to them by the old guard. The boiling point was reached in 1968, when Mexico experienced its first serious political unrest in 40 years. While there is some dispute as to whether this unrest was simply a copy of the student disturbances in Europe, or a genuine expression of discontent by the Mexican people, it clearly led to the end of the policy of "stabilized growth."

The six-year administration of President Echeverria (1970–1976) marked a fundamental change in Mexico's economic policy. These incoming governmental officials hailed from a new generation of professionals who considered themselves the heirs of President Cardenas's nationalistic socialism. Frustrated with the unequal distribution of Mexico's wealth, these new officials abandoned the existing economic policy. Their new policy involved channeling resources toward specific social needs, and substantial direct participation by the state in the economy. Foreign debt was used to finance this state-initiated growth—a process that was propelled by the excessive liquidity of money in international money markets.

This new policy promptly resulted in serious economic problems. As governmental expenditures increased rapidly with the state's direct involvement in the economy, public revenues were declining. Moreover, given the government's strong political rhetoric against private capital and investment—which President Echeverria blamed for the unequal distribution of wealth—private economic activity declined and little hope existed that tax revenues would increase. A logical consequence followed: Mexico's deficit grew, and had to be covered by the issuance of money that had no backing. Double-digit inflation made its debut in Mexico during the following years. What little confidence existed in the private sector was shattered by the nationalization of large tracts of privately-held farm land during the waning days of the Echeverria administration.

The following six-year administration (1976–1982) of President Jose Lopez Portillo began with an avowed promise to break ranks with the policies of the Echeverria presidency and return to a more market-oriented economy. Mexico discovered large quantities of oil early during the Lopez Portillo administration, which it exported to a hungry world market. The revenues generated from these exports fueled strong economic growth and made Mexico a favorite of foreign lenders. Petroleum revenues also enabled the government to pay off an emergency loan granted in 1976 ahead of schedule, thus freeing the country from the dictates of the International Monetary Fund that it clean up public finances, privatize the economy, eliminate obstacles to international commerce and free the peso's rate of exchange. Following these events, populist flags returned with a fervor that exceeded even that of the prior administration.

Mexico's ability to sustain President Lopez Portillo's populist policies crumbled when world oil prices fell. Petroleum comprised more than 70 percent of Mexico's export earnings. Based on these earnings, Mexico's external debt quadrupled during the Lopez Portillo presidency, to the point where it exceeded $8 billion dollars (two thirds of Mexico's gross national product) at the end of 1982. The decline in oil prices caused Mexico to experience a severe liquidity crisis, resulting in the devaluation of the peso and a moratorium on payments of the country's external debt.

Nor was the private sector interested or able to be of much economic assistance. Domestic savings already were at a low level, and the devaluation of the peso and the nationalization of Mexico's banks in 1982 resulted in a further lack of confidence in the economy. Capital fled the country at unprecedented rates, and according to the estimates of the U.S. banking system, the assets and investments of Mexicans in the southern states of the United States surpassed $50 billion. The old strategy of generating domestic-based growth through import substitution no longer worked, and industry was laying off significant numbers of workers at a time when Mexico needed to create approximately one million new jobs per year.

President Lopez Portillo ended his presidency thoroughly discredited. His populist policies proved unable to provide a large sector of the population a minimum level of well-being, and even ended up increasing the inequality in Mexico's distribution of wealth. These economic catastrophes set the stage for Mexico's economic rebirth.

II. Mexico's Economic Transformation

President de la Madrid took power in late 1982 with an urgent call for corrective action to halt the process of continued economic deterioration. The characteristics of the economy at that time included triple-digit inflation, a rapidly-devaluing peso, a bloated government bureaucracy, government ownership of many important companies and industries, a crippling foreign debt, a large deficit, a need to generate substantial employment for the country's growing population, industry that was accustomed to protection from foreign imports and poorly equipped to compete in world markets, and a complete lack of confidence.

The de la Madrid administration took a number of steps to solve these problems. These steps included a government austerity program, privatization of certain government-held companies, renegotiating Mexico's foreign debt, reducing the federal work force, and opening the country up to foreign trade. These steps occurred in fits and starts, but made gradual progress toward eliminating the root causes of many of Mexico's economic problems. Perhaps most significantly, they raised public confidence to a level that made real progress possible.

Toward the end of his administration, President de la Madrid introduced the Pact of Economic Solidarity (PSE), which continues to this day as a principal element of Mexico's economic policy. The PSE is a pact between Mexico's government and labor, business, and agriculture. It represents a combination of conventional medicine, such as governmental austerity, and price and wage freezes, and unorthodox measures designed to generate public confidence and participation. In its simplest form, the PSE represents an annual agreement between its participants to hold the line on price increases, wage increases, and government spending. In addition, the government usually commits to adhere to a variety of other economic policies, such as defending the peso, that are perceived to be necessary to promote the desired goals of stable economic growth, increased employment and a manageable rate of inflation.

When President Salinas took office in 1988, he inherited a better situation than had his predecessor, but the Mexican economy was still besieged with problems. He responded by increasing the pace of the reforms initiated by the de la Madrid administration. Government austerity programs were adhered to with a vengeance, and business and particularly labor made significant contributions to the fight against inflation. Mexico launched a determined campaign to generate employment by attracting foreign investment through the liberalization of Mexico's foreign investment laws. Virtually all major governmental holdings, except for those in very sensitive political areas such as oil, have been slated for privatization.

The net result: Mexico has wiped out its deficit and brought inflation down to single-digit figures. The economy now appears to be on a strong footing and in a position to address its historic problems of poverty among the lower classes and the need to create vast numbers of new jobs each year to keep pace with the ever-expanding size of the work force.

III. NAFTA and Mexico's Economic Future

President Salinas may well be best known for his efforts to promote the North American Free Trade Agreement ("NAFTA"). NAFTA, as discussed in greater detail in the following chapters, will integrate the economies of Mexico, the United States, and Canada over a 15-year period. It will do so, not just by eliminating tariffs, but also by harmonizing the laws of the three countries and institutionalizing (and furthering) the current Mexican policies of openness toward foreign investment. This fact alone should go a long way toward preserving the favorable climate that exists for U.S. companies wishing to do business in Mexico.

CHAPTER 2

Cultural Considerations for Doing Business in Mexico*

William E. Mooz, Jr., Esq.
Holland & Hart

I. Introduction

The recent passage of the North American Free Trade Agreement ("NAFTA") undoubtedly will add momentum to the desire of U.S. companies to do business with Mexico. NAFTA makes it easier for such companies to carry out this desire by gradually eliminating most tariffs, barring most discrimination against foreign investment, and establishing a mechanism for harmonizing many of the signatory nations' laws and standards that affect trade.

There are some things, however, that NAFTA will not change. Paramount is the fact that Mexico and the United States will remain independent countries, with their own unique traditions, languages, cultures, and ways of doing business. These differences have a tremendous impact on the day-to-day aspects of doing business with Mexico and inevitably give rise to certain frustrations on the part of both the U.S. businessperson and his or her Mexican counterpart.

* Reprinted with permission, *Preventive Law Reporter* (Mar. 1994).

At worst, these frustrations mount to the point where otherwise-desirable ventures fall apart, at great cost to all participants. By recognizing and understanding the differences in the ways in which business is conducted in the United States and in Mexico, cross-cultural frustrations can be kept to a minimum, increasing the chance of success.

This chapter does not attempt to provide a complete answer to all cross-cultural issues that arise when persons from the United States do business in Mexico. Such a definitive work would require a lifetime of study and hundreds of pages. Rather, it provides an overview of some of the cultural differences that may be encountered and offers some simple suggestions to guide a foreigner doing business in Mexico around some of the most common pitfalls.

II. Ten Tips on Dealing With Your Mexican Counterpart

A. Avoid Misunderstandings

Misunderstandings between U.S. businesses and their Mexican counterparts generally fall into two categories: substantive misunderstandings and incidental misunderstandings. A substantive misunderstanding arises when one party fails to agree on the general purpose of a joint activity or ignores the consensus that is reached. The classic and most extreme example occurs when one party acts to build a successful long-term enterprise out of the venture, while the other treats the venture as a vehicle for immediate personal enrichment.

Substantive misunderstandings typically occur when the parties fail to perform reasonable due diligence or fail to take the normal precautions that would prevail in a purely domestic commercial relationship. Surprising numbers of sophisticated businesspeople in the United States tend to drop their guard when approached by a cultured foreigner speaking fluent English and promising great riches. Substantive misunderstandings generally can be avoided by realizing that doing business in Mexico poses the same risk of running into a bad apple as does doing business anywhere else and acting accordingly.

Incidental misunderstandings, which encompass genuine misunderstandings on incidental points, are far less significant, but much more likely to occur. Incidental misunderstandings generally flow from the different perspectives that each party brings to the relationship, and the fact that one party will be dealing in a foreign language.

The best remedies tend to be time, flexibility, and seeing that key personnel in both countries have sufficient contact with their counterparts to become familiar with each other's way of doing business. The comparatively nominal investment of bringing key Mexican personnel to one's U.S. office from time to time can pay handsome dividends, as can periodic travel in the other direction.

As for language, the first step toward solving the problem is to recognize it exists. Many Mexican professionals speak English with such a high degree of fluency that persons from the United States lose sight of the fact that a language barrier, albeit a very slight one, exists. This oversight can be dangerous. While everyone may appear to be on the same level in a fast-paced discussion, certain points may not always be understood by all parties. As a result, parties sometimes leave the conversation with different understandings of what is to occur.

There are at least two simple ways to minimize potential misunderstandings. First, before holding an important conversation (particularly where the conversation will occur by telephone), provide the participants in advance with a written outline of the points to be covered. This gives everyone an opportunity to think about the same issue—as opposed to figuring out what the issues are—when the conference begins. Second, following up with a written confirmation of the plan of action agreed upon, the advice given, etc. ensures that no miscommunication has occurred and that all parties are on the same page.

B. Learn the Local Business Schedule

Businesses in the United States operate on a fairly standard schedule of 8:00 a.m. to 5:00 p.m., Monday through Friday, with days off for well-known holidays. Businesses in Mexico also operate on a fairly standard schedule, but one that is different from that followed in the United States. The normal business day in Mexico City begins around 9:00 a.m. Lunch runs from 2:00 p.m. to 4:00 p.m. The day ends at 7:00 p.m. or later.

The holidays observed in Mexico also differ substantially. For example, while the United States celebrates its independence on July 4, Mexico's celebration occurs on September 16. Business in Mexico also tends to slow down significantly during the school holidays around Christmas and Easter. Persons doing business in Mexico are well advised to obtain a Mexican calendar and prepare for these differences.

C. Dress Appropriately

Mexicans tend to dress formally and are always well groomed. If you wish to make a good impression, it is important that you follow suit. This is particularly true at the outset of a relationship when each party is extremely attuned to the nonverbal signals given off by his or her potential partner. In Mexico, it generally is appropriate for men to wear suits to most events including informal, social gatherings. Women typically wear dresses. When in doubt, it is better to overdress.

D. Take the Time Necessary to Build Personal Relationships

This point cannot be stressed enough. The U.S. businessperson who fails to establish solid personal relationships in Mexico typically also fails to establish successful business relationships. Business in the United States is generally far more impersonal than business in Mexico. The U.S. businessperson usually is ready to get down to business without establishing a personal relationship with his or her counterpart. This approach is complemented by our devotion to extensive contracts that seek to cover every possible contingency and is facilitated by the comparative ease with which one can obtain information about companies in the United States.

Business in Mexico is less an objective in and of itself and more an extension of the businessperson's life as a whole. The Mexican businessperson is uncomfortable doing business with someone with whom he or she does not also have a personal relationship. The Mexican will rely less on negotiating a contract the size of a phone book and more on a simple contract coupled with a personal relationship of trust within which problems can be resolved.

Developing this trust can be somewhat difficult in light of the comparative dearth of information that is available about Mexican companies. In the end, the U.S. business is likely to have to leave some cards in the hands of its Mexican counterpart and have faith that any problems that arise can be worked out amicably.

Therefore, it is imperative that the U.S. businessperson take the time at the outset of a relationship to get to know his or her counterpart personally. This requires showing a genuine interest in your counterparts and in the personal aspects of their lives, such as their families. A chance to visit a counterpart's home, or to entertain in your own home, should not be missed.

The value of personal relationships extends far beyond a particular transaction or piece of business. A relationship with one person will extend to that person's circle of friends and business contacts. Thus, credibility established with a single person can expand itself exponentially, opening many doors for further ventures. Conversely, a bad relationship with a single businessperson can poison many other wells.

A personal relationship provides more than just credibility and trust. It also provides access and a special willingness to help. This can be particularly important when you need to cut through delays or bureaucracy. The more people you know personally, the more circles of contacts you will have access to in times of need.

E. Be Polite

Mexicans are extremely polite people. For example, it is considered a small honor to pick up a restaurant check or to let someone go through the door before you. Given the image of the "ugly American," it is particularly important for the U.S. businessperson to recognize the need to be more gracious than usual.

Being polite can take many different forms. If you are invited to someone's house, it is polite to bring a box of chocolates, a bottle of wine, or some other small gift. The value of the gift is far less important than the quality of the item selected.

It is also appropriate for the U.S. businessperson to make an effort to speak some Spanish. Even if your Spanish is quite limited, it is polite to try. Just about any gesture of politeness will be well-received so long as it is sincere.

The emphasis on politeness in Mexico makes for a very pleasant existence, but can result in frustrations. The need to be polite, and a genuine desire to be helpful, may sometimes make it difficult for your counterpart to say "no" or "I don't know" in as blunt a fashion as we are used to. Thus, the U.S. businessperson may feel an agreement has been reached when it has not or may experience uncertainty as to where he or she stands. This becomes less of a problem as one learns the culture and gets to know one's counterparts.

F. Expect Generosity Well Beyond What You Are Used to and Be Prepared to Reciprocate

Mexicans are among the world's most generous people. You may be greeted personally at the airport, provided with a car and driver to show you around the area, or entertained lavishly. It is important that you think of your Mexican colleagues as personal friends and show them the same courtesies that they extend to you. This is particularly true when your Mexican counterpart makes a visit to the United States and you have the opportunity to serve as the host. As a general rule, it is appropriate for you to pick up the tab for entertainment when your counterparts are visiting.

G. Understand the Importance of Meals and Other Social Events

In keeping with the importance of personal relationships, meals and other social events play a prominent role in the process of doing business in Mexico. What better way to develop a personal relationship than to share a leisurely meal, during which the parties can talk at length about the things in life that are most important.

Lunch is the big meal of the day in Mexico and fills this function beautifully. While not as leisurely, the "power breakfast" has become quite popular as well. Dinners tend to occur late in the evening by U.S.

standards and are less popular for meeting business associates. Opportunities to share a meal or attend a social event with a business colleague should be sought out and will generally prove highly productive over the long run, even if business is never discussed.

H. Select the Appropriate Means of Communication

Persons doing business in Mexico must learn to employ different means of communication than those they are used to in the United States. This difference is perhaps most pronounced in the role played by the postal service. In the United States, businesses and consumers routinely use the mails to do such things as pay bills, send correspondence, etc. In Mexico, the postal system is, quite rightly, regarded as inherently unreliable. Cross-town deliveries can take up to two weeks and international mailings have been known to get lost. For this reason, Mexican businesses typically require consumers to pay their bills at the bank (or in person) and otherwise eschew the mail. The U.S. business operating in Mexico should do the same.

There are a number of good alternatives to the postal system when communicating with a Mexican firm. Federal Express, United Parcel Service, and DHL all offer prompt and reliable service between the United States and Mexico. As with all international shipments, however, packages sent via private courier services are subject to inspection by customs. Large packages (as opposed to letters) are far more likely to be opened in customs, which can add a day or two to the delivery time.

The fax is probably simplest and most effective way to send routine correspondence. Faxes can, however, be affected by the quality of Mexico's phone system, which is in the process of being modernized. The current system is quite functional but cutoffs and poor connections occur with some regularity. Sometimes it is easier to get a clean line, particularly for use by a computer modem, by using a cellular phone.

Finally, personal meetings are used as a vehicle for communication with greater frequency in Mexico than in the United States. If the subject is at all important, a personal meeting, even if it is just to deliver significant documents, may be appropriate. Remember, this is another way to strengthen your personal relationships.

I. Prepare for Uncertainty and Delay

One of the most common frustrations expressed by persons from the United States doing business in Mexico is the difficulty in obtaining immediate and definitive answers from their Mexican counterparts. What the person in the United States does not understand is that there are myriad reasons for the delays and uncertainties. The better that the businessperson understands the reasons for these delays and uncertainties, the easier it will be to plan for them and lessen the attendant frustration.

1. Lack of Guidance

The United States has an incredibly well-developed body of commercial laws and procedures that makes it very easy to obtain concrete guidance about what one can and cannot do in virtually any situation. By contrast, Mexico's body of commercial laws and procedures is far less developed and is changing rapidly. Thus, in Mexico, getting a concrete answer to a specific question may require obtaining an opinion from the appropriate bureaucrat. While the foreign businessperson cannot change this lack of guidance, he or she, through proper communication with his or her Mexican counterpart, can at least understand that the problem exists and gain a sense of comfort in knowing how it is being resolved.

2. Need for Bureaucratic Approval

Many actions in Mexico require bureaucratic approval, creating yet another source of uncertainty and delay. The Salinas government has greatly decreased the number of approvals required for high-level decisions and the amount of time that it takes to get them. For example, many applications are now deemed approved if they are not acted on within 45 working days.

But other, more mundane, areas of bureaucratic control, such as customs, have yet to be streamlined. The best antidote to this problem is knowing what bureaucratic approvals are required. This enables you to budget the time necessary to accommodate the process and, where appropriate, to work through agents having the necessary personal relationships with the suitable officials to get the approval process handled as expeditiously as possible.

3. Need for High-Level Approval

Authority tends to be far more centralized in Mexico than in the United States. Accordingly, decisions in Mexico, whether governmental or in the private sector, often have to be made at higher levels than a U.S. businessperson may be accustomed to.

If you are dealing with a junior person, he or she is likely to equivocate until a firm decision is made at a higher level. The key to this problem is ascertaining the level at which the decision will be made and going to that level directly. Good personal relationships can ensure that you deal with the right people automatically. You should be careful, however, not to abuse your relationships by bothering high-level people with trivial matters.

4. Develop Realistic Time Lines

Foreigners doing business in Mexico often get frustrated because they do not have a good understanding of all the steps necessary to carry a plan into action. Sitting down with your Mexican counterparts or advisors prior to implementing a transaction and developing a comprehensive list of all of the major steps that must occur to put the plan into action can put the process into proper perspective.

Once you have such a list, it is a simple matter to come up with realistic deadlines for the completion of each step. While certain steps may involve inherent uncertainties, such as obtaining bureaucratic approvals, at least you will know what is involved and will have budgeted realistically for potential delays.

5. Need for Regular Follow-Up

If not watched over carefully, even the best laid plans of action have a tendency to slip. This is particularly true in a culture such as Mexico's where politeness makes it difficult to say no to someone's request, even if it means deviating from the schedule assigned to a preexisting obligation. In order to make sure that your project will be completed on time, it is important to monitor the matter carefully. Whether the matter is as simple as getting your car repaired, or as complicated as carrying out a large transaction, you will be better served by checking on the status of the matter periodically, well before the actual deadline arrives.

J. Allow More Time

Persons doing business in Mexico need to realize that things may take longer to accomplish than in the United States. This is no reflection on your Mexican counterpart who, if you have selected him or her carefully, will be extremely capable and hard-working. Rather, there are simply certain hurdles that must be overcome that do not exist in the United States.

The first hurdle to international business is that you will be dealing with two sets of holidays instead of one. Persons doing business in Mexico need to plan around the Mexican holidays. On those days, even if the professionals and business people are working, the bureaucrats whose approval you need probably will not be.

A second hurdle is that official documents must be presented in Spanish. Most businesses in the United States are not in a position to prepare and work with documents not drafted, at least in the first instance, in English. This means time must be allowed for time-consuming translation.

A third hurdle is the role occupied by the *Notario Publico* (Notary Public) in Mexico. Unlike in the United States, where notary publics merely attest to the authenticity of a signature, in Mexico the *Notario Publico* is a quasi-public official who plays a very substantive role. For many actions to have legal effect, the *Notario Publico* must review the relevant documents and certify that they have been prepared in accordance with Mexican law, an additional step that adds processing time. These actions include the granting of powers of attorney, the formation of corporations, the purchase of real estate, to name a few.

A fourth hurdle is the dense traffic that exists in some of Mexico's larger cities, and Mexico City in particular. You must allow sufficient time to get to meetings. Most Mexican business people carry a cellular telephone so that travel time can be used productively. Many hotels and cellular telephone companies have rental services that provide visiting business people with the same capability.

Finally, the foreign businessperson needs to be aware that meetings may not start or finish exactly as scheduled. Because businesspersons from the United States have a reputation for being critical about meetings not starting on time, it is important that *you* arrive in a timely fashion. If you get caught in traffic, the polite thing to do is to call ahead by cellular telephone and notify your appointment of the delay.

No matter what you do, the possibility still exists that the person you are scheduled to meet with will not be ready on time, particularly if the meeting is with a government official. Accept this gracefully and come prepared with a briefcase full of work to occupy you in the event of a delay.

III. Conclusion

U.S. companies have been doing business in Mexico for over a century. Many have succeeded, while others have failed. The recent passage of NAFTA provides the best opportunity in modern history for more companies to expand their operations to the south. Like the companies that came before them, these companies will experience a greater likelihood of success if they realize that Mexico is not the United States and come prepared to adapt to the many differences that exist.

CHAPTER 3

Mexico's Legal System*

Professor William J. Bridge
School of Law
Southern Methodist University

Lic. Lionel Pereznieto Castro
Ogarrio y Diaz, Abogados

Professor James F. Smith
School of Law
University of California, Davis

I. Introduction

Mexico's legal system is both similar and dissimilar to that of the United States. Like the United States, Mexico has a federal system of government, with executive, legislative, and judicial branches that are analogous to the United States' counterparts. Unlike the United States, Mexico adheres to the civil law system, and not the common law system. This means that certain legal issues are likely to be resolved in a manner different from that to which businesspeople and lawyers in the United States are accustomed. Similarly, the players involved in the legal

* Parts I, III, IV, and V were written by Prof. William J. Bridge; parts II and VI were written by Lic. Lionel Pereznieto Castro and Prof. James F. Smith. The chapter was edited and supplemented by William E. Mooz, Jr.

process—judges, lawyers, and legislators—will play somewhat different roles than do their counterparts in the United States.

II. The Primary Sources of Mexico's Laws

A. Constitution and Legislation

Mexico's federal government is divided into legislative, executive, and judicial branches.[1] These branches are neither completely separate nor equal.[2] The executive branch dominates.[3] The president is the chief of the armed services[4] and the leader of his political party. He appoints diplomats, Supreme Court Justices and other judges.[5] He has special legislative and judicial powers, and he decides the most important matters of the nation.[6] This was most vividly illustrated by President Salinas' promulgation of new regulations regarding foreign investment and transfers of technology without the approval of Congress. It is doubtful that the president's power to do so could be effectively challenged even though the regulations may significantly modify previously existing statutory law.[7]

---

[1] Mex. Const., Art. 49. For an excellent overview of Mexican law, see H.L. Wright, *Foreign Enterprise in Mexico: Laws and Policies* (1971).

[2] F.T. Ramirez, *Derecho Constitucional Mexicano* 219 (Editorial Porrúa, Mexico D.F., 1984) (referring to the need for flexibility in the separation of powers doctrine); see also J. Carpizo, *El Presidencialismo Mexicano* 12–13 (Siglio Veintiuno Editores, Mexico D.F., 1976).

[3] In Mexico, the president has the power to affect all aspects of everyday life, and it is he who guides the destiny of Mexico. The president occupies the place of a European king in the 18th century. His powers are extensive, and in many areas, he acts almost without restriction. J. Carpizo, *La Constitucion Mexicana de 1917* 294 (Septima Edición, Editorial Porrúa, Mexico D.F., 1986).

[4] Mex. Const., Art. 89, §§ IV–VIII.

[5] Mex. Const., Art. 89, §§ 111, XVII, and XVIII.

[6] See generally Carpizo, *El Presidencialismo Mexicano*, N. 2, *supra.*

[7] Although the president has the constitutional power to issue regulations (Art. 89, 1), they must not contradict the statutory scheme. Carpizo, *El Presidencialismo Mexicano* 107, N. 2, *supra,* ("A regulation has to respect the law and cannot contradict, add to, modify or alter it but only develop those principals that it contains.") However, litigation challenging such regulation would only apply to the litigants as Supreme Court rulings have no stare decisis effect over executive agencies. Mex. Const., Arts. 107, 2; Amparo Law § 191–195.

Mexico has a federal system. Each of the 31 states exercises local police powers and has a civil code, code of civil procedure, penal code, and code of criminal procedure. These state codes typically follow their counterparts in the Federal District quite closely.[8] Beyond these areas, the states' power to legislate is quite limited.

Article 133 of the Federal Constitution provides that the Constitution and federal laws are the supreme law of the nation. Indeed, the Constitution itself is the primary source of public law as it contains detailed regulations of state enterprises, monopolies, agriculture, mining, natural resources, criminal procedure, education, election law, citizenship and immigration, jurisdiction of the courts, and the powers of the municipalities and states.

The federal government has exclusive jurisdiction over hydrocarbons, mining, commerce, electric and nuclear power, banking, labor (Article 73, § X), maritime laws, citizenship and nationality, economic planning, foreign investment, ecological protection (Article 73, §§ XII–XXIX–H) and virtually all other matters of national import. Congress has exclusive power to legislate on matters affecting the Federal District, which is governed by the president and, on certain matters, a local assembly of representatives (Article 73, §§ V and VI). The Constitution vests Congress with the exclusive power to levy taxes (Article 73, §§ VII and XXIX), and to borrow money (Article 73, § VIII). In short, most significant matters other than those of purely local interest are governed either by the federal constitution or a federal statute.

B. Treatises of Distinguished Scholars

The published writings of distinguished legal scholars, or treatises, form a primary source of law roughly analogous to case law in the United States. Accordingly, treatises often are cited as authority along with the relevant code sections or constitutional provisions. Annotated versions of a code or the constitution typically emphasize the historic antecedents of the provisions, and may include the comments of the treatise writers,

---

[8] Lyon L. Brinsmade, "Mexican Law—An Outline and Bibliography of English Source Materials Relating to Certain Aspects Thereof," 6 *Int'l Law.* 829, 831 (1972).

but are likely to have relatively scant references to case law.[9] In 1973, the U.S. Library of Congress published an excellent descriptive narrative of all Mexican law treatises then in print.[10]

C. Case Law in Mexico

Case law is a source of law in Mexico, but it is not nearly as important as in the United States. Neither the academician nor the practitioner is likely to devote considerable attention to case law. However, case law should not be ignored.

Individual opinions (*ejecutorias*) of the Supreme Court and the Circuit Courts are published but not widely circulated or cited.[11] Binding precedents (*jurisprudencia*) are published every ten years and supplemented periodically in the form of restatements by the courts of certain well-settled principles of law.[12] *Jurisprudencia* typically does no more than interpret (not construe) a particular facet of constitutional law or the codes. It is limited to cases brought under a Writ of Amparo[13] that

---

[9] See, e.g., *Los Derechos Del Pueblo Mexicano a Través de sus Constituciones* (Editorial Miguel Porrúa, 1986); Miguel Acosta Romero and Genaro David Góngora Pimental, *La Constitución Politica de los Estados Unidos Mexicanos* (Segunda Edición, Editorial Porrúa, México, 1989); Miguel Acosta Romero and Genaro David Góngora Pimentel, *Ley de Amparo* (Segunda Edición, Editorial Porrúa, México, 1985); Genaro David Góngora Pimentel and Miguel Acosta Romero, *Código Federal de Procedimientos Civiles, Ley Organica del Poder Judicial Federal* (Editorial Porrúa, México, 1986).

[10] H. Clagett and D. Valderrama, *A Revised Guide of the Law and Legal Literature of Mexico* (1973).

[11] These *ejecutorias*, which may be cited for their persuasive value, are published in the *Seminario Judicial de la Federación,* in both an official and a private version (Mayo Editoriales).

[12] *Apéndice* (1917–1985) *al Semanario Judicial de la Federación, Suprema Corte, Jurisprudencia Definida* (México, 1985). See also Lucio A. Cabrera, " 'History of the Mexican Judiciary' Inter-American Law issue: Symposium on Mexican Law," 11 *Miami L.Q.* 439–48 (1957).

[13] This all important procedural device is exclusively entrusted to the federal courts. It can be used to protect and ensure an individual's constitutional rights, challenge unconstitutional laws (*amparo contra leyes*), resolve conflicts stemming from administrative acts and decisions (*amparo administrativo*), and to appeal judicial decisions (*amparo casación*). See generally Richard D. Baker, *Judicial Review in Mexico* (1971); Hector Fix-Zamudio, "A Brief Introduction to the Mexican Writ of *AMPARO*," 9 *Cal. W. Int'l L. Rev.* 306 (1979); Pedro Pablo Camargo, "The Claim of "Amparo" in Mexico:

have been decided the same way in five consecutive cases, by a certain prescribed majority vote, without an inconsistent ruling by that particular court or a superior federal court.[14] *Jurisprudencia* is binding only on lower courts and certain quasi-judicial administrative courts, and not on administrative agencies.[15]

III. The Civil Law System

Perhaps the most instructive parallel to the civil codes for a lawyer from the United States is a constitution. Like a constitution, the codes include specific detail when necessary. For example, the U.S. Constitution is quite detailed regarding the election of Congress and the President. Mexico's codes are similarly detailed in the regulation of matrimonial regimes, and the law of succession. Just as the Constitution uses broad language in other areas, each code has provisions in general language which have been broadly interpreted. Specific statutes that derogate from the general structure are strictly interpreted, using the general framework and the concepts from the general document.

Mexico's codes are usually as stable as the U.S. Constitution, and survive successive changes in the country's political structure. Of course, a code will reflect the political philosophy which dominates at the time of its drafting, and its interpretation may also be subject to the vicissitudes of political change. The basic principles, however, have remained surprisingly stable.

Codification, long considered the hallmark of civil law systems,[16] has declined in significance as a distinction between common law and civil law. One reason is the increased use of codes or similar devices in the common law. It is necessary only to mention the Uniform Commercial

---

Constitutional Protection of Human Rights," 6 *Cal. W.L. Rev.* 201 (1970); and H.L. Clagett, "The Mexican Suit of Amparo," 33 *Geo. L.J.* 418–437 (1945).

[14] The Supreme Court (*en banc*), a Chamber of the Supreme Court (administrative, labor, civil, or penal) or one of the Circuit Courts.

[15] Law of Amparo (*Ley de Amparo*) § 191–195.

[16] A few civil law countries, e.g., Scotland and South Africa, have never codified their laws, but they are nevertheless considered to have civil systems because of their derivation from Roman law. See F. Lawson, *A Common Lawyer Looks at the Civil Law* 50 (1955).

Code and the Restatements and model codes of the American Law Institute.[17] The differences between civil law and common law may lie in the susceptibility to and the acceptability of codification.

These differences are continuing to narrow as the United States becomes somewhat more code-oriented and Mexico updates a number of its laws by effectively codifying much of the U.S. common law on particular subjects.[18] It would be a mistake, however, to underestimate the differences between the two legal systems and their approaches to legal analysis.

IV. Differences in Legal Approaches

In the common law, the judge is acknowledged to have a law-making function, especially when there is no statute, or precedent on point. The common law lawyer, using prior cases, will devote a good deal of effort to discovering the facts, and to relating the facts of prior cases to the facts of this case.[19] While a jury may determine the facts, the judge will control the ultimate outcome of the case — largely on the basis of *stare decisis.*

The legal approach taken in Mexico is very different, and reflects the diminished role that judges occupy in civil law countries. Even though many civil law countries — including Mexico — are developing bodies of case law, it is only recently that decisions of even the highest courts have been reported,[20] and judicial opinions are flat syllogistic statements, without lengthy explanation, and without published dissent.[21] If the problem has arisen before, the civilian judge will examine prior cases, if the judge can find them, and if he can ascertain the policy as well as the

---

[17] But see J. Merryman, *The Civil Law Tradition* 33–34 (1969).

[18] See, e.g., *Ley Federal de Competencia Económica* (largely codifying U.S. antitrust law).

[19] See Pound, "What Is the Common Law?," *The Future of the Common Law* 3–23 (1937).

[20] See J. Dawson, *The Oracles of the Law* 405.

[21] See Bellet, "A Cour de Cessation," 19 *Revue Internationals de Droit Compare* 213–15 (1978); Jalger, *"La Cour Federate de Justice de la Republique Federale d'Allemagne,"* *id.* at 311, 340–41. See also, Zwergert and Kotz, *An Introduction to Comparative Law* 267–68 (1977).

reasoning contained therein. Nonetheless, for the civilian judge the legislative solution remains paramount, followed by the general principles of the legal system articulated by the scholars.

Typically, in a civil case, a judge will be appointed to act as a reporter for the case. He will guide the development of the case file, the narrowing of issues and the marshalling of evidence. When the file is ready for decision, in many civil law countries, lawyers will argue before a panel of judges (usually three) who will decide the case. The reporting judge will then brief his colleagues during deliberations, and will often propose a decision. The role of the lawyer is to ensure that the judges see evidence favorable to his client, and that the issues are narrowed in the best possible way for his side. Since the trial is often discontinuous, rather than concentrated, there is less of a premium upon preparation and command of the facts.

In deciding the case, the civil law judge has only to place the proper label upon a disputed question, and then apply the relevant statutory provision or legal concept. The law is not only "a seamless web," but also a rational system. Since it is rational, and since the judge may not distort the system, the function of predictability served by *stare decisis* at common law, is at least as well served in the civil law approach.

Making the law more systematic is thought to make it more certain, legislatively. Legislation, it is thought, should have no ambiguities, no inconsistencies, and no gaps. The judge has only to apply the law, and may not allow considerations of equity to lead to a different decision. Individual instances of injustice are regrettable, but unavoidable if certainty is to be maintained.[22]

Since legal disputes most often require the management of uncertainty, and the judge is required to decide the case,[23] the judge must reason by analogy to other legislative provisions, or by extending the principle implicit in a statute to a new situation, or by resorting to doctrinal writing. The legal scholars are not uniform, and judges may select one school of thought over another. When the decision appears

---

[22] Merryman, *The Civil Law Tradition* 50–58, N. 17, *supra.*

[23] *Id.* at 89–91.

inconsistent, then the scholars must work to design a new solution, to be implemented by the legislators.[24]

V. The Legal Profession in Mexico[25]

A. The Mexican *Notoriate*[26]

A Notary Public in Mexico is a lawyer, appointed by a state or the Federal District, who is a public official of considerable importance. Notaries may practice law, but as a practical matter usually find their time consumed by notarial duties. Notaries are authorized to authenticate facts, making them irrebuttable, without the necessity of other witnesses. Authentication that witnesses made certain statements, however, does not irrebuttably establish the underlying facts. Notaries also are exclusively authorized to check wills or contracts as to their proper form, to do real estate title searches and to act as a public recorder. Accordingly, transactions that require the recording of documents invariably require a notary's services.

B. The Bar

Law graduates who have acquired their "licensure in law" may practice law throughout Mexico once they have obtained their title from the Bureau of Professions. Membership in a bar association is voluntary. However, organizations do exist in Mexico in which lawyers from various specialties may meet and where courses or seminars on various themes are presented. The "Illustrious Attorneys' Bar" is an organization of very ancient origins with a broad membership. However, the Mexican Bar of Lawyers is a more important organization in terms of size and influence.

---

[24] See *id.* at 86–91.

[25] For an entertaining commentary on American stereotypes of Mexico, see Michael Wallace Gordon, "Mythical Stereotypes—Dealing with Mexico as a Lawyer," 38 *J. Legal Ed.* 279–284 (1988). ("These Mexicans come carrying, not large hats, but diplomas from UNAM or Escuela Libre, and often from Michigan or Harvard as well. They embarrass us with their fluent English, their knowledge of our legal system, and their familiarity with our culture." *Id.* at 281). See also Guillermo F. Margadant, "Mexico and the United States: the Need for Frankness," 18 *Tex. Int'l L.J.* 455–474 (1983).

[26] See generally Dr. Guillermo Floris Margadant, "The Mexican *Notariate*, 1970 Mexican Law Symposium," 6 *Cal. W.L. Rev.* 201 (1970).

Generally, in every state or large city there are similar associations or bar groups. Others may have a more specialized membership such as the Mexican Academy of Private International Law, or the Mexican Academy of Labor Law, etc.

C. Legal Education in Mexico

Mexico's education system varies significantly from that in the United States. Formal primary education (*primaria*) is completed in six years, followed by three years of secondary education (*secundaria*) and three years in preparatory school (*preparatoria*). The student would then commence a university career by entering law school, often as early as age 17, after having completed 12 years of formal education. This system of education comes from continental Europe, specifically from France and Spain.

The law curriculum consists of five years of academic studies. Normally, the student takes five or more courses, two to three hours per week. Required courses include history, economics, political science, and sociology. Indeed, law often is studied in the same way that one would pursue a bachelor degree in liberal arts in the United States. Examinations are oral. After completing his studies, the student must prepare a thesis of law and present this work before a jury composed of three to five scholars. This exam, which is called the "professional exam," is necessary to obtain the academic degree of *licenciado en derecho*, which entitles the law graduate to the professional title of *Licenciado* and the right to practice law throughout Mexico. Lawyers who intend to specialize, as well as academics, commonly pursue post-graduate degrees of Master or Doctor of Law.[27]

Foreigners may practice law if their studies are undertaken in Mexico and their immigration status qualifies them for a professional

---

[27] See generally Richard C. Maxwell and Marvin S. Goldman, "Mexican Legal Education," 16 *J. Legal Ed.* 155 (1963); Fred V. Perry, "Understanding the Mexican Attorney: Legal Education and the Practice of Law in Mexico," 10 *Int'l Law.* 167 (1976).

license.[28] Otherwise, foreign attorneys are limited to consulting or teaching. The right to act as a foreign legal consultant is guaranteed in the North American Free Trade Agreement ("NAFTA").[29]

---

[28] Although the Mexican Constitution guarantees qualified foreigners the right to engage in the professions (Arts. 1, 4, 5, and 33), governing statutory and regulatory provisions restrict foreigners from such activities. Accordingly, a writ of amparo must be filed to guarantee such rights although countless cases have found such restrictions to be unconstitutional. See Len Davis Callahan Lashley, 60 SJF6a 1: 159 (1962) (reprinted and translated in Woodfin L. Butte, *Selected Mexican Cases* 17 (1970)) (unanimous Supreme Court ruling declaring unconstitutional the absolute prohibition foreigners engaging in licit professions, industry and commerce). Such apparent inefficiency appears anomalous to most American lawyers but follows logically from the effect of constitutional rulings. See Mex. Const., Art. 107, § II.

[29] See NAFTA, Annex 1210, § B.

CHAPTER 4

Legal Formalities Associated With Doing Business in Mexico*

Lic. Manuel Garcia Barragán
Garcia Barragán, Hamdan y Sanchez Reyes, S.C.

I. Introduction

The legal aspects of business transactions in Mexico are subject to far more formalities than those in the United States. This chapter highlights some of the more important formalities that might catch the uninitiated off guard.

II. Powers of Attorney

Powers of attorney take on far more importance in Mexico than in the United States. Corporate officers in the United States are automatically vested with the necessary authority to do such things as retain legal counsel, enter into transactions on behalf of the corporation, and the like. In Mexico, by contrast, any such action is likely to be subject to challenge if the person acting on behalf of the corporation does not have a properly-issued power of attorney. This is true even if the person acting on behalf of the company is its highest ranking officer.

* This chapter was edited and supplemented by William E. Mooz, Jr.

Powers of attorney will be valid only if they comply with the strict requirements imposed by Mexican law. This means that they typically must be issued before a notary public, in accordance with all of the requirements for being a public deed.[1] Where a corporation is issuing the power of attorney, the notary must be provided with official copies of the documents necessary for the notary to perform, in essence, a due diligence review. This means that the notary will need to see the documents forming the company, vesting the person or body granting the power of attorney with the authority to do so, and the grant of the power of attorney itself. In addition, powers of attorney must have the relevant provisions of the Civil Code repeated within their text.

An additional set of issues arises when the power of attorney is issued abroad. Powers of attorney issued abroad, which under Mexican law are required to be in the form of a public deed, may be granted before the Mexican Consul or before a U.S. notary public (or other authority authorized by the law of the country of issuance to authorize powers of attorney). Where the power of attorney is issued before a U.S. notary, the notary's signature must be legalized by the Mexican Consul,[2] whose signature, in turn, must be legalized by the Ministry of Foreign Relations.

The foreign power of attorney then must be protocolized before a Mexican notary public. This means that the power of attorney must be translated into Spanish by an official expert and must comply substantively with the requirements for issuing a power of attorney under Mexican law. In other words, the foreign power of attorney must be drafted to include the data required to be set forth by a Mexican notary public in a public deed regarding the appearing parties. In addition, if the grantor is a corporation, the issuing authority abroad (the Mexican Consul or the foreign notary) must recite in the power of attorney that he reviewed all of the documents necessary to determine that the power was properly issued by the company.

---

[1] The role of the notary public in Mexico and the requirements for obtaining a public deed are discussed in Part V, below. See also Ch. 2, Part II.J., and Ch. 3, Part V.A.

[2] See Part VII, below.

Mexico and the United States are parties to the Protocol on Uniformity of the Legal Regime of Powers of Attorney; hence, powers of attorney issued in one country have to comply with the requisites imposed by such Protocol in order to produce effects in another country. Those requisites basically are the same as the requirements imposed by Mexican law.

The importance of complying with these formalities cannot be overestimated. Failure to do so can be disastrous, particularly in the case of litigation, where, if the attorney is not properly authorized to represent the client, all documents filed by the attorney will be deemed not to have been filed. Consequently, a party could lose a case by default simply because it did not follow the proper formalities to provide its attorney with a valid power of attorney to represent it in the litigation.

III. Contracts

A. The Differences Between Civil and Commercial Contracts

The substantive and procedural requirements that one must satisfy to have a binding contract in Mexico depend in part upon whether the contract at issue is of a civil or commercial nature. Civil contracts are governed by the provisions of the applicable Civil Code. Commercial contracts are governed by the Commercial Code to the extent that it provides specific guidance, and by the Civil Code to the extent that the Commercial Code is silent. As a general rule, commercial contracts are those that relate to business, and civil contracts are those that relate to all else.

Certain areas are expressly designated as commercial in the Commercial Code or other commercial laws, such as the General Law of Commercial Companies and the General Law of Negotiable Instruments and Credit Transactions. Matters expressly designated as commercial in these laws include the following: purchases, sales, and leases of personal property entered into for business purposes; purchases and sales of real estate for commercial purposes; purchases and sales of shares and debentures of corporations; agreements involving debentures or other negotiable instruments issued by the government; the operations of corporations devoted to sales, construction, manufacturing, transportation, tourism, sales of books, editorial activities, public shows, or devoted to acting as commission agents or that have officers devoted to commercial transactions; the operations of banks; agreements regarding commercial transactions; insurance companies and the contracts entered into by them; deposits made in bonded warehouses and transactions regarding certificates of deposit and bonds of pledge issued by such warehouses; checks; bills of exchange; the remittance of money from one city to another; negotiable instruments issued in bearer or registered form; transactions between merchants and banks, contracts entered into between merchants regarding their commercial activities and sales by farmers or producers of their crops.

Even if a contract relates to a matter that is not expressly designated as commercial by law, it will still be considered a commercial contract if it is entered into for a business purpose. This inquiry, which turns on the parties' intent, is necessarily less precise.

The Civil Code operates in much the same way. There are certain areas, such as lease contracts for real estate, that clearly are regulated only under the Civil Code. In such circumstances, the contract will be civil in nature irrespective of whether the parties intend the contract to be for a business purpose. In all other areas, a contract will be deemed civil in nature if it is not regulated by a commercial law, and it is entered into for a purpose other than business.

It is entirely possible under the "business purpose" rule for a contract to be commercial with respect to one party and civil with respect to the other. Such is the case where a person who buys goods from an established merchant (a department store or the like) for personal use. When carrying out such a sale, the merchant is doing so as part of its usual business activities, while the private party, when buying such merchandise, is doing so with the intent of satisfying a personal need.

Where a transaction is of a civil nature for one party, and of a commercial nature for the other party, the Commercial Code provides that in the event of default, the defendant's circumstances will determine whether the contract is subject to enforcement under civil law or commercial law. This is significant because the commercial laws generally tend to be far more pro-creditor than the civil laws.

Accordingly, in order to avoid the possibility of being subject to civil law, established merchants commonly require the purchaser to issue a negotiable instrument as part of the transaction. Negotiable instruments are considered to be of a commercial nature and are therefore subject to commercial law, regardless of whether the purchaser entered into the contract for business purposes.

B. General Requirements for the Formation of a Valid Contract

The general requirements for the formation of a valid contract appear in the Commercial and Civil Codes.[3] With regard to commercial contracts, the general principle is that each party obligates itself in the manner and terms in which it appears to have wanted to become obligated without the requirement that any particular formalities be satisfied.[4] There are, as one would expect, numerous exceptions to this general principle.

The Commercial Code, and other laws, expressly provide that a wide variety of contracts must be in writing or comply with other formalistic requirements in order to be valid. This exception, which is sufficiently broad to at least seriously dent the general rule, is discussed at Part C, below. Similarly, where a contract is entered into in a foreign country, the formalities required to have a valid contract under that country's laws must be complied with, even if the contract would otherwise be valid under Mexican law. Failure to comply with either of these requirements, if applicable, renders the contract void.

Even where the contract is commercial in nature, one also must be aware of the requirements set forth in the Civil Code. The Civil Code applies to commercial contracts on all issues where the Commercial Code is silent and with regard to the capacity of the parties to enter into a contract and the causes that render a contract void or voidable.[5]

---

[3] Other laws, of course, may impose additional, more area-specific requirements.

[4] This general principle simply means that commercial contracts are binding upon the parties irrespective of whether all formalities are complied with. It does not mean that they will have any effect on third parties, or that third parties will be deemed to have notice of them, if the proper formalities are not followed.

[5] Commercial Code, Arts. 2, 81.

One of the most important areas implicitly delegated by the Commercial Code to the Civil Code has to do with the formation of contracts. The essential elements of a contract are established in Articles 1794 and 1824 of the Civil Code. Article 1794 provides that: "For the existence of a contract the following are required: I. consent; and II. an object to which the contract relates." Article 1824 provides that: "The following are the objects of contracts: (I) the thing that the obligor must give; and (II) the act which the obligor must do or not do." Consent is the act of the parties agreeing on the object. The object of a contract is the creation of duties between the parties. If these essential elements do not exist, a contract is not formed or created.

The Civil Code also controls when a contract may be declared void. As set forth in Article 1795, contracts are voidable:

(1) due to lack of legal capacity of one or both of the contracting parties;

(2) due to defects in the granting of consent;

(3) because their objective, motive, or purpose is illegal; and

(4) because consent has not been expressed in the form required by law.

The Civil Code takes a harder line than the Commercial Code on the form of documents. Article 1795 expressly provides that the form of a contract is an element of its validity. Article 1833 repeats this theme by providing that when the law requires a specific form or formality for an agreement, and this formality is not given to it, the agreement will not be valid, unless the law provides to the contrary.

Lack of the requisite formality, however, is not always immediately fatal. If the parties' intent to enter into the contract appears in an unequivocal manner, any of them may request that the agreement be vested with the required form or formality. Therefore, even when an agreement lacks the form or formality required by law, the agreement will exist and a party will be entitled to request of the other party that the contract be changed to the required form or formality so that the agreement is no longer voidable.

At bottom, it is extremely important that the parties be aware of any and all formalistic requirements that apply to the particular contract at issue. These requirements can appear in either general laws such as the Civil or Commercial Codes, or in narrower laws applicable to the particular transaction in question. The formalistic requirements that can apply to a transaction may be as simple as requiring that the contract be in writing, to requiring that it be a public deed, to requiring the performance of certain duties in order to perfect the agreement.

C. Formalistic Requirements

Mexican law provides that a wide variety of contracts must appear in a particular form in order to be valid. There are two different levels of formality that may be required.

The highest level of formality that may be required is that the contract appear in the form of a public deed issued before a notary public or a public commercial broker.[6] The types of contracts that must meet the public deed requirement include the following: the formation of a corporation (there are, however, some legal authors who maintain that the setting up of a corporation does not have the nature of a contract); most transfers, purchases, and sales of real estate in excess of $5,000; mortgages; purchases of ships and aircraft; and most powers of attorney.

The second, and lower, level of formality that may apply to a contract is simply that it be in writing in order to be valid. The types of contracts subject to this lesser requirement include the following: the commission agency, which, although it may be orally granted, has to be ratified in writing prior to the termination of its subject matter; leases; a temporary association for commercial purposes without incorporation; pledges of securities; letters of credit; confirmed credit; chattel mortgages; firm loans; promises to contract or preparatory contracts; powers of attorney not subject to the public deed requirement; and all contracts that are

---

[6] The requirements for obtaining a public deed are discussed at Part V, below.

required to be recorded with a Registry and are not subject to a higher level of formality.

IV. Public Registration of Documents and Title

Mexican law, like that of many countries, requires that a wide variety of documents be registered publicly in order for them to be fully effective against third parties. Registration of such documents will typically occur in one of two different places.

The first is the Public Registry of Property. The Registry of Property is an office of the local government, and thus, its procedures may differ from state to state. As its name implies, this Registry exists primarily for the registration of matters affecting the title to real estate.

The second Registry is the Public Registry of Commerce. This Registry is federal in nature, and is governed by both the Commercial Code and the Regulations for the Public Registry of Commerce. Consequently, it is regulated in a uniform manner through out the country. The Public Registry of Commerce is kept by the same person who is in charge of the Public Registry of Property (the "Registrar").

The Public Registry of Commerce is divided into three different books. The first book is where documents affecting the status of "merchants," both individuals and corporations, are recorded. Such documents include commercial registrations, all acts related to the formation of a company, the amendment of its charter and by-laws, its dissolution and liquidation, the appointment of officers, and the granting of powers of attorney. Transactions involving real estate owned by a company also will be registered in this book, but the registration will simply refer the reader to the appropriate entry in the Public Registry of Property.

The second book is for the recording of debt instruments such as debentures, industrial mortgages, mortgages on airplanes, bonds, and chattel mortgage loans. This book also serves as a catch-all repository where any other acts or contracts that have to be recorded are kept.

The third book is for the recording of judicial decrees pertaining to the bankruptcy of merchants, the suspension of payments, and attachments.

Mexico has, by way of Spain, adopted the French system of recording. Under this system, registration is not necessary for an act or contract to be valid between the parties. However, until such acts or contracts are recorded, they will be ineffective against third parties. Once recorded, the contract or act is a matter of public record and will be enforceable against third parties. Recording will also prevent a third party from claiming to have acted as a bona fide party without knowledge of the recorded item. As one would expect, the Public Registries are open to the public, with all recorded documents subject to inspection.

Acts and contracts submitted for registration start to produce effects as of the date they are filed for recording, even though the actual recording may not occur for several days. The Registrar is empowered to determine the legality of documents presented for registration and may suspend, deny, or admit registration of acts or contracts that lack the requisite legality. In the event the Registrar suspends registration because of a defect in the title that may be cured, the suspension does not interrupt the priority as of the date of the original filing, provided the defect is cured within ten working days following the date on which the interested party is notified of the determination of the Registrar. In the event the Registrar refuses the registration, the interested party may file a suit to appeal such determination. If this suit is successful, and a judicial decree issues ordering the recording of the act or contract, the date of registration is retroactive to the date on which the act or contract was originally filed for recording.

V. Role of the Notary Public Under Mexican Law

One of the biggest differences between legal practice in the United States and legal practice in Mexico is the role of the notary public. While the notary public in the United States typically is a secretary who performs a largely ministerial function, the notary public in Mexico is a professional who acts as a quasi public official. As indicated above, a wide variety of common business documents or actions will not be valid in Mexico unless they are taken or granted in front of a notary. This means that the notary reviews such actions or documents and certifies that they are in compliance with all applicable laws. The transactions subject to notarial review encompass virtually all facets of commercial life, including the issuance of powers of attorney, the sale of real estate, and the formation of a company. In addition, the notary public has the power to provide facts or acts with an almost conclusive presumption of validity for the purpose of litigation.

The notary public's power in Mexico traces back to its origins in Europe. At the outset, notaries served as mere domestic servants who assisted their masters in drafting documents or contracts. These domestic servants became experts in such activities, and their status rose rapidly. Now, notaries are regarded as public officers whose blessing is required for many kinds of documents to have full legal effect.

The activities and appointment of notary publics in Mexico are governed by the federal district and the individual states. While the role of the notary public, in theory, could differ from state-to-state, in practice all of the Mexican states largely follow the Notarial Law for the Federal District. For this reason, and the fact that a disproportionate amount of commerce is centered in Mexico City, the following discussion focuses on the law of the federal district.

The Notarial Law defines a notary public as a public officer who is vested with public faith. This means that the formalistic blessing of a notary public will endow facts or acts with an almost conclusive presumption of authenticity. The notary public is also authorized to bestow legal form on documents and other legal acts. The notary public is entrusted with the safekeeping of the documents and annexes thereto that the notary authorizes, and may issue certified (i.e., official) copies of such documents.

A. Requisites to Become a Notary Public

Only attorneys are eligible to become notary publics. The first step in making the leap from private attorney to notary public is becoming an "Applicant to Become a Notary Public." This requires that the attorney satisfy the following criteria:

(1) be a Mexican national between the ages of 28 and 60 who has observed good behavior;

(2) be an attorney-at-law, with at least three years of practice after having passed the Bar examination;

(3) have at least eight uninterrupted months of practice under the supervision of a licensed notary public prior to the date of taking the exam;

(4) not have been convicted of an intentional criminal offense; and

(5) pass an examination.

After obtaining the status of applicant, the interested party has to pass a second exam in order to become a notary. This exam is partly oral and partly written and covers the most complicated subjects of notarial activity. The exams are given by a jury composed of officers of the Federal District Government and licensed notary publics.

The number of notaries in the Federal District is limited to 200, and government may add up to ten additional notarial offices per year to meet the needs of the population.

B. Obligations and Supervision of the Notary Public

The notary public must post a bond in favor of the Government of the Federal District in an amount equal to 1,825 times the current daily minimum wage for the Federal District. The bond guarantees payment of fines or other tax liabilities that the notary may incur and payment of amounts that the notary may be ordered to pay to private parties for having incurred liabilities.

In addition, the notary must obtain, at his own expense, the Protocol (i.e., book of documents) assigned to him and his seal. He must record his seal and signature with the government of the Federal District, the Registry of Public Property, and the Association of Notaries. The notary must establish an office within a designated section of the Federal

District, and notify the above-mentioned authorities and the Association of Notaries of the opening of the notary's office for business.

Notaries are required to maintain professional confidentiality except when they are required to render information to the authorities pursuant to law or in connection with acts that must be recorded in the Public Registry. They must advise and explain to the parties appearing before them the legal effects and consequences of the acts or contracts that the notaries authorize.

The notary is forbidden from acting in matters in which, for any reason, he cannot act in an impartial manner or in matters in which the notary's spouse or relatives are involved. The notary is also forbidden from receiving or keeping money, valuables, or negotiable instruments relating to the acts in which he intervenes, except in cases where the money kept is for the payment of taxes arising out of the transactions the notary handles.

Notaries are subject to the vigilance and inspection of the government of the Federal District, which observes the work of notaries in order to make sure that they are acting according to the law. Failure to act in accordance with the law can subject the notary to fines, suspension, or removal, depending on the seriousness of the violation.

C. The Book of Protocol

The notary records all of his or her acts under formalities prescribed by law in a set of books known as the "Protocol." These books are authorized by the government of the Federal District and will contain all of the public deeds and notarial acknowledgments granted before the notary. The notary may not authorize any act or contract without recording it in his Protocol.

The books comprising the Protocol are numbered consecutively. When a book is completed, the notary delivers it to the General Director of the Public Registry who closes the book out in accordance with the prescribed formalities. In addition, the Notary keeps a file for each book. This file is called the "Appendix," and contains all documents relating to the public deeds and notarial acknowledgments granted before the notary.

The Appendix is regarded as part of the Protocol and is delivered to the Public Registry together with the books for closing. After closing by the Public Registry, the notary may keep the books and appendixes for five years. During that time period, the notary may continue to issue certified copies of the public deeds and acknowledgments contained in such books and appendixes. When the five-year period expires, the books are delivered to the Public Registry where they are filed at the Archives of Notaries. Thereafter, certified copies are issued by the General Director of the Archives of Notaries.

D. Public Deeds

Many contracts, as elaborated on more fully early in this chapter, must be in the form of a public deed in order to be valid in Mexico. A public deed, generally speaking, is an original document issued before a notary that complies will all legal formalities and is made part of the notary's book.

The legal formalities associated with public deeds are extensive. For example, all such documents must bear the signatures of the parties and the notary on each page and at the end of the document and must also bear the seal of the notary. In addition, the names of the parties involved, their nationality, date of birth, place of birth, marital status, occupation, and domicile have to be stated. Public deeds must be in Spanish, and ancillary documents that are required to be part of the public deed must be translated into Spanish if the original appears in a different language. Both the original document and the translation, which must be prepared by an official expert, are attached to the Appendix to the notary's book of Protocol.

In addition to the general requirements applicable to all public deeds, specific types of transactions may give rise to a number of other requirements. For example, when any person acts as an agent in connection with the matter covered by the public deed, the notary must include a description of the source of the agent's authority. Where real estate is involved, the public deed must include the notary's transcription of the last certified copy of the public deed or document relating to the seller's title and the date that such document was recorded with the Public Registry.

When all the legal requirements have been complied with by the parties, the notary then authorizes the public deed.

E. Minutes or Notarial Acknowledgments

The minutes or notarial acknowledgments are the original documents written down in the book of the notary containing important facts or legal acts. It is prepared by the notary at the request of the interested party.

Among the acts that the notary is required to write down in his book as notarial acknowledgments are the following: notices; summonses; demands for payment; protests of negotiable instruments; the existence, identity, legal capacity, and acknowledgment of signatures of persons identified by the notary; material facts, such as the deterioration of a building due to an adjacent and newer building; comparisons of documents; the existence of maps, photographs, and other documents; the delivery of documents; and in general, facts, acts, or omissions involving persons or things that may be judged objectively.

F. Certified Copies

Certified copies are the copies prepared by the notary in which he fully transcribes a public deed or notarial acknowledgment, including the documents relating thereto kept in the Appendix. The notary is required to issue to the interested parties certified copies of the public deeds and notarial acknowledgments granted before him. It is often convenient to have the notary provide one with several certified copies at the same time that the notary issues the original.

VI. The Commercial Public Broker

In addition to the notary public, the commercial public broker occupies an important position under Mexican law. Commercial public brokers, like notaries, are vested with the public faith and can perform many of the same activities as notaries. The principal difference between the two offices is that the commercial public broker can act only with regard to matters of a commercial nature. Notaries, by contrast, can act with regard to all matters, including those of a commercial nature.

VII. Legalization of Documents

Documents issued or authenticated by foreign authorities will not produce effects in Mexico unless the signatures of the foreign authorities are legalized by the Mexican Consul with jurisdiction over the region where the foreign authority resides. In turn, the signature of the Mexican Consul has to be legalized by the Ministry of Foreign Relations in Mexico City. The Mexican Consuls in the United States are very familiar with this process, and generally are able to provide prompt assistance. The fee for this service in 1993 was $USD25.

Under Article 121 of the Mexican Constitution, the official actions of a Mexican state are entitled to full faith and credit throughout the Mexican Republic. A prerequisite to receiving this treatment is that the signatures authorizing the act be legalized by the Governor of such state or the Governor's delegate.

Likewise, letters rogatory issued by Mexican judicial authorities must be legalized by the Governor of the state where such judicial authorities are located, if they are local, or by the Ministry of the Interior, if such judicial authorities are federal. Finally the signature of the Governor or the officer of the Ministry of the Interior must be legalized by the Ministry of Foreign Relations.

With regard to documents issued by private parties, it is not required that their signatures be authenticated by a notary public or by any authority of the place of residence of the parties, unless such documents are required to be recorded in a Public Registry. In such cases, the signatures of the parties to such documents have to be authenticated by a notary public or the corresponding authority. If the authenticating party is foreign, its signature must be legalized by the nearest Mexican Consul, whose signature must be authenticated by the Ministry of Foreign Relations.

CHAPTER 5

Restrictions on Foreign Investment*

Lic. Jorge Camil
Camil y Treviño

William E. Mooz, Jr., Esq.
Holland & Hart

Elizabeth R. Carney, Esq.
Holland & Hart

I. Introduction

Foreigners do not have an automatic right to invest in Mexico. What foreigners can and cannot do in Mexico is the subject of many different laws. The most important of these laws are the Foreign Investment Law of 1993 (the "1993 FIL"), the Foreign Investment Regulations of 1989 (the "1989 Regulations") and Mexico's Constitution (the "1917 Constitution"). In addition to these laws, which apply to foreigners from all countries, investors from the United States and Canada should be aware of the provisions of the North American Free Trade Agreement ("NAFTA") that relate to foreign investment.

* Part II is reprinted by permission of the *Houston Int'l L.J.*

II. Constitutional Limits on Foreign Investment

Mexico passed a new constitution in 1917 that imposed the first set of restrictions on foreign investment. The 1917 Constitution claimed direct government ownership over land, waters, and petroleum and other subsurface mineral deposits.[1] Nonetheless, certain ownership rights were recognized in favor of foreigners willing to waive the diplomatic protection of their home governments.[2] The 1917 Constitution also banned foreign acquisition of land in the so-called "restricted areas," which are located within 100 kilometers from the borders and 50 kilometers from the seacoasts.[3]

These restrictions form the bedrock of Mexico's foreign investment laws. While subsequent laws have either expanded these limitations through embellishment, or, as has been the case in recent years, curtailed them through interpretation, the 1917 Constitution remains the starting point of all such laws.

Mexico's initial approach to the foreign investment restrictions contained in the 1917 Constitution, was to expand them considerably. Over the next 50 years, the Mexican government, gradually, but persistently, claimed a larger role in the economic process, either nationalizing or subjecting to "Mexicanization" a number of economic endeavors. By 1970, activities such as sulphur mining, oil and gas exploration and production, petrochemical production, mining, forestry and fishing, transportation, radio and television broadcasting, electric power generation, and automotive parts manufacturing, all were either closed to foreign participation or severely restricted. These restrictions were imposed in a piecemeal fashion, and dampened, but did not extinguish foreign investment in Mexico's booming economy.

In 1973, President Echeverria passed Mexico's first general law on foreign investment (the "1973 FIL"). The 1973 FIL basically collected the principal restrictions on foreign investment existing in 1973. Consequently, the statute reasserted a ban on foreign participation in

---

[1] Mex. Const., Art. 27.
[2] Mex. Const., Art. 27., § I.
[3] Mex. Const., Art. 27, § I.

economic activities previously reserved for the federal government or Mexican investors. The 1973 FIL also set forth the general principle that foreign investment should not exceed 49 percent in any case, and set even more restrictive levels for certain industries such as mining and auto parts. Management contracts could not be used to circumvent these limitations. The Foreign Investment Commission (FIC) was empowered to grant exceptions to the limitations on foreign ownership if the project involved had certain special characteristics,[4] but such exceptions were rarely granted and extremely cumbersome to obtain.

The foreign investment pendulum began to swing in the opposite direction under President de la Madrid, who governed Mexico from 1982 until 1988. This pro-foreign investment momentum took concrete form during the succeeding administration of President Salinas when Mexico published the 1989 Regulations.[5] While the Regulations technically did not supersede the 1973 FIL, in practical effect they greatly liberalized foreigners' rights to invest in Mexico. In 1993, the FIL itself was replaced, with the 1989 Regulations being kept in effect to the extent that they do not conflict with the 1993 FIL. At about the same time, Mexico subscribed to NAFTA, with its further commitments to liberalizing foreign investment. Under these new laws, Mexico's constitutional limits on foreign investment have been interpreted much more narrowly than in the past, and virtually all sectors of the Mexican economy are now open to foreign investment.

III. The Foreign Investment Law of 1993

The 1993 FIL was published on December 27, 1993 and applies to all foreign investors, whether or not they are residents of a NAFTA country.[6] The general principle of the 1993 FIL is that foreign investors can engage in any activity, or acquire any asset, unless the 1993 FIL

---

[4] These characteristics included the project's impact on jobs, training of Mexican personnel, technology, and location.

[5] *Reglamento de la Ley para Promover la Inversión Extranjera, Diario Oficial* [*D.O.*], May 16, 1989.

[6] The 1989 Regulations remain in effect under the 1993 FIL to the extent that they are consistent with the law. 1993 FIL, Fourth Transitory Article. All investments legally made prior to the 1993 FIL's effective date are exempt from the 1993 FIL's requirements. 1993 FIL, Fifth Transitory Article.

provides otherwise.[7] This general grant of freedom to invest applies to most industries, but some industries continue to be restricted, and certain bureaucratic requirements still must be complied with.

A. Restricted Activities

Activities that are not completely open to foreign investors under the 1993 FIL are subject to one of three different types of restrictions. The first class of restrictions reserves the enumerated activities to the Mexican government. The activities subject to this level of restriction largely parallel those listed in the 1917 Constitution and include, *inter alia*, petroleum and hydrocarbons, basic petrochemicals, electricity, railroads, satellite communications, the postal system, and radioactive minerals.[8] How each of these activities is defined will have a big impact on the scope of the restriction. Additional guidance on this point may be available in the 1989 Regulations, which remain in effect for the purpose of supplementing the 1993 FIL, and in interpretations issued under those regulations.

The second level of restriction reserves the enumerated activities to Mexicans and Mexican companies that exclude foreign participation. These areas include: national ground transportation of passengers; tourism and cargo excluding courier services and express package services; the retail sale of gasoline and liquid petroleum gas; radio broadcasting services and other radio and television services, with the exception of cable television; credit unions; institutions of development banking; and certain professional and technical services.[9]

The third level of restriction allows for foreign investment, but limits it to a fixed minority percentage. For example, there is a limit of 25 percent on foreign investment in the area of national air transportation and a 30 percent limit with respect to companies controlled by financial groups, credit institutions of multiple banks, brokerage houses, and stock exchange specialists.[10] A limit of 49 percent still exists with respect to

---

[7] 1993 FIL, Art. 4.

[8] 1993 FIL, Art. 5.

[9] 1993 FIL, Art. 6.

[10] 1993 FIL, Art. 7.

many activities, including: insurance institutions, bond institutions, financial lenders, cable television, and basic telephone service.[11] The FIC may grant approval for a higher level of foreign investment in certain of these sectors, such as cellular telephone services, petroleum pipeline construction, and the drilling of petroleum and gas wells.[12]

Irrespective of the type of company involved, one further restriction is generally applicable. FIC approval is required whenever foreigners will own more than 49 percent of the capital of a Mexican company, either directly or indirectly, if the value of the fixed assets of the company at the moment of acquisition of the shares exceeds a threshold amount that will be set by the FIC annually.[13] The threshold amount is 85 million new pesos (approximately $26.56 million USD).[14]

Through the NAFTA process, Mexico has committed to lifting a number of these restrictions over time. In recognition of this fact, the 1993 FIL itself provides for the phase-out of some of these limits. For instance, while international ground transportation of passengers, tourism and cargo between points within the territory of Mexico as well as central passenger trucking and auxiliary services are currently reserved to Mexicans or Mexican companies which exclude foreign participation, up to 100 percent foreign participation will be allowed with respect to such activities after a ten-year phase-in period.[15] One hundred percent foreign participation without prior government approval will be allowed after a five-year period with respect to building construction activities[16] as well as the manufacture and assembly of parts and accessories for the automobile industry.[17] By incorporating these provisions into the 1993 FIL, Mexico has extended the benefits of these portions of NAFTA to all foreign investors.

The 1993 FIL does not contain all of the adjustments necessary to achieve compliance with NAFTA. For example, as part of NAFTA

---

[11] 1993 FIL, Art. 7

[12] 1993 FIL, Art. 8; 1993 FIL, Ninth Transitory Art., § III.

[13] 1993 FIL, Art. 9.

[14] 1993 FIL, Tenth Transitory Art.

[15] 1993 FIL, Sixth Transitory Art.

[16] 1993 FIL, Ninth Transitory Art.

[17] 1993 FIL, Seventh Transitory Art.

Mexico has committed to opening up its financial sector over time to investment from the United States and Canada.[18] The 1993 FIL does not attempt to incorporate these provisions and, instead, defers to the specific laws for those activities.[19] Thus, before concluding that an activity is off-limits to foreign investment, it may be worth consulting the provisions of NAFTA and any other, more specific, Mexican law regulating the activity.

The 1993 FIL generally prohibits the use of any device to avoid its limitations on foreign investment.[20] Indirect foreign investment will be allowed, however, where it is approved by the FIC or, in certain circumstances, through the use of "neutral investment."[21] Under the neutral investment provisions of the 1993 FIL, Mexican companies and fiduciary institutions may issue nonvoting stock/investment instruments upon approval of the Ministry of Commerce and Industrial Development.[22] Moreover, with government approval, neutral investment will be permitted in fiduciary institutions controlled by financial groups, institutions of multiple banks, and brokerage houses.[23] Government approval will also be required in order for international financial development companies to make neutral investments.[24] The advantage of the neutral investment provisions of the 1993 FIL is that the neutral shares/investment instruments will not be counted in determining the percentage of foreign investment in the capital stock of Mexican companies.[25] Thus, the neutral investment provisions of the 1993 FIL may provide a method for circumventing the sectoral and percentage restrictions on foreign investment.

B. Real Property

In keeping with the 1917 Constitution, the 1993 FIL continues to recognize the limitation of foreign ownership of land within 100

---

[18] See NAFTA, Ch. 14.
[19] 1993 FIL, Art. 4.
[20] 1993 FIL, Arts. 6–7.
[21] 1993 FIL, Arts. 18–22.
[22] 1993 FIL, Arts. 20–21.
[23] 1993 FIL, Art. 21.
[24] 1993 FIL, Art. 22.
[25] 1993 FIL, Art. 18.

kilometers of Mexico's borders and within 50 kilometers of its beaches, albeit in a more limited fashion than in the past. The 1993 FIL permits Mexican companies that do not exclude foreign participation to own real property in the restricted zone provided that such property is acquired for industrial or commercial use and is registered with the Foreign Ministry.[26] In addition, the 1993 FIL explicitly authorizes the use of Mexican trusts for the purpose of allowing Mexican companies that do not exclude foreign participation to acquire beneficial title to residential real property within the restricted zone upon approval of the Foreign Ministry.[27] Upon approval of the Foreign Ministry, Mexican trusts may also be used to permit foreign investors to acquire the rights of use and enjoyment to real property located in the restricted zone.[28] All acquisitions of real property in the restricted zone that are subject to the approval of the Foreign Ministry will be examined with regard to their economic and social benefit.[29] The Foreign Ministry must take action with respect to any application for approval of the acquisition of land in the restricted zone within 35 working days from the date such application is filed.[30] Otherwise, the application will be deemed approved. Under the 1993 FIL, trusts are limited to a maximum period of 30 years, but this term can be extended upon request of the interested party.[31]

C. Bureaucratic Requirements

The 1993 FIL does away with much of the bureaucracy that foreign investors previously had to negotiate in Mexico. Nonetheless, certain reporting and other obligations continue to exist, even for basic investments that do not otherwise require governmental approval. For example, all foreign companies that habitually do business in Mexico must be inscribed in the Public Registry of Commerce.[32] Requests for permission to be inscribed must be acted upon within 15 working days, or will be deemed granted automatically.[33] Similarly, all Mexican

---

[26] 1993 FIL, Art. 10.
[27] 1993 FIL, Arts. 10–12.
[28] 1993 FIL, Art. 12.
[29] 1993 FIL, Art. 14.
[30] 1993 FIL, Art. 14.
[31] 1993 FIL, Art. 13.
[32] 1993 FIL, Art. 17.
[33] 1993 FIL, Art. 17.

companies or trusts with foreign investors or beneficiaries, and all foreigners habitually doing business in Mexico, must register themselves in the National Registry of Foreign Investment.[34] This involves providing a variety of basic information, which must be updated periodically.[35]

IV. Protections Provided to Foreign Investors Under NAFTA

NAFTA seeks to promote foreign investment among the three member countries in a number of different ways. Most importantly, it requires that each country accord to investors of other member countries the same treatment that is provided to domestic investors.[36] This requirement, in most cases, is carried out in the 1993 FIL.

In addition to calling for the elimination of direct restrictions of foreign investment, NAFTA eliminates performance requirements in connection with foreign investment, such as domestic sales restrictions, export quotas, local content regulations, preferences for domestic sourcing, trade balancing, technology transfer, or product mandating.[37] NAFTA also allows investors to have the right to transfer payments relating to the investment, such as dividends, interest, or royalty payments without delay and in freely convertible currency at the market rate of exchange.[38] Further, under NAFTA an investment may not be expropriated except for a public purpose, and should expropriation occur, compensation must be paid promptly, in the amount of the fair market value of the investment.[39]

In the event that a member country violates these protections, the investor may seek to have them enforced in arbitration.[40] The arbitration will be supervised by the International Centre for Settlement of

---

[34] 1993 FIL, Art. 32.
[35] 1993 FIL, Arts. 33–35.
[36] NAFTA, Art. 1102.
[37] NAFTA, Art. 1106.
[38] NAFTA, Art. 1109.
[39] NAFTA, Art. 1110.
[40] NAFTA, Art. 1116(1)(a).

Investment Disputes (ICSID), and be decided by a non-partisan tribunal.[41] The arbitration will be governed by either the ICSID rules or the arbitration rules of the United Nations Commission on International Trade Law.[42] A member country's failure to abide by the arbitral decision, which can include the payment of a monetary award, can result in the suspension of benefits to that country under NAFTA.[43]

V. Conclusion

With the advent of NAFTA and the 1993 FIL, Mexico has removed many of its pre-existing obstacles to foreign investment. This opening of Mexico's economy to foreign investment will continue as NAFTA is phased in over the next 15 years.

---

[41] See NAFTA, Arts. 1124–25.
[42] NAFTA, Arts. 1120, 1124.
[43] See NAFTA, Arts. 1134, 1135, 2008–19.

CHAPTER 6

Mexican Law on Business Entities*

Beverly May Carl
Former Professor of Law
Southern Methodist University

I. Introduction

Business entities in Mexico are governed by the General Law on Business Entities.[1] This law identifies the specific entities recognized in Mexico and defines their characteristics. It also sets out the general legal provisions applicable to all entities.

II. Matters of General Application to the Formation of All Business Entities

The first chapter of this law lays down rules that apply to all business entities operating in Mexico. For instance, the documents establishing the

* This chapter was edited and supplemented by Elizabeth R. Carney and William E. Mooz, Jr., Holland & Hart.

[1] *Ley General de Sociedades Mercantiles, D.O.*, Aug. 4, 1934, as amended June 11, 1992.

company must be executed before a notary public.[2] Then, such documents must be approved by the civil court of the place where the company is domiciled, after which they must be recorded in the Public Commercial Registry.[3]

The organizational documents or agreements are required to contain the following information:

(1) The names, nationalities, and domiciles of the individuals or companies forming the entity.

(2) The purpose of the entity.

(3) The name of the entity.

(4) The duration of the entity.

(5) The amount of capital.

(6) A description of the contribution of each participant, whether in cash or property, together with the value of each contribution in kind, and an explanation of the means used to arrive at such valuation. If the association is formed with variable capital, this fact must be stated as well as the minimum authorized capital.

(7) The domicile of the entity.

(8) A description of the form of administration (e.g., a sole director board or a board of directors).

(9) The names of the initial directors or managers and a statement indicating which of them are authorized to act on behalf of the entity.

---

[2] *Ley General de Sociedades Mercantiles, D.O.*, Aug. 4, 1934, as amended June 11, 1992, Art. 5.

[3] *Id.*, Art. 260; Commercial Code, Art. 19.

(10) The method of distributing the profits and losses of the entity.

(11) The amount of the reserve fund.

(12) The grounds for liquidation of the entity.

(13) The procedures for liquidating the entity.[4]

Every Mexican business entity must transfer at least 5 percent of its net profits each year to a reserve fund until that reserve equals 2 percent of the entity's capital. If the reserve falls below that percentage for any reason, it must be subsequently replenished from the net earnings.[5]

III. Entities Recognized Under Mexican Law

The General Law on Business Entities establishes six kinds of business entities:

(1) the "*sociedad en nombre colectivo*";

(2) "*sociedad en comandita*";

(3) "*sociedad en comandita por acciones*";

(4) the "*sociedad cooperativa*";

(5) "*sociedad de responsabilidad limitada*"; and

(6) the "*sociedad anónima.*"

It also provides that these types of business associations, with the exception of the "*sociedad cooperativa,*" may be formed with variable capital[6] provided that certain requirements are satisfied.[7] In addition, this

---

[4] *Id.*, Art. 6.

[5] *Id.*, Art. 20.

[6] *Ley General de Sociedades Mercantiles, D.O.*, Aug. 4, 1934, as amended June 11, 1992, Art. 1.

[7] Discussed at Part X, Notes 175–181, below, and accompanying text.

statute governs the operation of branches of foreign companies. The entities of most interest to foreign investors tend to be the "*sociedad de responsabilidad limitada*" or limited liability company and the *"sociedad anónima"* or corporation.

IV. The *"Sucursal"* (Branch)

A foreign company may qualify to do business in Mexico as a branch if it obtains an authorization of the Department of National Economy and if it registers in the Public Commercial Registry. To obtain such approval the foreign company must satisfy the following requirements:

(1) prove that it was duly organized in accord with the laws of its place of origin by submitting a certified copy of its organizational documents (e.g., articles of incorporation) and a certification of the Mexican Consular Office that the company was duly organized under the laws of such place;

(2) indicate that the organizational documents are not contrary to Mexican law or public order; and

(3) affirm that a branch or agency of that company will be established in Mexico.

A branch must publish an annual balance sheet approved by a certified public accountant.[8] Because of various tax disadvantages and restrictions on owning real property, a branch of a foreign company is not usually the preferred vehicle for doing business in Mexico.

V. The "*Sociedad en Nombre Colectivo*" (General Partnership)[9]

This business entity is similar to the general partnership in the United States. Each partner is jointly and severally liable for the partnership

---

[8] *Ley General de Sociedades Mercantiles, D.O.*, Aug. 4, 1934, as amended June 11, 1992, Art. 251.

[9] *Ley General de Sociedades Mercantiles, D.O.*, Aug. 4, 1934, as amended June 11, 1992, Arts. 25–50.

debts; his liability is unlimited.[10] The name of at least one partner must appear in the firm's name. If the names of all the partners are not used in the firm's name, the words "*y compañia*" or their equivalent must be added.[11] These associations are legal entities which may transact business, as well as sue and be sued, in their own names.[12] Normally the death of a partner dissolves the partnership.[13] However, the partnership agreement may provide that the partnership may be continued with the heirs.[14] In addition, a partner may transfer his interest only upon consent of all the partners unless the partnership agreement provides for transfer upon majority consent.[15]

VI. The "*Sociedad en Comandita Simple*" (Limited Partnership)

This kind of association is composed of both general and limited partners. The liability of the former is unlimited. Normally, a limited partner's liability may not exceed his capital contribution;[16] however, he becomes personally liable for the company's debts if he permits his name to be used in the firm's name, if the designation "*sociedad en comandita*" or its abbreviation, "*S. en C.*" is omitted from the firm's name,[17] or if he actively participates in the management of the company.[18] Where, however, the sole managing partner dies or becomes incapacitated, a limited partner may perform necessary actions during a period of one month following the death or incapacity of such general partner[19] in the event that the partnership agreement does not provide for the replacement of the managing partner and no general partner is available to take on such role. In this case, the limited partner does not incur unlimited

---

10 *Id.*, Arts. 25, 26.
11 *Id.*, Art. 27.
12 *Id.*, Art. 2.
13 *Id.*, Arts. 32, 230.
14 *Id.*
15 *Id.*, Art. 31.
16 *Id.*, Art. 51.
17 *Id.*, Art. 53.
18 *Id.*, Art. 55.
19 *Id.*, Art. 56.

liability. In other respects, the rules governing these limited partnerships are similar to those for general partnerships.[20]

VII. The "*Sociedad en Comandita por Acciones*" (Limited Partnerships With Shares)

This type of business entity is also composed of both general and limited partners.[21] The partners' contributions, however, are represented by shares of stock. Bearer shares are prohibited and shares may not be transferred without the consent of all the general partners and two thirds of the limited partners.[22] The company's name may include the name of one or more of the general partners; if not all the general partners' names are included in the company's name, then the name must be followed by the words "*y compañia*." In any event, the company's name must be followed by the phrase "*sociedad en comandita por acciones,*" or its abbreviation, "*S. en C. por A.*"[23] The remaining aspects of these associations are governed by the principles of partnership law in some situations[24] and those of corporate law in others.[25] This is not a popular form of business organization in Mexico because of its unlimited liability feature.

VIII. The "*Sociedad de Responsabilidad Limitada*" (Limited Liability Company)

The limited liability company displays features of both corporations and partnerships. Its members are liable only to the extent of their contributions, but their ownership interests may not be represented by negotiable certificates or shares of stock.[26] Unless the bylaws require a greater voting margin, the transfer of any ownership thereof and the admission of new members requires the consent of the members whose contributions comprise a majority of the capital stock of the company.

---

[20] *Id.*, Art. 57.
[21] *Id.*, Art. 207.
[22] *Id.*, Art. 209.
[23] *Id.*, Art. 210.
[24] *Id.*, Art. 211.
[25] *Id.*, Art. 208.
[26] *Id.*, Art. 58.

The company may not sell shares or any ownership interest to the public.[27] It is a legal entity which may transact business, as well as sue and be sued, in its own name. The legal document creating such a company will be herein referred to as the "agreement of association."

A. Company Name

The name of the company must consist of the name of one or more of its members followed with the designation "*sociedad de responsabilidad limitada*," or its abbreviation, "*S. de R.L.*"[28] Failure to comply with this requirement subjects its members to unlimited liability.[29] Any nonmember of the company who permits his name to appear in the company's name is liable for the company's debts up to an amount equal to the largest capital contribution.[30]

B. Members

There may not be more than 50 members of a limited liability company.[31] Each member holds an undivided interest in the company[32] that is proportionate to his capital contribution.[33] Nevertheless, the company's agreement of association may provide for partition of interests and partial transfers under stipulated circumstances.[34]

C. Capital

The minimum capital required to form a limited liability company, as established in the 1992 amendments to the General Law of Business Entities, is 3 million old pesos, or slightly less than $1,000 USD.[35] Companies formed prior to June 12, 1992 remain subject to the previous

---

27 *Id.*, Art. 63.
28 *Id.*, Art. 59.
29 *Id.*
30 *Id.*, Art. 60.
31 *Id.*, Art. 61.
32 *Id.*, Art. 69.
33 *Id.*, Art. 68.
34 *Id.*, Arts. 61, 62, 65, 66, 69.
35 *Id.*, Art. 62.

minimum capital requirement of 5,000 old pesos.[36] The stated value of each member's interest must be 1,000 old pesos or a whole multiple thereof.[37] Nevertheless, different classes and different values for such classes of interests may be created.[38] At the time of formation, the capital must be fully subscribed and at least 50 percent of each member's interest must have been paid in.[39] In the event of a capital increase, existing members enjoy a preferential right to acquire the newly issued interests in proportion to their present ownership.[40] If so provided in the agreement of association, members may be required to make pro-rata supplementary contributions if the members' assembly passes a resolution to that effect.[41]

The agreement of association may provide for redemption of a member's interest out of net profits available for payment of dividends. The agreement may also permit the exchange of a member's interest for a participating certificate that entitles him to future distributions of profits.[42]

D. Distribution of Profits

The Assembly of the members is empowered to authorize the distribution of profits of the company.[43] Unless otherwise agreed, members share in profits and losses in proportion to their ownership interest.[44] The agreement of association may give members the right to receive annual interest not in excess of 9 percent on their capital contributions even though there are not yet any profits. Such interest payments may only be made during the period of construction of facilities necessary for start-up of the operation; in no case may this time period exceed three years.[45]

---

[36] *Id.*, Second Transitory Article.
[37] *Id.*
[38] *Id.*, Art. 62.
[39] *Id.*, Art. 64.
[40] *Id.*, Art. 72.
[41] *Id.*, Arts. 70, 78(6).
[42] *Id.*, Arts. 71, 137.
[43] *Id.*, Art. 78(2).
[44] *Id.*, Art. 16.
[45] *Id.*, Art. 85.

E. Transfers of Member's Interest

Unless a larger voting margin is specified in the agreement of association, the consent of the members holding a majority of the capital stock is required for a member to transfer his ownership interest or for a new member to be admitted.[46] If transfer to an outsider is authorized, the existing members have a preferential right to acquire the interest within 15 days from the date the transfer is authorized.[47]

Ordinarily, consent of the members is not required to transfer a deceased member's interest to his heirs. The agreement of association may, however, provide that upon death of a member the company shall be dissolved and his share of the proceeds paid to his heirs.[48]

F. Assembly Meetings of the Members

The ultimate authority of the company is vested in the Assembly of the members.[49] This body is empowered to appoint and dismiss managers, approve the balance sheet, determine the distribution of profits, appoint a board of examiners, divide and amortize members' interests in the capital, require supplementary contributions from members, bring a derivative suit against the association's executives or members, increase or reduce the capital of the association, approve transfers of ownership interests in the capital and the admission of new members, amend the articles, and dissolve the company.[50]

The Assembly must meet once a year at the domicile of the Company.[51] The Assembly may be called together by the managers, the board of examiners, or by members representing one third of the capital. Written notice must be sent to each member at least eight days before the meeting.[52] The agreement of association may designate situations in

---

[46] *Id.*, Art. 65.
[47] *Id.*, Art. 66.
[48] *Id.*, Art. 67.
[49] *Id.*, Art. 77.
[50] *Id.*, Art. 78.
[51] *Id.*, Art. 80.
[52] *Id.*, Art. 81.

which a mail ballot may be used.[53] However, if the members representing one third of the capital request a meeting of the Assembly, a meeting must be called even if the agreement of association would permit the matter to be voted on by mail ballot.[54] Usually, a member has one vote for each 1,000 old pesos ownership interest.[55] For an Assembly meeting held on the first call, decisions on ordinary matters must be adopted by votes representing at least one half of the capital unless a greater percentage is required by the agreement of association. If a meeting is held on the second call, decisions may be made by a majority of those present.[56] Normally, an amendment to the agreement of association requires a favorable vote representing three quarters of the capital. Nevertheless, any amendment that would change the purpose of the company or increase the obligations of the members requires a unanimous vote.[57]

G. Management of the Company

Managers are appointed and may be removed by the Assembly.[58] Managers may but need not be members, and they may be appointed for either a specified term or an indefinite period.[59] Ordinarily, they act by majority vote, unless the agreement of association requires joint action in which case unanimity is required.[60] If no managers are appointed, the company is managed by its members.[61]

H. Liability of Management

A derivative suit on behalf of the company may be brought by any member or by the Assembly against a manager to recover company funds or property. Managers who had no knowledge of a decision or who voted against it incur no liability therefor. In addition, a manager may

---

[53] *Id.*, Art. 82.
[54] *Id.*
[55] *Id.*, Art. 79.
[56] *Id.*, Art. 77.
[57] *Id.*, Art. 83.
[58] *Id.*, Art. 78.
[59] *Id.*, Art. 73.
[60] *Id.*, Art. 75.
[61] *Id.*, Art. 73.

be absolved from liability by vote of the Assembly representing three fourths of the capital.[62]

I. Financial Surveillance

Managers are required to submit to the members specified financial statements, such as the yearly balance sheet.[63] In addition, the agreement of association may provide for a board of examiners composed of members or nonmembers.[64]

IX. The "*Sociedad Anónima*" (Corporation)

The "*sociedad anónima*" is similar to the corporation in the United States. It is the only form permitted for publicly-held companies. A separate legal entity, it may own real estate, transact business, and sue or be sued, in its own name. The liability of its shareholders is limited to the amount of their respective capital contributions.[65] Their interest in the company is represented by stock certificates and at least two shareholders are required.[66]

A. Company Name

The name of the company must be different from that of any other concern. In all cases the name must be followed by the words "*sociedad anónima*" or its abbreviation, "*S.A.*"[67]

B. Formation of the Company

Two alternative methods of forming a Mexican corporation exist. If the shares are to be privately subscribed, the incorporators, who must be shareholders, may form the company by executing the organizational

---

[62] *Id.*, Art. 76.

[63] *Id.*, Art. 78(I); Commercial Code, Art. 33.

[64] *Ley General de Sociedades Mercantiles, D.O.*, Aug. 4, 1934, as amended June 11, 1992, Art. 84.

[65] *Id.*, 87.

[66] *Id.*, Art. 89.

[67] *Id.*, Art. 88.

documents (articles of incorporation) before a notary public.[68] As indicated above, such documents must also be approved by the civil court where the company is domiciled and recorded in the Public Commercial Registry.[69]

Alternatively, a corporation may be formed through public subscription.[70] In this case, not only will it be necessary to satisfy the requirements of the Mexican securities laws, but the promoters must also record the proposed articles of incorporation and bylaws in the Public Commercial Registry.[71] Only after such recordation may the company accept subscriptions. All shares must be subscribed within one year;[72] if the shares are not fully subscribed within this period, the existing shareholders may withdraw their contribution.[73] (An exception to the rule requiring fully subscribed shares exists for companies with a "variable capital" structure. See Part X, below.)

After the capital stock has been subscribed, the promoters of the company must call a shareholders' meeting within 15 days.[74] At that meeting the shareholders shall:

(1) verify the initial payment of the stock subscription;

(2) evaluate and approve the valuation placed on contributions in kind;

(3) discuss the promoter's profit participation; and

(4) select the initial directors and "*comisario(s)*"(examiner(s)).[75]

---

[68] *Id.*, Art. 90.
[69] *Id.*, Arts. 260 *et. seq.*
[70] *Id.*, Art. 90.
[71] *Id.*, Art. 92.
[72] *Id.*, Art. 97.
[73] *Id.*, Art. 98.
[74] *Id.*, Art. 99.
[75] *Id.*, Art. 100. The *comisario* is somewhat akin to a statutorily-mandated corporate auditor.

C. The Articles of Incorporation

In addition to the data required in the organizational documents of all Mexican business entities, the articles organizing a corporation must also contain the following information:

(1) a statement as to the paid-up portion of the share capital;

(2) the number of shares, their par (or no par) value, and the characteristics of the shares into which the capital is divided;

(3) the terms and conditions under which the uncalled portion of the shares is to be paid;

(4) the participation in profits granted to the promoters;

(5) a provision for selection of one or more *comisario(s)*;

(6) the power and authorities of the shareholders when meeting together; and

(7) quorum and voting requirements for shareholders' meetings to the extent the pertinent legal provisions may be modified by agreement between the shareholders.[76]

After formation of the company has been approved at the initial shareholders' meeting, the minutes thereof and the bylaws of the company must be authenticated and registered.[77]

The articles of incorporation may be amended only at an extraordinary meeting of the shareholders called for that purpose.[78] Thereafter, such amendments must be notarized, approved by the appropriate court, and recorded in the Public Commercial Registry.

---

[76] *Id.*, Art. 91.

[77] *Id.*, Art. 101.

[78] *Id.*, Art. 182(XI).

D. Capital Requirements

The minimum capital required to form a corporation is 50 million old pesos (approximately $16,000 USD).[79] Shares may be issued in exchange for either cash or property. If a share is to be issued, in whole or part, for property, full payment must be made at the time of subscription.[80] Moreover, such shares must be deposited with the company for two years. If during this time the property is appraised at a value of less than 75 percent of the amount for which it was contributed, the shareholder must pay the corporation the difference.[81]

A share payable in cash may be paid for over time, but a down payment of at least 20 percent must be paid upon subscription.[82] Subscribers of shares that are not fully paid up remain liable for the uncalled amount for five years. Such shares must also be nominative and participate in profit distributions only in proportion to the amount that has been paid.[83] In the event of default, the company may sue to collect the difference or to sell the shares to a third party.[84]

Shares may not be issued for less than par value.[85] However, it is not necessary to place a par value on the certificates.[86] The capital may be divided into different classes of stock, but all shares within a class must be of equal value and confer equal rights on their owners.[87]

New shares of stock may not be issued until all the outstanding shares have been fully paid up.[88] Existing shareholders enjoy a preferential right to purchase new issues in proportion to their existing interests in the company.[89] When a company decides to reduce its capital

---

[79] *Id.*, Art. 89(II).
[80] *Id.*, Art. 89(IV).
[81] *Id.*, Art. 141.
[82] *Id.*, Art. 89 (III).
[83] *Id.*, Art. 117.
[84] *Id.*, Art. 118.
[85] *Id.*, Art. 115.
[86] *Id.*, Art. 125(VI).
[87] *Id.*, Art. 112.
[88] *Id.*, Art. 133.
[89] *Id.*, Art. 132.

by repurchasing shares, the selection of the shares to be redeemed is determined by a drawing in the presence of a notary public or licensed broker.[90]

E. Stock

1. Common Stock

This stock, which represents the residual ownership in the company, carries no preference in the areas of dividends or rights upon liquidation. Each share is entitled to one vote.[91] A company's capital must be represented by nominative shares.[92] A transfer of shares other than by endorsement must be recorded on the shares. The articles of incorporation may provide that the transfer of shares shall require approval of the board of directors. That board may withhold its consent and designate a purchaser for the shares at the current market price.[93]

Corporations are also required to maintain a registry of shares that contains the following information:

(1) name, nationality, and address of each stockholder;

(2) a statement of the number of shares held by each shareholder along with a description of the numbers, series, classes, etc., of such stock;

(3) a statement of the amount paid up on the shares of each stockholder; and

(4) a record of transfers of stock.[94]

---

[90] *Id.*, Art. 135.
[91] *Id.*, Art. 113.
[92] *Id.*, Art. 111.
[93] *Id.*, Art. 130.
[94] *Id.*, Art. 128.

The name recorded in the register shall be considered the owner of the nominative shares. The company must list in the registry any transfers made at the request of the holder.[95]

The bylaws may provide for annual interest payments to shareholders on their contributions. Such payments, chargeable to general expenses, may not exceed 9 percent per annum and are limited to a three-year period.[96] Attached to the stock certificate must be coupons that are used to collect dividends and interest.[97]

2. Preferred Stock

The articles of incorporation may create preferred shares that combine restricted voting rights with priorities in distribution of profits and liquidation of assets. No dividends may be declared on the common shares until a 5 percent dividend has been paid on the preferred shares. This requirement is cumulative and any shortfall must be made up in subsequent years. The articles of incorporation may also provide that holders of preferred shares will be paid a higher rate of dividends than owners of the common shares.

Despite their limited voting rights, preferred shareholders may not be deprived of the right to vote on certain major questions, such as dissolution, merger, or consolidation. Finally, preferred shareholders enjoy many of the same rights as minority shareholders, such as the right to select one director and one "*comisario*" where more than one position is being filled.[98]

3. Promoter's Certificates

The company's promoters or organizers may be granted certain rights in the future profits of the company. These rights are represented by certificates called "founders' bonds."[99] The value of these certificates is

---

[95] *Id.*, Art. 129.
[96] *Id.*, Art. 123.
[97] *Id.*, Art. 127.
[98] *Id.*, Art. 113.
[99] *Id.*, Art. 106.

not included in the company's capital; such certificates carry no rights to participate in the management of the company nor to share in the assets upon liquidation.[100] Such certificates, however, may confer upon the promoters the right to receive up to 10 percent of the company's profit for a period not in excess of ten years. No payments can be made on these certificates until the shareholders have received a 5 percent dividend on their shares.[101]

4. Redemption of Shares

When so authorized by the articles of incorporation and a resolution of a general meeting of the shareholders, a company may redeem its shares out of distributable profits. Only fully-paid shares may be redeemed. If the articles of incorporation or the shareholders' resolution provide for redemption at a fixed price, the shares to be redeemed shall be determined by a drawing before a notary public or licensed broker. The results of the drawing must be published in the official gazette of the state where the company is domiciled. As an alternative procedure, the shares to be redeemed may be purchased on the stock exchange.[102]

Such redeemed shares must be cancelled. In place of the redeemed shares, the company may issue "benefit" shares when so authorized by the articles of incorporation. These benefit shares may participate in whatever cash profits are available after payment of the stipulated dividends on the redeemable shares and may be given voting rights if so provided in the articles of incorporation. In case of liquidation, benefit shares also enjoy certain rights in the company's assets.[103]

5. Treasury Stock

Corporations may not buy their own shares except pursuant to judicial execution for payment of a debt.[104] Members of the board of directors who authorize an illegal purchase of the corporation's own stock will be

---

[100] *Id.*, Art. 107.
[101] *Id.*, Art. 105.
[102] *Id.*, Art. 136.
[103] *Id.*, Art. 137.
[104] *Id.*, Art. 134.

jointly and severally liable to the corporation and its creditors.[105] In the latter case, the company has three months within which to sell such shares; failure to do so requires that the corporation reduce its capital. While the company holds these shares, they may not be voted.[106]

G. Debentures

A Mexican corporation may also issue debentures to finance its operations. The issuance and use of debentures is governed by the General Law of Credit Instruments and Transactions of August 26, 1932, Articles 208 through 228. A 1964 amendment to that law also authorizes corporations to issue convertible debentures.

H. Governance

1. Shareholders' Meetings

The ultimate authority of the company is vested in the shareholders.[107] Shareholders' meetings are held at the company's domicile.[108] They are divided into general meetings and special meetings. If more than one class of shares exists, special meetings are held to deal with matters affecting a particular class.[109] General meetings treat subjects of interest to all classes.

General meetings are in turn divided into ordinary general meetings and extraordinary general meetings.[110] Ordinary meetings are those called to deal with any topic other than those specifically reserved for extraordinary general meetings.[111] An ordinary general meeting must be held at least once annually and within four months after the end of the fiscal year. In addition to other items on the agenda, that meeting shall approve, disapprove, or modify the balance sheet or take other

---

[105] *Id.*, Art. 138.
[106] *Id.*, Art. 134.
[107] *Id.*, Art. 178.
[108] *Id.*, Art. 179.
[109] *Id.*, Art. 195.
[110] *Id.*, Art. 180.
[111] *Id.*, Art. 180.

appropriate action, after hearing a report from the *comisario*; select the director or directors, as well as the *comisario(s)*; and set the compensation to be paid the directors and *comisario(s)* if such is not established in the bylaws.[112]

A quorum for an ordinary meeting is one half of the outstanding capital stock. A majority vote of the stock represented at the meeting is sufficient to pass a resolution.[113] If a quorum is not present at the first meeting, a second meeting shall be called at which meeting the quorum requirements are treated as waived.[114]

To constitute a quorum at an extraordinary meeting, at least three fourths of the outstanding capital stock must be represented; the articles of incorporation may require an even higher percentage.[115] If a quorum is not present at the first meeting, a second meeting may be called. Resolutions may be passed at extraordinary meetings held on the second call only if at least one half the outstanding capital shares are represented.[116]

The following matters may be dealt with only at an extraordinary general meeting of the shareholders:

(1) extension of the company's duration;

(2) dissolution of the company;

(3) an increase or decrease in capital stock;

(4) changes in the purpose or nationality of the company;

(5) a change in the basic structure or transformation of the company;

---

112 *Id.*, Art. 180.
113 *Id.*, Art. 189.
114 *Id.*, Art. 190.
115 *Id.*, Art. 191.
116 *Id.*, Art. 190.

(6) merger with another company;

(7) issuance of preferred shares;

(8) issuance of debentures;

(9) redemption by the company of its own shares and the issuance of profit sharing certificates;

(10) amendments to the articles of incorporation; and

(11) any other matter for which the law or the articles of incorporation requires a special quorum.[117]

Normally, shareholders' meetings are called by the sole director or by the board of directors; if they fail to do so, the *comisario(s)* may call a meeting.[118] In addition, shareholders representing not less than 33 percent of the company's capital may demand that a meeting be called. If both the directors and the *comisario(s)* still fail to call the meeting, the shareholders can enforce this right through court action.[119] Finally, a demand for a meeting may be made by the holder of only one share of stock, if no general meeting of shareholders has been held for two consecutive years, or if the meetings held during that time have not dealt with matters required by law to be considered at the annual general ordinary meeting.[120]

Notices of general meetings must be published at least 15 days in advance in the official gazette of the state where the corporation is domiciled or in a newspaper of wide circulation in the area. The bylaws may establish a different notice period. No personal notice is necessary. During the period of notice required before the meeting, the books of the company shall be open to inspection by the shareholders at the company's offices.[121] The notices of the meetings must contain the agenda and must

---

[117] *Id.*, Art. 182.
[118] *Id.*, Art. 183.
[119] *Id.*, Art. 184.
[120] *Id.*, Art. 185.
[121] *Id.*, Art. 186.

be signed by the person calling the meeting.[122] Any resolution passed at a meeting convoked in violation of the rules about call and notice is void, unless the entire capital stock is represented at the meeting.[123]

2. Voting

Shareholders may be represented at meetings by proxies, who need not be shareholders. Neither a director nor a *comisario* may act as a proxy.[124] A shareholder may not vote on any transaction in which he has a conflicting interest.[125] Any shareholder voting despite a conflict of interest will be liable in damages to the company if his vote was necessary to achieve the required majority for the passage of the resolution.[126] Directors and *comisarios* may not vote on questions concerning the financial report or on motions affecting their liability.[127]

3. Rights of Minority Shareholders

When there are three or more directors on the board, the minority shareholders representing 25 percent of the capital are entitled to select at least one director.[128] If, however, the corporation is listed on the stock exchange, the minority shareholders representing only 10 percent of the capital are entitled to select at least one director.[129] Shareholders representing one third of the outstanding shares may postpone the vote on any subject for three days. Such right may be exercised only once for the same matter.[130]

Shareholders representing one third of the capital may bring suit to enjoin implementation of a shareholders' resolution, if such resolution is contrary to the law or articles of incorporation. To bring such a suit, the moving parties must have either voted against the resolution or have been

---

122 *Id.*, Art. 187.
123 *Id.*, Art. 188.
124 *Id.*, Art. 192.
125 *Id.*, Art. 196.
126 *Id.*
127 *Id.*, Art. 197.
128 *Id.*, Art. 144.
129 *Id.*
130 *Id.*, Art. 198.

absent from the meeting at which it was adopted, and suit must be initiated within 15 days of the meeting at which the resolution was adopted.[131] A preliminary injunction may be issued suspending the resolution provided plaintiffs have posted a bond to cover damages to the company should the resolution be upheld.[132] In addition, the complainants must deposit their shares either with a notary public or a credit institution, such as a bank.[133]

If a shareholders' meeting approves a resolution that changes the company's purpose, its nationality, or basic structure, any dissenting shareholder may withdraw from the company. He may then compel the company to purchase his shares at their book value as shown on the last balance sheet, provided that such request is made within 15 days of the shareholders' meeting.[134]

4. The Board of Directors

One or more directors, who do not have to be shareholders, are charged with the administration of the company.[135] Frequently, this function is performed by one person, the sole director. Where there are two or more directors, they constitute a board.[136] The duties of a director are personal and may not be delegated to another.[137]

The initial directors are selected at the organizational meeting of the shareholders.[138] Unless otherwise provided in the articles, the first director selected shall serve as chairman of the board. Thereafter, directors shall be chairman in order of their entry onto the board.[139]

The time and place of meetings of the board, as well as the requirements for a call, are normally established in the articles of

---

131 *Id.*, Art. 201.
132 *Id.*, Art. 202.
133 *Id.*, Art. 205.
134 *Id.*, Art. 206.
135 *Id.*, Art. 142.
136 *Id.*, Art. 143.
137 *Id.*, Art. 147.
138 *Id.*, Art. 100.
139 *Id.*, Art. 143.

incorporation. To constitute a quorum, at least one half the directors must be present. Decisions of the board require a majority vote, and the chairman is authorized to break a tie.[140] The board may designate one of its members to implement its decisions; if no member is so named, this duty devolves on the chairman.[141]

A director who has a conflict of interest must disclose such conflict to the other directors. He is not allowed to discuss or vote on any resolution concerning that interest. Should he fail to disclose such conflict, or should he vote on such matter, he is personally liable for any loss or damages the company thereby incurs.[142]

Directors may be removed without cause at any time by the shareholders; however, the director chosen by the minority shareholders may only be removed if all the directors are removed.[143] If, after a director is removed, the number of remaining directors is sufficient to form a quorum, they may carry on the company's business until the next election. Otherwise, the *comisario(s)* shall appoint the necessary, temporary directors.[144]

5. Liability of Directors

The bylaws may require directors to post a bond as security for any liability that may be incurred while acting in their official capacity.[145] Directors are liable to the company for payment of capital contributions by the shareholders, for the lawfulness of dividends paid, for proper maintenance of the legally required books and records, and for compliance with shareholder resolutions.[146] They are also responsible for matters inherently within the scope of their authority and for obligations imposed upon them by law, the articles, and the bylaws.[147]

---

140 *Id.*
141 *Id.*, Art. 148.
142 *Id.*, Art. 156.
143 *Id.*, Art. 144.
144 *Id.*, Art. 155.
145 *Id.*, Art. 152.
146 *Id.*, Art. 158.
147 *Id.*, Art. 157.

A director, who is otherwise without fault, will be relieved of liability arising from passage of a board resolution if such director opposed it.[148] Directors are jointly liable with their predecessors for any irregularities of past directors, if the current directors discover such violations and fail to report them to the *comisarios.*[149] A general meeting of the shareholders may impose liability upon a director and designate the person to enforce such decision through court action.[150] If liability is so imposed, the director's authority immediately ceases. A director removed by the shareholders because of such liability may not be renamed as a director, unless a court finds the decision of the shareholders was without foundation.[151]

Shareholders representing at least 33 percent of the capital may also bring suit against the directors on behalf of the company, provided that the plaintiffs did not vote in favor of a shareholders' resolution absolving the directors of liability. Any property recovered in such a lawsuit belongs to the company.[152]

6. Managers

To carry on the everyday business of the company, general, as well as special managers may be elected by a general meeting of the shareholders or appointed by the board of directors. The managers do not need to be shareholders. The appointment of such managers is terminable at the will of the directors or the shareholders.[153] Once the shareholders or directors have delegated general authority to the managers, no additional authorization is required for them to carry out specific functions.[154] The bylaws may require managers to post a bond as security for any liability incurred while performing their duties.[155]

---

148 *Id.*, Art. 159.
149 *Id.*, Art. 160.
150 *Id.*, Art. 161.
151 *Id.*, Art. 162.
152 *Id.*, Art. 163.
153 *Id.*, Art. 145.
154 *Id.*, Art. 146.
155 *Id.*, Art. 152.

7. The *Comisario(s)*

The shareholders are required to select one or more *comisario(s)*, who do not have to be shareholders.[156] A *comisario* may not be an employee of the company or a close relative of any director. Moreover, a *comisario* may not be an employee of another company that owns more than 25 percent of the corporation in question. Nor may he be an employee of a company in which the corporation involved owns more than 50 percent of the shares.[157] If three or more *comisarios* are to be selected, at least one must be chosen by minority shareholders representing one fourth of the outstanding capital stock.[158]

Comisarios are charged with ensuring that managers and directors post the requisite bonds, with inspecting the books and records of the company, with reviewing the balance sheets, and generally with "unlimited surveillance" over the company. A *comisario* may call ordinary or extraordinary general meetings of shareholders at any time and is obligated to attend meetings of the board of directors.[159]

The *comisarios* must ensure that the directors submit to them a monthly financial statement.[160] The *comisarios* must submit to the shareholders' general meeting, a report commenting on the financial statements presented by management and on the policies being followed.[161] Failure to comply with these requirements is grounds for removal by the shareholders of the *comisarios* or the directors from office and may form the basis of civil liability.[162] Fifteen days after the shareholders have approved the balance sheet, it shall be published in the official gazette of the state where the company is located and recorded in the Public Commercial Registry. Where a company has offices or branches in various states, the publication must be in the *Diario Oficial* of Mexico.[163]

---

156 *Id.*, Art. 164.
157 *Id.*, Art. 165.
158 *Id.*, Art. 171.
159 *Id.*, Art. 166.
160 *Id.*
161 *Id.*
162 *Id.*, Arts. 170, 171, 176.
163 *Id.*, Art. 177.

The *comisario* has no vote. The *comisario* does not have to be an accountant, but usually is.

A *comisario* may be required by the bylaws to post a bond similar to that required for directors and managers.[164] He must abstain from participating in any transaction where he has a conflict of interest.[165] The *comisario* is personally liable if he fails to perform the duties imposed upon him by law, the articles and the bylaws.[166] A *comisario* is also liable for the irregularities of his predecessors if, upon discovery thereof, he fails to report such violations to the shareholders.[167] Any shareholders may complain to the *comisario* about an irregular act on the part of the management or the directors. At the shareholders' general meeting, the *comisario* must report such complaints and make a recommendation thereon.[168]

Although the *comisarios* may be removed without cause by the shareholders, any *comisario* chosen by the minority shareholders may be removed only if all the *comisarios* are removed.[169] If a vacancy occurs in a *comisario* position, the board of directors must within three days call a general shareholders' meeting to fill the vacancy. If the board fails to do so, any stockholders may request the appropriate court to call the meeting. Should such meeting not be held, or the vacancy not be filled, the court, upon the request of any shareholders, may appoint a *comisario* to fill the vacancy until the next general meeting of the shareholders.[170]

A general shareholders' meeting may impose liability upon a *comisario* for failure to perform his duties properly; such a resolution automatically suspends the *comisario* from office. Alteratively, a suit may be instituted by shareholders representing one third of the capital stock.[171]

---

[164] *Id.*, Art. 171.
[165] *Id.*, Art. 169.
[166] *Id.*
[167] *Id.*, Art. 171.
[168] *Id.*, Art. 167.
[169] *Id.*, Art. 171.
[170] *Id.*, Art. 168.
[171] *Id.*, Art. 171.

I. Dividends

Dividends may only be paid out of profits.[172] If there has been any loss of capital, such deficiency must be made up before any dividends can be distributed.[173] The articles may establish the method of distributing dividends among shareholders, but any stipulation excluding stockholders from participating in dividends is void.[174]

X. "*Sociedades de Capital Variable*" (Companies With Variable Capital)

Any of the business entities described above may be organized as a variable capital company. Ordinarily Mexican companies have a fixed capital. A variable capital company also has a minimum fixed capital that must be fully subscribed.[175] Nevertheless, it may also have variable capital for which shares or interest may be authorized and held by the company to be subscribed and paid for when and if needed.[176]

Where the articles of incorporation so permit, the variable portion of the capital may be increased or decreased without amending the articles,[177] but any increases or decreases must be shown in the special register kept for this purpose.[178]

Corporations and limited partnerships with shares (*sociedad en comandita por acciones*) with variable capital may not advertise an increase in capital without also setting forth the amount of the company's minimum fixed capital.[179]

A company using the variable capital structure must follow its names with the words *"capital variable"* or it's abbreviation, "C.V." For instance,

---

172 *Id.*, Art. 19.
173 *Id.*, Art. 18.
174 *Id.*, Arts. 17, 112.
175 *Id.*, Art. 217.
176 *Id.*, Art. 216.
177 *Id.*
178 *Id.*, Art. 219.
179 *Id.*, Art. 217.

a corporation with variable capital would be designated as *"sociedad anónima de capital variable"* or the initials, *"S.A. de C.V."* [180]

XI. Dissolution of Business Entities

A company must be dissolved if:

(1) the term fixed for its duration expires;

(2) the purpose for which it was formed has been fulfilled or has become impossible to fulfill;

(3) the owners, in accord with law and organizational documents, decide to dissolve the company;

(4) the number of shareholders falls below the minimum required by law or all the ownership interests become the property of one person; or

(5) the company loses two thirds of its capital.[181]

Partnerships are dissolved by the death, incapacity, exclusion, or withdrawal of any partner, unless otherwise agreed in the partnership agreement. A partnership, after death of a partner, may be continued with his heirs only if they so consent; otherwise, the deceased partner's interest must be liquidated and paid to his heirs.[182]

A dissolution must be registered in the Public Commercial Registry.[183] After dissolution, the directors or managers may not transact any new business.[184]

---

[180] *Id.*, Art. 215.
[181] *Id.*, Art. 229.
[182] *Id.*, Art. 230.
[183] *Id.*, Art. 232.
[184] *Id.*, Art. 233.

XII. Liquidation of Business Entities

Upon dissolution, a company must be wound up by liquidators who will be appointed as prescribed in the organizational documents or chosen by the owners of the company.[185] In the event a liquidator is not so selected, he may be appointed by a court upon request of an owner.[186] The selection of a liquidator must be recorded in the Commercial Public Registry.[187] Liquidators are required to collect amounts due, sell the company's property, pay all debts and distribute the remaining assets to the company's owners.[188] With respect to the liquidation of general partnerships, limited partnerships or limited liability companies, unless otherwise provided in the organizational documents, the remaining assets are distributed in accordance with a statutory schedule that provides for distribution on the basis of each owner's proportionate capital interest.[189]

XIII. Reorganizations

The 1992 amendments included two new provisions that provide previously-lacking guidance on mergers and spin-offs.

A. Mergers

Before a company can undertake a merger, the resolutions of merger must be recorded in the Public Commercial Registry. In addition, each company taking part in the proposed merger must publish its last balance sheet. Companies that will be merged into another entity must also publish their procedure for extinguishing liabilities.[190] There is a three month waiting period after registration in the Public Commercial Registry before the merger may be consummated. During this waiting period, any creditor of the companies involved in the merger may commence summary proceedings to oppose the merger, in which case the merger will be suspended until judicial authorization of the merger can be

---

185 *Id.*, Arts. 234–236.
186 *Id.*, Art. 236.
187 *Id.*, Art. 237.
188 *Id.*, Art. 242.
189 *Id.*, Arts. 246, 247.
190 *Id.*, Art. 223.

obtained. In the event that opposition to the merger is not filed within the three-month waiting period, the merger may be consummated and the resulting company will assume all rights and obligations of the companies which have been absorbed as a result of the merger.[191] However, a merger may take immediate effect upon recordation in the Public Commercial Registry if:

(1) it is stipulated that all liabilities of the merging companies are met;

(2) an amount sufficient to cover such debts is deposited in a credit institution; or

(3) the consent of all creditors is obtained.[192]

B. Spin-Offs

There are two situations in which a spin-off may occur: (1) when a company decides to dissolve and divides all or part of its assets, liabilities, and capital stock into two or more parts that are transferred to newly created companies known as beneficiary companies; or (2) when the original company transfers a portion of its assets, liabilities, and capital stock to one or more newly-created companies but does not dissolve.[193]

In order for a spin-off to occur, the shares of stock or partnership shares of the company to be spun-off must be totally paid up. Moreover, initially, each member of the original company shall hold a proportion of the capital stock of the beneficiary companies equal to that which is held in the original company.[194]

A spin-off must be approved by the required voting margin of shareholders or partners necessary to amend the articles of association.[195]

---

[191] *Id.*, Art. 224.
[192] *Id.*, Art. 225.
[193] *Id.*, Art. 228.
[194] *Id.*
[195] *Id.*

Any shareholder or partner who votes against the resolution of spin-off shall have the right to withdraw from the company. Any shareholder exercising such withdrawal right may then compel the company to purchase his shares at their book value as shown on the last balance sheet, provided that such request is made within 15 days of the meeting in which the resolution of spin-off is adopted.[196]

The resolution of the shareholders or partners approving the spin-off must contain:

(1) a description of the form, time frame and manner in which the various assets, liabilities and capital stock shall be transferred;

(2) a description of the portions of the assets, liabilities and capital stock which will be transferred to each beneficiary company as well as a description of those portions which will remain with the original company, if applicable;

(3) financial statements certified by an external auditor of the original company which include at a minimum the transactions carried out during the last fiscal year;

(4) a statement of the obligations which each beneficiary company will assume as a result of the spin-off;[197] and

(5) a draft of the bylaws of the beneficiary companies.[198]

The resolution of spin-off must be notarized and recorded in the Public Commercial Registry, the Official Gazette and a periodical of widespread circulation within the domicile of the original company. In

---

[196] *Id.*

[197] If a beneficiary company fails to comply with any of the obligations assumed as a result of the spin-off, all beneficiary companies will be jointly and severally liable up to the amount of the net assets allotted to the company as a result of the spin-off with all other beneficiary companies to creditors who did not consent to the spin-off for a period of three years after publication of the resolution approving the spin-off in the Public Commercial Registry. If the original company still exists, it shall be liable for the entire obligation. *Id.*

[198] *Id.*

addition, a summary of the resolution must be kept in the business domicile of the company and made available to associates and creditors for a period of 45 days from the date of registration of the resolution and publication of the resolution in the Official Gazette and a periodical of widespread circulation. This summary must contain, at a minimum, a description of the form, time frame and manner in which the various assets, liabilities and capital stock shall be transferred by the original company as well as a description of the obligations that each beneficiary company will assume as a result of the spin-off.[199]

During the 45-day period in which a summary of the resolution of spin-off is available for inspection at the business domicile of the company, a creditor or any member or group of members representing at least 20 percent of the capital stock of the company may judicially contest the spin-off. In the event of such a contest, the spin-off shall be suspended until judicial authorization is received or an agreement is reached; provided, however, that the contesting party must post a bond in an amount sufficient to cover any damages that may be sustained by the company as a result of the delay in effecting the spin-off.[200]

Once all requirements are fulfilled, if the 45-day inspection period has elapsed without contest by any party, the spin-off may be consummated. The bylaws of the beneficiary companies which are formed as a result of the spin-off must be registered with the Public Commercial Registry. If the spin-off is to result in the dissolution of the original company, a request to cancel the articles of association of the original company must be filed with the Public Commercial Registry once the spin-off has been effected.[201]

---

[199] *Id.*

[200] *Id.*

[201] *Id.*

CHAPTER 7

Export Promotion Programs*

Lic. Carlos Angulo
Angulo, Calvo, Enriquez y Gonzalez, S.C.

Lic. Jorge Vazquez
Barrera, Siqueiros y Torres Landa, S.C.

Export promotion programs have been a part of the Mexican landscape at least since World War II. These programs took on a new level of prominence in 1965 when Mexico introduced its "Border Industrialization Program." While the "maquiladora" program has attracted the most attention, other export promotion programs exist can provide foreign investors with important benefits.

Mexico's export promotion programs are an important part of Mexico's economy. They are a source of employment and training for Mexican nationals, a vehicle for the development and transfer of technology, and a generator of foreign currency. The maquiladora program alone currently includes more than 2,155 establishments, employing approximately 544,500 workers.

The advent of the North American Free Trade Agreement ("NAFTA") has impacted, but in no way eliminated, the export promotion programs.

* This chapter was edited by William E. Mooz, Jr.

I. The Maquiladora Program

A. What Is a Maquiladora?

A maquiladora company is a Mexican company operating under a program of special customs treatment. This special customs treatment permits the company to temporarily import into Mexico machinery, equipment, replacement parts, raw materials, and, in general, everything needed to carry out its production activities. Because the import is a temporary one, it is exempt from customs duties.

A number of restrictions apply to companies operating as maquiladoras. For example, due to the existing high level of industrialization and congestion, maquiladoras cannot be located in Mexico City and its suburbs. This restriction, however, does not apply to already-existing companies that intend to perform maquiladora activities with their idle production capability, or to companies that do not generate pollution in their production processes.

Prior to NAFTA, maquiladoras were required to export all of their production. This requirement served to protect Mexican industry and to justify the exemption from customs that maquiladoras receive. Nevertheless, even prior to NAFTA, maquiladoras could, under certain conditions, sell their products in the Mexican market in quantities representing up to 50 percent of the value of their exports during the preceding 12 months, provided that a permit for such sales is obtained from the Ministry of Commerce and Industrial Promotion ("SECOFI").

With the passage of NAFTA, the mandatory export requirement has been softened somewhat. Beginning in 1994, a maquiladora may sell domestically 55 percent of the total value of its annual exports for the previous year. This 55 percent limitation is increased by an additional 5 percent each year through the year 2000, with such limitations being removed entirely by the year 2001. Local sales by maquiladoras must be reported bi-monthly to SECOFI.

B. Requirements to Qualify as a Maquiladora Company

In addition to the standard requirements associated with forming any company in Mexico, maquiladora companies must apply for and obtain what is called a Maquiladora Working Program ("*Programade Maquila*"). This Program is a document containing general data of the maquiladora company, describing the manufacturing process, and setting forth the characteristics of the products that the maquiladora will manufacture. The Program also contains a listing of the necessary equipment and raw materials to be temporarily imported into Mexico or bought in the Mexican market, states the amount of labor to be employed, and describes the company's export program.

Maquiladora Working Programs must be approved by SECOFI. This approval may be obtained locally, since SECOFI has offices in all major cities where maquiladoras are located. Applications filed with SECOFI will be carefully analyzed. SECOFI will inform the customs authorities when a maquiladora application has been approved so that the maquiladora may import the covered items into Mexico on a temporary basis. When a Maquiladora Working Program is approved, the applicant receives a Maquiladora Registry Number. This number must be used in any and all governmental matters.

C. Temporary Importations

As mentioned above, the distinctive characteristic of any maquiladora company in Mexico is that it is capable of importing, on a temporary basis, machinery and equipment, replacement parts, raw materials, and in general, anything needed to carry out its activities and fulfill its production goals, without paying the otherwise-applicable customs duties.

It should be noted that in order to carry out the importation procedures, a customs broker, or an attorney-in-fact for customs purposes, must handle such matters in the name and on behalf of the maquiladora company. In keeping with the temporary nature of the importations by maquiladora companies, Mexican Customs requires the posting of a bond or similar collateral to guarantee that the temporarily imported items leave the country in due time.

Effective as of July 1, 1988, the relevant authorities issued a general ruling exempting importations of raw materials from the requirement of posting a bond or collateral. Instead, the maquiladora company may deliver a "guaranty letter," whereby the company formally agrees to re-export the raw materials when the prescribed time arrives or to pay the applicable duties. In general terms, there are three types of temporary importations related to maquiladora companies:

(1) initial importations, which are those authorized for the initiation of the Maquiladora Working Program;

(2) subsequent importations, which are those necessary to continue fulfilling the Maquiladora Working Program; and

(3) emergency importations, which are those imports needed at any given moment, that are not included in the Maquiladora Working Program.

Specifically, Mexico's customs regulations provide for the following temporary imports by a maquiladora company:

(1) raw and auxiliary materials required for the fulfillment of the manufacturing or assembly operations, pursuant to an approved Maquiladora Working Program and any additions or increases thereto;

(2) machinery, apparatuses, instruments, and equipment necessary to carry out manufacturing or assembly operations, together with those required for the quality control of its products;

(3) spare parts for the items referred to in the foregoing subsection;

(4) tools and ancillary production and safety equipment, as well as environmental pollution control devices, telecommunication and computing equipment, work manuals, and industrial blueprints; and

(5) containers, trailers, packaging material, tags, and pamphlets.

D. Other Authorizations

Obtaining an approved Maquiladora Working Program simply means that a company has qualified for treatment as a maquiladora. As with any other company, it may require additional authorizations in order to conduct its intended operations. Such authorizations may include environmental permits, among others.

II. The PITEX Program

The "PITEX" program is an export promotion program regulated by the Decree to Establish Temporary Importation Programs to Produce Goods to be Exported, dated May 3, 1990. Authorization to operate under a PITEX program must be obtained from SECOFI. Both existing Mexican companies, and companies to be established in Mexico, are eligible to obtain this authorization so long as they meet one of the following two criteria:

(1) the company exports, directly or through third parties, more than 10 percent of its net sales; or

(2) the company's exports are at least US$500,000 annually.

A. General Requirements and Benefits

The PITEX program offers differing levels of benefits, with access to a certain level of benefits being dependent upon compliance with various threshold requirements. The more important of these benefits, and the corresponding requirements, are set forth below. The actual level of benefits authorized will appear in the company-specific PITEX plan approved by SECOFI.

(1) All companies that meet either of the eligibility criteria for the PITEX program will be allowed to temporarily import a number of items. These items include raw materials, parts, components, packing materials, containers, fuel, tools, auxiliaries, and other materials to be used or consumed directly in the production process for goods to be exported.

(2) Companies with annual exports equaling at least 30 percent of their total sales will be allowed to temporarily import a number of additional items, including machinery, equipment, instruments, tools, molds, equipment and accessories for industrial security, or quality control, communications equipment, computers, and training of personnel and others related directly with the production process of the goods to be exported.

As with the maquiladora program, the advantage of importing goods temporarily is that the importing company does not have to pay import duties on the goods imported. All goods imported temporarily under a PITEX program may stay in Mexico during the term of the PITEX program. The initial term of a PITEX program is five years. Upon compliance with the requirements of SECOFI and the program itself, a PITEX program may be extended for one or more five-year terms.

In order to prove their compliance with the terms of the PITEX program, companies operating under a PITEX program must submit to SECOFI reports of their exports made under the PITEX program. These reports must be filed during the months of January and July of each year.

B. Sales Into the Mexican Market

A company authorized to operate under a PITEX program is not required to export 100 percent of its production. It also may sell in Mexico goods produced or manufactured with the materials imported under the PITEX program, subject to certain limitations. These limitations include a ceiling on such sales equal to 30 percent of the exports made under the PITEX program, and a requirement that the company obtain the prior authorization of SECOFI to permanently import the inputs used in this production and pay the corresponding import duties.

III. Impact of NAFTA on Export Promotion Programs

Mexico's export promotion programs have been overtaken somewhat by NAFTA. The primary benefit offered by these programs is the ability to temporarily import the equipment and materials used in production without having to pay import duties. NAFTA erodes this benefit by eliminating virtually all tariffs between the member countries of NAFTA over a 15-year period. As NAFTA's schedule of tariff reductions take effect, the ability to temporarily import goods into Mexico duty-free becomes less important.

NAFTA, however, does not reduce all tariffs to zero overnight, and NAFTA's tariff reductions apply only to goods that are "sourced" to a member country. Thus, Mexico's export promotion programs will be of continued significance over the short run, and for companies needing to import goods sourced to countries other than the United States and Canada.

Over the long run, the maquiladora and PITEX programs have the potential to serve as a facilitating vehicle for taking advantage of the comparative advantages of the three NAFTA countries. Japan now produces approximately 35 percent of its export goods through similar production sharing arrangements with countries such as Malaysia and Thailand. By contrast, such arrangements currently account for approximately 5 percent of the U.S. production of export goods.

CHAPTER 8

U.S. Tax Considerations for Doing Business in Mexico*

Randolph M. Karsh, Esq.
Holland & Hart

I. Overview

A. Scope of Discussion

This chapter will address U.S. income tax issues that are likely to be encountered by a U.S. business when it chooses to operate in Mexico. The discussion assumes that the business to be conducted will be an active trade or business and that the income derived from the Mexican business operations will not be attributable to passive activities. Therefore, the U.S. tax rules concerning foreign personal holding companies and passive foreign investment companies are beyond the scope of this discussion.[1] In addition, the discussion that follows assumes that the U.S. business desiring to conduct business in Mexico is a U.S. corporation. With few exceptions, the applicable rules for U.S. and Mexican taxation are the same for individuals.

---

1 See generally Sections 551–558, 1296 of the Internal Revenue Code of 1986, as amended (hereinafter "IRC").

B. Sources of Law

1. U.S. Provisions

The controlling rules for imposition of U.S. income taxation are contained in the Internal Revenue Code of 1986, as amended (the "Code") and as interpreted by the U.S. Treasury Department and the federal courts of the United States who have jurisdiction over federal tax matters. Administration and enforcement of U.S. domestic tax law is generally performed by or under the supervision of the Secretary of the Treasury who in turn has the power to delegate to the Commissioner of Internal Revenue.[2]

2. Mexican Provisions

The rules for imposition of Mexico's domestic tax are generally set out in the *Ley del Impuesto Sobre la Renta ("LISR")*, supplemented by regulations.[3] The Mexican agency in charge of applying, interpreting and enforcing the *LISR* is the *Secretaria de Hacienda y Credito Publico* (the "*Hacienda*").

3. Tax Treaty

In addition to the above primary law sources, the U.S. taxation of cross-border operations in Mexico are to a great extent affected by the Income Tax Convention between the Government of the United States of America and the Government of the United Mexican States which, with Protocols attached, became effective as of January 1, 1994 (the "Treaty").[4] The principal purposes of the Treaty are to reduce or eliminate double taxation of income earned by residents of either country from sources within the other country, and to prevent income tax avoidance or evasion. The Treaty is intended to promote close economic

---

[2] IRC §§ 7801 and 7802.

[3] See Ch. 9 for a general discussion of Mexico's domestic tax laws.

[4] For a general discussion and interpretation of the Treaty, see Joint Committee on Taxation, *Explanation of Proposed Income Tax Treaty (and Proposed Protocol) between the United States and Mexico* (JCS–16–93), Oct. 26, 1993; and *Treasury Department Technical Explanation of U.S.–Mexico Income Tax Treaty* (Nov. 30, 1993).

cooperation between the two countries, and to eliminate possible trade barriers caused by their overlapping taxing jurisdiction.

C. Scope of U.S. Taxation

1. General Principle of U.S. Taxation

The controlling principle of U.S. taxation is that a "U.S. person," be it an individual or some form of business entity, is taxed on its worldwide income, no matter where derived.[5] The operative rules for U.S. taxation of foreign source income derived by foreign entities controlled by U.S. persons do not offer a significant opportunity to "avoid" U.S. taxes. Often the most effective tax planning for U.S. taxpayers dictates a game-plan designed to avoid double taxation whereby the U.S. taxpayer will generally attempt to defer recognition of U.S. taxation, and if deferral cannot be achieved and double taxation is imposed, then effective utilization of the foreign tax credit becomes imperative.

2. Common Tax Objectives

The tax objectives of the U.S. taxpayer include: avoidance of U.S. tax on the formation and funding of the Mexican operations; minimization of taxation by Mexico of the income attributable to the foreign operations; the utilization of losses from the foreign operation; avoidance of current U.S. taxation of the Mexican source income; utilization in the U.S. of the foreign tax credit for taxes imposed by Mexico on the foreign source income; and, the minimization of U.S. taxes on the repatriation of the income or assets attributable to the Mexican operations. In addition, if funds are borrowed to finance the foreign operations, consideration should be given to means of fully deducting any interest payable on such borrowings and the avoidance of complexity in the structuring of such borrowings. Realization of these tax objectives to a large extent depends upon choosing the proper form of entity for conducting the foreign operations which requires a consideration of both the tax and business aspects of the different business forms. Both aspects will be affected not only by U.S. law, but also by Mexican law, and the

---

[5] See Treasury Regulations § 1.1–1(b) (hereinafter "Treas. Reg.").

Treaty will also affect the tax considerations in choosing the form of business entity.

D. Choice of Entity

The entity chosen by a U.S. business to conduct operations in Mexico will not normally affect the manner in which Mexico will tax such business operations because under the *LISR* the entity will be treated as a separate enterprise subject to the current Mexican income tax rate of 34 percent.[6] In addition, because Mexico operates under an integrated tax system, the distribution of after-tax profits to the equity owners of the Mexican enterprise will not be subject to a second level of taxation. However, the characterization of the Mexican entity will affect the manner in which the U.S. equity owner will be taxed under the Code. Given Mexico's taxation of corporations and partnerships as entities separate and apart from their equity owners, it is even possible to have a "hybrid" entity whereby the Mexican operations would be taxed as a corporation under Mexican domestic law, and treated as a partnership for U.S. tax purposes. There are a number of advantages and disadvantages to such partnership classification.

1. Advantages

As a partnership, the losses of the Mexican enterprise can be passed through directly to the U.S. equity owner and claimed as a deduction on its U.S. income tax return, thereby offsetting or reducing its overall U.S. taxable income.[7] Similarly, if the Mexican entity is profitable, the net income derived therefrom would pass through to the U.S. equity owner and be offset by losses incurred by such owner from other business sources. The character of the losses and the income would be retained when passed through to the U.S. owner.[8] Thus, partnership classification permits the U.S. equity owner to achieve consolidated reporting with a foreign entity, even though the U.S. owner may own less than 80 percent

---

[6] See Ch. 9.

[7] IRC §702(a).

[8] IRC § 702(b).

of such foreign entity.[9] In addition, partnership classification eliminates certain complexities with respect to the ability of a U.S. parent corporation to claim the foreign tax credit attributable to Mexican taxes paid. Under U.S. tax principles, the credit is directly passed through to the members of the partnership, each of whom may separately elect the allowance of same.[10]

2. Disadvantages

Income of a foreign corporation generally is not recognized until distributed, unless special rules come into play.[11] However, partnership income is required to be recognized currently and thus control over the timing of recognition is difficult to achieve. In addition, certain expenses incurred in Mexico would be subjected to special limitations, thereby limiting the deductions allowable for U.S. tax purposes. For example, restrictions are placed on the deductibility of intangible drilling costs, and foreign mining exploration and development expenses;[12] depreciation would be allowable over a longer recovery period;[13] certain foreign deductions would either be subject to recapture or reclassification as U.S. source income;[14] and, if the partner has an overall foreign loss, or is in an excess foreign tax credit position, it may not fully benefit from the pass through of deductions.[15] Finally, in order to take advantage of certain elections and to properly determine the income of a U.S. partner, the foreign partnership may be required to file a U.S. income tax return.[16]

---

[9] Generally, a U.S. corporation may not file a consolidated return with a foreign entity. IRC § 1504(a). But see, IRC § 1504(d).

[10] IRC § 703(b)(3).

[11] See Part III.D, *infra*.

[12] IRC §§ 263(i), 616(d), and 617(h).

[13] IRC § 168(g)(i)(a)(4).

[14] IRC §§ 904(f), 907.

[15] IRC § 904(f).

[16] IRC §§ 703(b), 6031; Reg. § 1.6031–1(d)(2); *Atlantic Veneer Corp. v. Commissioner*, 812 F.2d 158 (4th Cir. 1987). See also, Prop. Reg. § 1.6031–1(d)(2), which would require a foreign partnership to file a U.S. return if 25% or more of the foreign partnership's income is allocable to U.S. partners.

E. Capitalization of Foreign Operations

1. Transfer of U.S.-Based Assets

Once the entity form has been selected, the mere starting up of the foreign entity can yield some unexpected tax results because the Code reflects a philosophy designed to protect the erosion of the U.S. tax base. The Code is concerned that an outbound transfer of appreciated U.S.-based assets could present an opportunity to avoid U.S. taxes on the initial transfer and, absent an obligation to repatriate, the U.S. might never get its fair share of income taxes. In the formation of domestic businesses, IRC §§ 351 and 721 generally apply to yield nonrecognition of gain for incorporation of U.S. businesses and formation of U.S. partnerships. However, the nonrecognition rules for transfers to foreign entities are more restrictive. Here, the general rule calls either for gain recognition or imposition of an excise tax on the outbound transfer, with a few specified exceptions.[17] In addition, repatriation of assets either through current distributions or distributions upon dissolution can also result in income recognition to the U.S. owner of the foreign entity.

2. Capitalization With Debt

Prior to the effective date of the Treaty, it was common to avoid capitalizing a Mexican subsidiary with debt. At that time, inflation rates in Mexico were high, and accordingly any deduction for interest was limited since under Mexican law an interest deduction is reduced by an inflation factor. In addition, without the Treaty, the withholding tax on interest was 35 percent. *LISR* § 154(III). However, a shareholder's basis in its stock is increased for inflation. *LISR* § 19. Thus, capitalizing a Mexican subsidiary with equity rather than debt results in a lower gain upon the eventual sale of the stock in the subsidiary. Recently, however, inflation rates have declined to single digits, and the Treaty has reduced the withholding tax on interest to 15 percent in most cases.[18] Although it may generally be better to capitalize a Mexican subsidiary with equity, these changes will require an in-depth analysis before the best method of capitalization can be selected.

---

[17] IRC §§ 367, 1491.

[18] Treaty, Art. 11(2)(c).

II. Branch Operations

A. Noncomplexity

From a U.S. tax perspective, creation of a Mexican branch is the least complicated form of doing business. Because a branch is part of the same corporate entity, the U.S. taxpayer can transfer appreciated property to the branch without triggering any U.S: tax consequences. Similarly, the repatriation of assets to the U.S. at a later date is not likely to result in a U.S. taxable event.

1. Mexican Taxation

In general, the branch operations income would be subject to Mexican taxation at the normal business tax rate of 34 percent. Mexican branches of U.S. corporations are not presently subject to a branch profits tax on earnings remitted to its home office.

2. Mexican Deduction Limitations

Under the LISR, branches of foreign companies are not generally permitted to deduct royalties, fees or interest payments made to their home office.[19] However, the Treaty permits a permanent establishment to deduct such expenses to the extent the payments reimburse actual expenses of the home office.[20] Nonetheless, subject to Mexican transfer pricing limitations, it may be possible to structure transactions with the home office so that payments abroad may constitute fully deductible expenses. For example, the interposition of an intermediary foreign affiliate could yield a full deduction, although such payments would then be subjected to a Mexican withholding tax as well as potential taxation in the intermediary's host country.

3. U.S. Taxation

Because a U.S. corporation is taxed by the U.S. on its worldwide income, no matter how derived, the branch operations income would be

---

[19] *LISR* § 23.

[20] Treaty, Art. 7(3).

included in the U.S. corporation's gross income and thereby potentially subjected to double tax absent the availability of the foreign tax credit. Operation through a branch can offer a distinct advantage because any taxable losses that the Mexican branch incurs in its start-up years can be used to offset income from the U.S. corporation's profitable U.S. operations. However, U.S. corporations which are part of a consolidated group should carefully review whether the use of such losses may be disallowed in the U.S. under IRC § 1503(d)[c] dealing with dual consolidated losses.[21]

4. Scope of Mexican Audit

Even though for U.S. tax purposes the branch is the least complicated of the entity choices, it may yield some undesirable complications or results. For example, because the branch will cause the U.S. corporation to be engaged in a business within Mexico, this will require the U.S. corporation to file a Mexican tax return, and may subject the U.S. corporation's books and records to scrutiny by Mexican tax authorities. In addition, engagement by the U.S. corporation of a business in Mexico could cause some of the U.S. corporation's investment or portfolio income to become taxable by Mexico to the extent such income is associated with the branch operations.

B. Incorporation of Branch

The subsequent incorporation of a Mexican branch is a taxable event in Mexico. In addition, incorporation would result in U.S. gain recognition to the extent branch historical losses have exceeded the branch's historical taxable income.[22] Therefore, if a branch is used, the branch may be incorporated free of U.S. tax once the branch's income equals or exceeds its prior losses.

---

[21] See Treas. Reg. § 1.1503–2A.

[22] IRC § 367(a)(3)(C).

III. Mexican Subsidiary of U.S. Corporation

A. Gain Recognition on Capitalization

Operation through a Mexican subsidiary brings into play special Code rules applicable to the contribution of appreciated property to the subsidiary. The starting point is IRC § 367(a), which provides that the general nonrecognition provisions of IRC Subchapter C do not apply to foreign corporations. Therefore, the affected transactions include not only incorporation transactions, but also liquidations and reorganizations of the foreign subsidiary.[23] Obviously, of special concern to a start-up operation is the potential IRC § 367(a) override of IRC § 351, the latter of which ordinarily results in nonrecognition of gain or loss on the contribution of property to a controlled corporation.

1. Avoidance of Gain Recognition

Subject to a number of special rules and exceptions, assets may generally be transferred tax-free to a Mexican corporation if the IRC § 351 principles are otherwise satisfied, and the assets are used by the corporation in the active conduct of a trade or business outside the United States.[24] This test for nonrecognition is applied on an asset-by-asset basis and, therefore, even though the Mexican corporation may engage in an active trade or business, it must be shown that the specific asset will in fact be used in that business.[25] However, even if the asset is used in the active conduct of a trade or business, certain "tainted" assets do not qualify for nonrecognition treatment, e.g., inventory, accounts receivable, installment obligations, certain leased property, foreign currency, and intangible property.[26] Finally, to obtain Section 351 treatment for qualifying assets, the U.S. parent must comply with the reporting requirements of IRC § 6038B.[27] The transferor's failure to comply with the information reporting requirements will result in the imposition of a

---

[23] See IRC §§ 332, 354, 356, and 361.
[24] IRC § 367(a)(3)(A).
[25] Temp. Reg. § 1.367(a)–2(T)(b)(5).
[26] IRC § 367(a)(3)(B).
[27] Temp. Reg. § 1.367(a)–2T(a)(2).

penalty equal to 25 percent of the amount of the gain realized on the exchange, unless reasonable cause is shown for such failure.[28]

2. Loss Recognition and Asset Basis

As previously indicated, the purpose of IRC § 367(a) essentially is to prohibit the use of IRC § 351 to remove appreciated assets from the U.S. tax base. It should be noted that while the Section 367(a) override requires the recognition of built-in gains, it does not allow the recognition of built-in losses. In addition, while the Internal Revenue Service ("IRS")[29] has ruled that the foreign corporation is entitled to a basis step-up for gain recognized by the U.S. transferor,[30] this may be of questionable value if the Mexican tax laws do not recognize such basis step-up.

3. Intangibles

If intangibles are transferred, IRC § 367(d) displaces the general recognition rule of IRC § 367(a) which imposes one-time gain recognition. Under IRC § 367(d), a U.S. corporation transferring the intangible to the Mexican corporation is treated as having sold the property in exchange for a series of payments contingent upon the productivity, use, or disposition of the property.[31] Furthermore, the amount of the deemed payments shall be "commensurate with the income attributable to the intangible," thereby resulting in the direct imputation to the U.S. parent of the income produced during the life of the intangible.[32] Finally, the payments includible in the U.S. parent's income by reason of IRC § 367(d) are treated as U.S.-source ordinary income.[33] Avoiding the impact of IRC § 367(d) requires consideration of alternative means for transferring the assets to the Mexican corporation, which could include the sale of technology at a fixed price, a deferred payment sale, or a licensing arrangement.

---

[28] IRC § 6038B(b)(1).

[29] The IRS has the duty of interpreting and enforcing the U.S. tax laws.

[30] Rev. Rul. 78–201, 1978–1 C.B. 91.

[31] IRC § 367(d)(2)(A)(i).

[32] See IRC § 367(d)(2)(A)(ii).

[33] IRC § 367(d)(2)(C).

B. Mexican Taxation

The Mexican corporation will automatically be subject to Mexican taxation on its worldwide income.[34]

C. U.S. Tax Consolidation

Generally, foreign corporations are not permitted to join with their U.S. affiliated corporations in filing consolidated income tax returns.[35] Therefore, under normal circumstances the U.S. parent of a Mexican subsidiary corporation is precluded from utilizing any operational losses which may be incurred by the Mexican subsidiary, and is not entitled to a direct pass through of the foreign tax credit for Mexican taxes paid by the subsidiary when the business operations turn profitable. However, an exception is allowed under IRC § 1504(d), which permits the filing of a consolidated return for Mexican corporations wholly owned by a U.S. parent corporation if the Mexican corporation is organized and maintained "solely for the purpose of complying with the [Mexican] laws . . . as to title and operation of property . . . ." If these circumstances exist, then the U.S. parent corporation may elect to treat the Mexican subsidiary as a domestic corporation for tax purposes and include its operations in a consolidated return filed by the U.S. parent. Recent revisions to Mexico's Foreign Investment Law[36] have eliminated substantially all of such property ownership restrictions and will diminish the significance of a Section 1504(d) election. However, the election will remain of value as long as certain activity specific Mexican laws require the use of a Mexican corporation, e.g., the mining law which requires a Mexican corporation to be formed in order to achieve 100 percent ownership of mining concessions in Mexico.[37]

---

[34] *LISR* § 1–II. For a discussion of the Mexican taxation of Mexican corporations, see Ch. 9.

[35] IRC § 1504(b)(3).

[36] *Ley de Inversion Extranjera,* published in the *Diario Oficial* on Dec. 28, 1993.

[37] Mining Law of Mexico § 10.

D. Potential U.S. Taxation of Mexican Corporate Income—Subpart F Rules

Normally the income of a Mexican corporation will not be subject to U.S. taxation unless it has business activities or other operations in the United States.[38] However, assuming the Mexican corporation is a wholly-owned[39] subsidiary of a U.S. parent, under the Code the Mexican corporation will be classified as a Controlled Foreign Corporation ("CFC").[40] As a CFC, for U.S. tax purposes the U.S. parent could be subject to immediate U.S. taxation on the combined amount of the subsidiary's "Subpart F income," the investment of the subsidiary's earnings in U.S. property, and the subsidiary's "956A amount."[41] This inclusion takes place even though the U.S. parent does not receive any distributions from the subsidiary. The CFC's income is included in the U.S. shareholder's return as a dividend which does not qualify for the dividend deduction otherwise available to corporations.[42] The U.S. shareholder is allowed to adjust its basis in the subsidiary corporation's stock resulting from this inclusion of CFC income.[43]

---

[38] See IRC §§ 881 and 882.

[39] Technically, under Mexican corporate law, there cannot be a "wholly-owned" subsidiary corporation because the formation and maintenance of corporate status requires no less than two shareholders. See *Ley General de Sociedades Mercantiles* § 6I. Compliance with this rule can be achieved by having a related or controlled party of the U.S. corporation serve as the second shareholder.

[40] A CFC is defined as any foreign corporation in which more than 50% of the total combined voting power or value of all classes of stock is owned by "United States shareholders" on any day during the corporation's tax year. IRC § 957(a)(1) and (a)(2). A "United States shareholder" is a U.S. person who owns 10% or more of all classes of such stock. IRC § 951(b).

[41] This rule of inclusion applies to any U.S. person who owns or is considered as owning 10% or more of the total combined voting power of all classes of voting stock. IRC § 951(b).

[42] IRC § 245.

[43] IRC § 961.

1. Subpart F Component

The includible Subpart F income consists of a number of different items,[44] the broadest category being "foreign base company income," which includes the following items:

(1) *Foreign Personal Holding Company Income*—generally includes all forms of passive income, *e.g.*, dividends, interests, rents, royalties, foreign currency gains, and similar items.[45]

(2) *Foreign Base Company Sales Income*—includes profits, commissions, and other income or gain derived in connection with the purchase and sale of personal property by, from, or on behalf of a related person, but only if the property purchased or sold (as the case may be), is manufactured, produced, grown or extracted outside of Mexico and such property is sold for use, consumption or disposition outside of Mexico.[46]

(3) *Foreign Base Company Services Income*—includes income derived in connection with the performance of technical, managerial, engineering, architectural, scientific, skilled, industrial, commercial or like services performed by, for, or on behalf of a related party and outside of Mexico.[47] Such a situation could arise whenever the Mexican corporation provides, for example, warranty services on behalf of its U.S. parent for products sold to customers outside of Mexico.

(4) *Industry Oriented Subpart F Income*—which is an all inclusive category consisting of insurance income,[48] foreign base shipping company income,[49] and oil and gas income derived from the manufacture and distribution of oil and gas products outside the

---

[44] Also included are certain illegal payments under the Foreign Corrupt Practices Act of 1977, certain income from countries engaged in international boycotts, insurance income related to U.S. risks, and foreign base company income. IRC § 952.

[45] IRC § 954(c).

[46] IRC § 954(d).

[47] IRC § 954(e).

[48] IRC § 953(a)(1)(A), 952(a)(1).

[49] IRC § 954(f).

United States, unless such products are extracted from or used in the foreign country.[50]

The Code grants two exceptions for inclusion of the Foreign Base Company Income. The first is a "de minimis" exception, which generally provides that if the foreign base income is less than the lesser of 5 percent of the Mexican corporation's gross income or $1 million then no part of the Mexican gross income will be treated as foreign base company income.[51] The second exception applies whenever it is established that the income was subject to creditable income taxes imposed by Mexico at an effective rate that is greater than 90 percent of the maximum U.S. corporate tax rate, then at the election of the U.S. parent the foreign base company income will be excluded from the computation of Subpart F income.[52] The current Mexican business tax rate of 34 percent would certainly qualify for this second exception.[53]

2. Investment in U.S. Property

The second category of income inclusion consists of an increase of investments by the CFC in U.S. property, to the extent the amount would have been a dividend if distributed.[54] This increase is measured by the excess of the level of investment in U.S. property at the end of the taxable year over the level of investment in U.S. property at the end of the previous taxable year, reduced by certain distributions made during the year.[55] Such reinvestment can take on many indirect forms, such as the acquisition of tangible personal property or stock of U.S. corporations, loans from the CFC to the U.S. parent corporation, any right to use certain of the CFC's intangible assets in the U.S., and guarantees and pledges by the CFC of the U.S. parent's debt. The breadth of this rule effectively precludes attempts to avoid U.S. taxation by failing to have the CFC pay dividends to the U.S. parent. Presently, the comparability

---

[50] IRC § 954(g).

[51] IRC § 954(b)(3)(A).

[52] IRC § 954(b)(4), Temp. Reg. § 1.954–1T(d)(1).

[53] See *Ley del Impuesto Sobre la Renta, Articulo 10,* as amended.

[54] IRC § 956(a)(1).

[55] IRC § 956(a)(2).

of the Mexican tax rates and the indirect foreign tax credit eliminate the need of U.S. corporation's to utilize such schemes.

3. The 956A Amount

The third includible component consists of the value of the CFC's "excess passive assets."[56] The "excess" is the amount by which the CFC's passive assets exceed 25 percent of the corporation's assets. Once this threshold is reached, the U.S. parent is required to annually include as dividend income the lesser of its pro rata share of (i) the "excess" amount, or (ii) the CFC's post-September 30, 1993 earnings.

4. Impact on U.S. Foreign Tax Credit

Although the Mexican subsidiary CFC status might preclude the deferral of U.S. income taxes on the Mexican corporation's Subpart F income, this can be beneficial for foreign tax credit purposes because even though the CFC income is treated as a dividend, the foreign tax credit "basket" is determined by looking through to the Mexican corporation's underlying operations. Thus, for example, if the Mexican corporation is engaged in the manufacture of products, the deemed dividends from the Mexican corporation would be placed in the U.S. parent's "general" basket rather than in its "passive" basket.[57]

E. Foreign Sales Corporation

Under the U.S. tax laws, a foreign sales corporation ("FSC") is a foreign corporation engaged in selling U.S.-made goods outside the United States. If numerous qualification rules are met,[58] a portion of the FSC's income is exempt from current U.S. taxation and can be distributed to a corporate U.S. shareholder without the imposition of a U.S. tax. Even though the United States and Mexico have entered into the Treaty and entered into an exchange of information agreement addressing

---

[56] IRC § 956A.

[57] IRC § 904(d)(3).

[58] See IRC § 922.

enforcement of their tax laws,[59] which agreements would appear to meet the exchange of information Code requirement imposed upon FSCs,[60] at the present time the comparability of the Mexican and U.S. business tax rates do not appear to justify the use of a FSC. In addition, even without such comparability of tax rates, one might question whether all the administrative burdens related to the maintenance of such entities are worth the tax savings.

IV. Formation of Mexican Partnership

A. Significance of Partnership Status

For U.S. income tax purposes, the U.S. investor may find it advantageous to conduct its business operations either through a joint venture or other partnership arrangement in order to have the foreign entity treated as a partnership for U.S. tax purposes and not an "association" taxable as a corporation. As previously indicated herein, the significance of this classification is that as a partnership there is an automatic pass-through of income and losses to the U.S. partner whereas, if classified as an association, there is no automatic pass-through and the corporate tax provisions discussed above will be applied. In addition, classification determines which rules will apply with respect to the tax impact of capitalization of the foreign entity.

B. Classification of Foreign Entities

Generally, in making the determination of partnership status for foreign entities, the same tests are applied as in making the classification for a U.S. partnership.[61] Under these enunciated tests, the analysis requires a review of four principal corporate characteristics — continuity of life, centralized management, limited liability, and free transferability of interest. An incorporated organization, and even a partnership under local law, will be classified as an association taxable as a corporation if

---

[59] Agreement between the United States of America and the United Mexican States for the exchange of information with respect to taxes (Nov. 9, 1989).

[60] See IRC § 927(e)(3)(a) and Treaty, Art. 27.

[61] See Rev. Rul. 73–254, 1973–1 C.B. 613; Reg. § 301.7701–2(a)(2).

the entity has three of these four corporate characteristics.[62] In establishing the presence of the corporate characteristics, the local law of the foreign jurisdiction must be applied to determine the legal relationships of the members among themselves and the public at large, as well as the interests of the members in the organization's assets.[63] For purposes of applying IRC § 7701, the IRS has established a presumption that all foreign entities are considered to be "unincorporated organizations."[64]

For U.S. companies seeking to do business in Mexico who desire to limit their legal liability and yet obtain pass-through tax treatment, the Mexican *Sociedad de Responsibilidad Limitada* may be the entity of choice. The *Limitada* exhibits characteristics of both a corporation and a partnership under applicable U.S. Treasury Regulations, and therefore if the organizational documents are properly drafted, it should receive recognition by the U.S. as a "partnership."[65]

---

[62] See Reg. § 301.7701–2(a)(3). It should be noted that the IRS recently proposed an "anti-abuse" regulation that would authorize it to recast partnership transactions to reflect the economic arrangements of its partners and prevent circumvention of the intended purpose of the Code partnership provisions. Prop. Reg. § 1.701–2. Under these proposed regulations, if a partnership is formed or availed of for a principal purpose of substantially reducing the present value of the partners' aggregate U.S. income tax liability in a manner inconsistent with the intent of the Code, the IRS can disregard the form of the transaction and, among other remedies, determine that the partnership should be disregarded in whole or in part.

[63] Reg. § 301.7701–1(c); Rev. Rul. 73–254, 1973–1 C.B. 613.

[64] Rev. Rul. 88–8, 1988-1 C.B. 403. The IRS has announced that it will not rule on whether a foreign corporation will be classified as a partnership. Rev. Proc. 94–7, 1994–1 I.R.B. 174, Section 4.23. However, this position may change in light of the willingness of the IRS to rule on the classification of foreign limited liability companies under certain circumstances. See Rev. Procs. 93–44, and 93–45.

[65] The IRS has announced the conditions under which it will consider ruling requests that relate to the U.S. tax classification of a foreign limited liability company as a partnership. Rev. Proc. 95–10, 1995–3 I.R.B. — (Jan. 17, 1995). This Rev. Proc. should be consulted as a drafting guide in the preparation of the *Limitada's* organizational documents. The IRS apparently has not issued any ruling with respect to the tax classification of a Mexican *Limitada*. It has been held in one reported case that a Mexican *Limitada* possessed three of the four characteristics and would therefore be treated as an association taxable as a corporation, but the reported facts indicate that with proper draftsmanship of the organizational documents, the entity could have lacked two of the four corporate characteristics. *Raffety Farms, Inc. v. U.S.*, 511 F.2d 1234 (8th Cir. 1975).

C. U.S. Taxation Upon Partnership Capitalization

The normal nonrecognition rules under IRC § 721 do not apply to foreign partnerships, and therefore capitalization of the foreign partnership could give rise to substantial adverse tax consequences to the U.S. company seeking to capitalize the Mexican subsidiary with property other than cash. Although IRC § 367 does not apply to transfers to partnerships, a 35 percent excise tax may be imposed on the built-in gain at the time of the transfer unless one or more elections are made before the transfer.[66]

1. The 1492 Election

The excise tax can be avoided if the transferor elects to apply the rules applicable to Sections 367 transfers, e.g., to recognize gain on the transfer of assets to the foreign partnership as if the property had been transferred to a foreign corporation.[67] However, this election must be made prior to the transfer. If the Section 1492 election is not made, the excise tax is determined on an asset-by-asset basis, thereby denying the ability to offset built-in gain in one transferred asset by the built-in losses of the other assets.[68] The excise tax cannot be offset by any foreign tax credit. In addition, the transferor is not considered to have recognized this gain on the asset for income tax purposes, and therefore the foreign partnership takes a carryover basis in the transferred assets.[69]

2. The Section 1057 Election

As an alternative to the Section 1492 election, the transferor may elect to recognize the built-in gain under IRC § 1057.[70] Under a Section 1057 election, gain is considered to have been recognized for income tax purposes, and therefore the foreign partnership will obtain a stepped-up basis in the transferred property. In addition, the gain recognized on the transfer of the assets may constitute foreign source income, thereby

---

[66] IRC § 1491.

[67] IRC § 1492.

[68] Rev. Rul. 71–433, 1971–2 C.B. 325.

[69] See IRC §§ 721(a), 723.

[70] IRC § 1492(3).

allowing the transferor to utilize excess foreign tax credits to reduce the U.S. tax liability imposed upon the recognized gain.

3. Transfers of Intangibles

If the foreign partnership is to be capitalized with intangibles, consideration should be given to the potential advantages of a Section 1057 election over the Section 1492 election. Because the Section 1492 election triggers the application of Section 367 principles, under this election the transfer of intangibles will result in the application of the rules of IRC § 367(d), which require the transferor to recognize income on the hypothetical stream of payments computed under the "commensurate with income" standard. However, making a Section 1057 election for all assets could trigger immediate gain on both tangible and intangible assets.

4. U.S. Taxation of Operations

After capitalization occurs and the Mexican partnership becomes operational, assuming it is classified as a partnership for U.S. tax purposes, the U.S. partners will be subject to immediate tax on the foreign partnership's distributive share of income or gain. As previously indicated, the inability to defer U.S. tax on this income may be a significant disadvantage to the use of the partnership form where the U.S. tax cannot be reduced through foreign tax credits.

V. Transfer Pricing

IRC § 482 permits the IRS to allocate income or deductions arising from transactions between related entities where such allocation is necessary to prevent evasion of tax or to clearly reflect the income of the entities. IRC § 482 applies when the entities engaging in the transactions are "owned or controlled directly or indirectly by the same interest." Transactions to which IRC § 482 may apply include:

(1) sales of tangible property;

(2) the licensing of intangible property;

(3) loans; and

(4) the performance of services.

The IRS's application of IRC § 482 and the results thereof are uncertain. The standards applied by the IRS are set out in a set of existing Section 482 regulations (the "Current Regulations"), partially withdrawn regulations proposed in 1992 (the "1992 Proposed Regulations"), and a set of Temporary Regulations published in 1993 (the "Temporary Regulations"). In addition, there is a significant body of case law that demonstrates the taxpayer's success in defending against IRS's Section 482 allocations, even though the taxpayers generally must prove the IRS's proposed allocation to be arbitrary.[71] In addition, the IRS has announced a procedure whereby taxpayers can apply for advance rulings on their transfer pricing methods, thereby avoiding a challenge by the IRS.[72]

The Temporary Regulations seek to establish an arm's-length standard whereby the taxpayer's transaction is to be judged against that of a person dealing at arm's-length with an uncontrolled taxpayer.[73] The standard is said to have been met if the results of a transaction are consistent with the results that would have been realized if two uncontrolled taxpayers had engaged in a comparable transaction under comparable circumstances.[74] The Temporary Regulations also provide three transfer pricing methods for intangibles and five for tangibles. The provisions of the 1992 Proposed Regulations dealing with cost-sharing arrangements have been retained.

---

[71] For a general discussion of these issues, see Glicklich and Goldstein, "New Transfer Pricing Regs. Adhere More Closely to an Arm's-Length Standard," 78 *J. Tax'n* 306 (May 1993).

[72] Rev. Proc. 91–22, 1991–1 C.B. 526.

[73] Temp. Reg. § 1.482–1T(b)(1). See also Temp. Regs. § 1.482–1T(a)(2).

[74] Temp. Reg. § 1.482–1T(c).

VI. Foreign Tax Credit

A. General Principles

To minimize double taxation, if the U.S. taxpayer chooses, a dollar-for-dollar credit is allowed against the U.S. tax liability for Mexican taxes paid or accrued on income derived from direct operations or investments in Mexico.[75] A "deemed paid credit" is also allowed with respect to dividends received by U.S. corporations from Mexican subsidiary corporations operating in Mexico. This credit is also available to offset U.S. tax on income of a controlled foreign corporation ("CFC") that is included in the income of its U.S. shareholders under Subpart F of the Code.[76]

1. The Credit

Under IRC § 901, the United States permits a U.S. taxpayer to claim a foreign tax credit ("FTC") for taxes paid to foreign countries with respect to foreign source income. The Treaty does not modify the FTC nor provide additional benefits under U.S. or Mexican laws.[77] If the FTC cannot be fully utilized in a given year, it may be carried back two years and carried forward five years.[78] The FTC is limited so that it will offset only U.S. taxes on foreign source taxable income, i.e., foreign source income net of expenses, as defined under U.S. tax laws. This limitation prevents a U.S. taxpayer from using FTCs to offset U.S. tax on U.S. source income. The limitation is calculated on an overall basis by multiplying the ratio of the taxpayer's foreign source taxable income to its worldwide taxable income by the taxpayer's total pre-credit U.S. tax.[79] However, the alternative minimum tax and certain other taxes may not be offset by the FTC.[80]

---

[75] IRC § 901(a).

[76] IRS § 960.

[77] Treaty, Art. 24.

[78] IRC § 904(c).

[79] IRC § 901(a).

[80] IRC § 26(b) The other noncreditable taxes are: environmental tax, § 59A; additional taxes on certain distributions, § 72(m)(5)(B), (q), (t), or (v); recaptures of federal subsidy from use of mortgage bonds, § 143(m); accumulated earnings tax, § 531; personal holding company tax, § 541; recoveries of foreign expatriation losses,

2. Optional Deduction

As an alternative to claiming the FTC, on an annual basis the U.S. corporation can elect to deduct the income taxes paid to Mexico. Such an election may be preferable for years in which the U.S. corporation has suffered an income tax loss because the Mexican taxes imposed could then become part of a net operating loss to be carried forward and backward.

3. Full Credit Utilization

Although the U.S. and Mexico are treaty partners, the FTC may not totally eliminate double taxation because of some unique U.S. tax principles. For example, U.S. tax laws require a U.S. corporation to allocate and apportion its expenses between U.S. and foreign sources.[81] Therefore, to the extent U.S. expenses are allocated against Mexican source income, double taxation may result since Mexico would likely not allow a deduction for such expenses when computing Mexican tax liability.[82]

4. "Basket" Limitations

In addition to the potential loss of the FTC attributable to deduction disparities, the Code imposes a number of separate FTC limitations for the various types of income earned by the U.S. company ("baskets") for determining the total FTC limitation. The separate baskets include:

(1) overall active income;

(2) passive income;

---

§ 1351(d)(1); built-in gains tax of S corporations, § 1374; certain passive income of S corporations, § 1375; nonqualified withdrawals from capital construction funds, § 7518(g)(6)(A); certain income of nonresident aliens and foreign corporations, §§ 871(a) and 881; taxes on certain residual interests, § 860E(e); the branch profits tax, § 884; and, interest on certain deferred liabilities, §§ 453(a)(3) and 453A(c).

[81] Reg. § 1.861–8.

[82] See *LISR* § 24.I and VIII.

(3) DISC dividends;

(4) FSC dividends;

(5) FSC taxable income attributable to foreign trade income;

(6) financial services income;

(7) shipping income;

(8) high withholding tax interest; and,

(9) dividends from each noncontrolled foreign corporation.[83]

In addition, the Code contains "look through" rules whereby dividends, interest, rents and royalties from CFCs are characterized as either active or separate limitation income, depending upon the character of the earnings and profits of a CFC.[84] These look-through rules apply to payments received by a U.S. shareholder of the CFC, and the regulations provide that the look-through rules also apply to payments and distributions from one CFC to a related CFC.[85]

The impact of the separate FTC basket is to segregate foreign income on a type of income basis. In many cases, this scheme creates excess FTCs in the active basket and excess limitations in many of the separate baskets, the scheme income from which would be subject to some U.S. tax. Generally, diversified companies will be adversely affected by the basket limitations, whereas companies deriving income abroad solely from a specific type of operations should not be adversely affected.

---

[83] See IRC § 904(d). Additional limitation rules apply to the use of creditable foreign taxes attributable to foreign oil and gas income. IRC §§ 907 and 901(e). See also, Reg. § 1.904–4(i).

[84] IRC § 904(d)(3).

[85] See Reg. § 1.904–5.

B. The Indirect Credit

An indirect FTC is available to a U.S. corporation for a proportionate amount of the Mexican taxes paid by the foreign corporation upon the receipt of a dividend from the foreign corporation.[86]

1. Scope of Indirect Credit

The indirect credit extends to Mexican taxes imposed on the income of a Mexican subsidiary whose income is included in the gross income of its U.S. parent under Subpart F of the Code, and on the portion of any gain that is taxed as dividend income under IRC § 1248 upon the sale of stock of the Mexican subsidiary.[87] This indirect credit works to equate the U.S. tax cost imposed on U.S. corporations operating through a Mexican subsidiary to the U.S. tax burden of a U.S. corporation doing business in Mexico through a branch.[88] First-and second-tier foreign corporations are deemed to have paid the foreign taxes of second- and third-tier corporations, respectively, upon the receipt of a dividend.[89]

2. Incomplete Utilization

As indicated, any dividend distributed will carry out a portion of the Mexican taxes paid in proportion to the distributed "earnings and profits." In the case of Mexico, a potential problem arises because the earnings and profits of the Mexican entity are required to be calculated in accordance with U.S. tax principles,[90] which do not mirror the deductions allowable under Mexican law, such as the current deduction for inventory costs. Consequently, the effective Mexican tax rate in relation to the U.S. calculation of earnings and profits could be lower than 34 percent,

---

[86] IRC § 902(a).

[87] IRC § 960; Reg. § 1.1248–1(d).

[88] See generally, Associated Telephone & Telegraph Co. v. U.S., 306 F.2d 824, 832 (1962), *cert. denied.*

[89] IRC § 902(b). It should be noted that foreign taxes paid by fourth- or lower-tier subsidiaries are not eligible for the indirect credit even though the earnings of such subsidiaries are eventually distributed to the U.S. parent through successive upstream distributions.

[90] IRC §§ 902(c)(1) and 964(a).

thereby likely yielding a residual tax to be paid to the U.S. upon the U.S. parent's receipt of the dividend distribution.

C. Carryback and Carryforward

Foreign taxes paid or accrued in excess of the applicable separate limitation first must be carried back two years or forward five years.[91] Foreign taxes utilized in the current year are first deemed to be the current year taxes and then taxes paid, accrued or deemed-paid in the earliest year.[92]

---

[91] IRC § 904(c).
[92] IRC § 904(c).

CHAPTER 9

Mexican Tax Considerations for Investing and Doing Business in Mexico*

Randolph M. Karsh, Esq.**
Holland & Hart

I. Mexican Taxation

A. Sources of Law and Enforcement

1. The *Codigo Fiscal*

Under authority granted by the Constitution, the *Codigo Fiscal de la Federacion*[1] (the "*Codigo Fiscal*") establishes the fundamental principle that individuals and business entities are obligated to contribute to the public expenses in accordance with fiscal laws.[2] These contributions can take the form of specifically imposed taxes, contributions to social security, contributions to public works, and contributions established

** The author gratefully acknowledges the assistance of Lic. Bernardo Ledesma U. of the Mexico City law firm of Barrera, Siqueiros y Torres Landa, S.C., whose instruction in the Mexican system of taxation was instrumental to the author in the preparation of this article.

[1] Published in the *Diario Oficial* on Dec. 31, 1981.

[2] *Codigo Fiscal* § 1.

under the law for the use and improvement of public property.[3] Titles II through VI of the *Codigo Fiscal* establish the rights and obligations of taxpayers; the powers of fiscal authorities; imposition of penalties for violation of the fiscal laws; administrative remedies; and, procedures for seeking administrative litigation.

2. Income Tax Code

Consistent with the authority granted by the Constitution and the *Codigo Fiscal*, the rules for the imposition of the income tax are set out in the *Ley del Impuesto Sobre la Renta*[4] ("*LISR*"), which is supplemented by relatively uncomplicated regulations.[5] The *LISR* is divided into a number of major topics under the following headings:

(1) *Title I: General Provisions,* e.g., definitions, persons or transactions subject to tax, foreign tax credit, treaty impact, inflationary adjustments with respect to interest paid on debt, joint ventures, and trusts.

(2) *Title II: Provisions Applicable to Artificial Persons,* i.e., business entities.

(3) *Title IIA: Simplified Provisions for the Taxation of Business Entities,* e.g., agricultural, cattle, forestry, and fishing activities.

(4) *Title III: Tax-Exempt Organizations.*

(5) *Title IV: Provisions Applicable to Individuals.*

(6) *Title V: Foreign Residents with Mexican Source Income.*

---

[3] *Codigo Fiscal* § 2.

[4] Published in the *Diario Oficial* on Dec. 30, 1980. Since its enactment in 1980, the *LISR* has undergone a number of annual amendments which are released and published as "Transitory Articles."

[5] *Reglamento de la Ley del Impuesto Sobre la Renta*, published in the *Diario Oficial* on Feb. 29, 1984.

(7) *Title VI: Personal Savings Accounts and Insurance Payments for Retirement.*

3. Other Tax Provisions

A number of other taxes are imposed upon persons conducting business in Mexico. These include payroll related taxes payable by the Mexican employer, a value added tax, an assets tax, and a special tax imposed on the initial acquisition of real estate.[6]

4. Judicial Authority

Historically, it has been very uncommon for taxpayers in Mexico to challenge the imposition of any taxes. Therefore, court rulings with respect to tax issues are virtually nonexistent.

5. Tax Conventions

As a developing country, Mexico has made a concerted effort to modernize its tax system to include tax conventions with other countries. Mexico's first treaty became effective with Canada, and subsequent tax conventions have been entered into with Belgium, Ecuador, France, Germany, Italy, Sweden, Switzerland, and the United States.[7] To a great extent such treaties modify the application of the Mexican tax laws to the citizens and residents of such countries who either invest in Mexican businesses, or engage in a trade or business in Mexico.

---

[6] See Part I.D, *infra.*

[7] The official title of this document is the *Convention Between the Government of the United States of America and the Government of the United Mexican States for the Avoidance of Double Taxation and the Prevention of Fiscal Evasion with Respect to Taxes on Income* (hereinafter "Treaty"), and by its terms became effective as of Jan. 1, 1994. For a discussion of selected provisions of the Treaty, see Part II, *infra.* A discussion of the provisions of treaties with other countries is considered to be beyond the scope of this chapter.

6. Enforcement of Tax Laws

The governmental agency in charge of applying, interpreting and enforcing the income tax laws is the *Secretaria de Hacienda y Credito Publico*[8] (the "*Hacienda*").

B. Persons Subject to Taxation

The *LISR* specifically establishes three characteristics or elements that determine the taxpayer for purposes of imposition of the income tax.[9] These consist of residency, permanent establishment, and source of enrichment.[10]

1. Residency

The *LISR* requires Mexican residents to report all income regardless of its source.[11] Individuals who have a residence in Mexico are treated as residents for tax purposes, except for a calendar year in which they stay more than 183 days in another country and are treated as having acquired a tax residence in the other country.[12] Business entities are treated as residents if they have established their principal place of business in Mexico.[13] A rebuttable presumption is created for individuals and business entities who are Mexican nationals.

2. Permanent Establishment

Foreign persons who have either a permanent establishment or a fixed base in Mexico are required to pay the Mexican income tax with respect to income derived from that permanent establishment or fixed base.[14] Although the *LISR* contains a comparatively broad definition of

---

[8] See generally *Codigo Fiscal.*

[9] *LISR,* §§ 1–4.

[10] Prior law provided that the basis for taxation consisted of nationality, residence, and source of enrichment. *Ley del Impuesto Sobre la Renta de Diciembre de 1964.*

[11] *LISR* § 1–I.

[12] *Codigo Fiscal* § 9.

[13] *Id.*

[14] *LISR* § 1–II.

permanent establishment,[15] it is overridden by any treaty provisions[16] that, generally, contain a narrower definition. In particular, under the *LISR* a foreign corporation is deemed to have a permanent establishment in Mexico if it acts through an individual or entity that performs any of the following tasks with respect to the foreign corporation:

— maintenance of inventory on behalf of the foreign resident;

— assumption of risk on behalf of the foreign resident;

— operation under the control of or pursuant to detailed instructions from the foreign resident;

— engaging in activities that economically correspond to the foreign resident; or

— receipt of a guaranteed fee.

Prior to the Treaty, one of the most troublesome tax problems for U.S. companies operating in Mexico was this somewhat ambiguous and overly broad definition of a "permanent establishment" for Mexican tax purposes. Following its agreement to a more limited "permanent establishment" definition in its treaties with the United States and Canada, in 1994 Mexico amended its domestic law to more closely conform to such treaty concepts.[17]

3. Source of Enrichment

The *LISR* subjects a foreign person, regardless of nationality or residence, to Mexican income taxes on income derived from Mexican sources.[18] Passive income paid by Mexican persons to foreigners is typically impacted by this provision, e.g., dividends, interest, and

[15] *LISR* § 2.

[16] *LISR* § 4–A.

[17] See Perez de Acha, "Mexico Amends Tax Legislation to Reflect Increased Global Trade, NAFTA," *Tax Notes Int'l* 623 (Mar. 7, 1994).

[18] *LISR* § 1–III.

royalties. Treaty provisions greatly limit the extent to which Mexico may tax such types of income.

C. Income Taxation of Business Activities[19]

1. Tax Rates

Mexican and foreign companies deriving income from business activities conducted in Mexico presently are taxed at a fixed rate of 34 percent of net taxable income.[20] This fixed tax rate applies to all corporations and most partnerships, as well as to individuals who directly engage in business activities.[21] Reduced tax rates are granted to businesses engaging in certain favored industries.[22] In addition, those businesses engaging in agricultural, cattle, fishing, and forestry activities may elect to be taxed under a simplified system.[23]

2. Gross Income

With few exceptions gross income items under the *LISR* are comparable to those found under the U.S. tax laws, but without many of the multiple complexities thereof.[24] Mexico does not have any tax provisions which exempt from taxation the transfer of assets to corporations in exchange for stock, i.e., unlike the U.S. there are no "tax-free incorporations."[25] This is an added cost of doing business to be anticipated in organizing corporations in Mexico. However, the

---

[19] For a general discussion of Mexican taxation of business activities, see del Castillo and Preciado, T.M. 972, *Business Operations in Mexico* (BNA 1992).

[20] *LISR* § 10.

[21] *LISR* § 107. Graduated tax rates, ranging from 3% to 35%, generally only apply to non-business income of individuals. *LISR* §141.

[22] Such special treatment is granted in the form of a percentage deduction from the regular rate. Thus, the reduction for the book publishing industry is 50%, and for agricultural, cattle, forestry, and fishing industries, 25% to 50%. *LISR* § 13.

[23] *LISR* § 67.

[24] See generally *LISR* §§ 15–21.

[25] See, e.g., U.S. Internal Revenue Code of 1986, as amended, § 351 (hereinafter "IRC").

recognized gain may be substantially reduced because of prior inflation adjustments to the bases of the contributed assets.[26]

3. Deductions

Business taxable income is calculated by subtracting "indispensable" expenses from gross income. If an expense item is not indispensable, which generally means it must be specifically described by statute or regulation, the deduction will be disallowed.[27] In addition to being indispensable to the conduct of a business activity, the expenses must be properly reflected in the books of the company, properly documented, and, in the case of deductions for payments from which the taxpayer is obligated to withhold taxes, the taxpayer must fulfill such withholding obligation and deliver to the other party a copy of the withholding documents showing payment of the withheld taxes.[28]

a. Shareholder Loans

As a general rule, interest is a deductible business expense.[29] However, the *Hacienda* is granted the authority to recharacterize interest paid to shareholders as a dividend whenever the loan is payable on demand; in the event of default by the debtor, the creditor may intervene in the management of the debtor; or the payment of the interest, or the amount thereof, is determined by the debtor's earnings or profits.[30]

b. Nondeductible Expenses

The *LISR* lists a number of expense items that are clearly nondeductible,[31] which include the following:

---

[26] See *LISR* § 18.
[27] See generally *LISR* §§ 22–31 and §§ 41–51A.
[28] See generally *LISR* § 24.
[29] *LISR* § 24 (VIII).
[30] *LISR* § 66.
[31] *LISR* § 25.

— the income tax, and the employer portion of social security contributions less those made on behalf of minimum-wage employees;[32]

— the value added tax and the special tax on production and services, except in limited circumstances;

— profit sharing contributions to employees to the extent they do not exceed other nontaxable benefits provided by the employer;[33]

— expenses incurred abroad and allocated to the Mexican taxpayer by persons who are not subject to Mexican income tax;[34]

— gifts and similar costs unless directly related to the sale of products or services generally offered to clients;[35]

— premiums paid by corporations to redeem their own shares, and losses derived from mergers, capital reduction, or liquidation of companies in which the taxpayer had any equity interest;[36]

— penalties, indemnification for injury or damages, and for contractual obligations, unless paid pursuant to the taxpayer's legal obligation and with respect to which the taxpayer was not at fault;[37]

— reserves established for the personal indemnification of third parties, for seniority payments or similar payments, with an exception for those specially permitted by law;[38] and

— business meals and entertainment expenses.[39]

---

32 *LISR* § 25–I.
33 *LISR* § 25–III.
34 *LISR* § 25–XIX.
35 *LISR* § 25–IV.
36 *LISR* § 25–XI, 25–XVII.
37 *LISR* § 25–VII.
38 *LISR* § 25–IX.
39 *LISR* § 25–XXI.

4. Inflation Adjustment Factor

The *LISR* contains a comprehensive system for indexing the impact of inflation to certain items of income and deduction affected by the passage of time, such as interest, exchange gains and losses, and depreciation.[40]

a. Interest

The taxpayer is required to make a monthly inflationary adjustment with respect to interest income and expense. With regard to interest income, the inflationary component with respect to the taxpayer's interest-earning assets is subtracted from the total income interest accrued. If the result is positive the taxpayer will have taxable interest income and, if negative, it is a deductible inflationary loss.[41] With respect to the inflationary component for the taxpayers's debt obligations, an inflationary component based on the outstanding balance of such debts is subtracted from total interest expense accrued for the month. If the result is positive, the taxpayer has a deductible interest expense and, if negative, it is included in income as an inflationary gain. Therefore, in effect, if the interest expense of the taxpayer exceeds the rate of inflation, the taxpayer is allowed a deduction, but if the interest expense rate is less than the inflationary rate, the taxpayer realizes a form of "phantom" income.

b. Depreciation[42]

The depreciation deduction is allowed only on a straight-line basis at statutory fixed rates. The maximum statutory rates may be used in each fiscal year, but the total accumulated depreciation may not exceed the cost of the asset. The rates for selected items are as follows:[43]

Real estate improvements	5%
Office furniture and equipment	10%

---

[40] See generally *LISR* § 7.

[41] *LISR* § 7–B.

[42] See generally *LISR* § 41.

[43] *LISR* § 44.

Airplanes (agricultural use)	25%
Airplanes (nonagricultural)	10%
Automobiles and trucks	25%
Electronic Computing Equipment	25%
Pollution control equipment	50%

The taxpayer may make a one-time election to claim depreciation at rates lower than that specified by statute. In addition, as an alternative to straight-line depreciation, the taxpayer may generally elect to claim in a single fiscal year a statutorily-prescribed present value of the normal depreciation deduction allowable over the life of the asset.[44] This election applies only to certain new assets[45] and is not allowed for assets located in Mexico City, Guadalajara, and Monterrey, or other highly industrialized communities. If the straight-line depreciation method is used, the depreciation deduction is adjusted for inflation through the application of indexing factors.

5. Cost of Goods

Unlike some countries, Mexico does not use an inventory method of accounting and does not require a taxpayer to determine the cost of goods sold. A deduction is allowed for the current year's actual cost of goods and, in the case of a manufacturer, the cost of raw materials and semi-finished products.[46] The cost of imported goods is generally deductible at the time in which the import duties have been paid.

6. Capital Gains

Corporate capital gains on the sale or exchange of capital assets normally are treated as ordinary income and taxed at the regular rates. The tax basis used to determine gain or loss is adjusted for inflation during the years elapsed between the acquisition and sale of the asset. This is accomplished by multiplying the acquisition cost by an inflation

---

[44] *LISR* § 51.

[45] A "new asset" is deemed to be a qualifying asset used for the first time in Mexico. The option is not available for office furnishings and equipment, automobiles, autobuses, cargo trucks, tractor-trailers, and airplanes. *Id.*

[46] See *LISR* § 22–II.

factor calculated using the National Consumer Price Index ("NCPI") published by the *Banco de Mexico*.

a. Stock Gains

A shareholder's tax basis in shares of stock is adjusted according to a complicated formula which accounts for inflation, for the taxable income or losses of the issuing company, and for dividends paid by the company during the period in which the taxpayer held the stock.[47] These adjustments are intended to make the taxation of capital gains consistent with Mexico's integrated tax structure for corporations and their shareholders. Gain from sales of securities on the Mexico Stock Exchange are generally exempt from tax.[48]

b. Stock Losses

Capital losses from the sale of securities may be deducted only to the extent of capital gains from other securities. Unused capital losses may be carried forward three years with appropriate adjustment for inflation.[49]

7. Fiscal Year and Tax Payments

All companies are required to use the calendar year as their fiscal year.[50] Businesses in Mexico must estimate their tax obligations and make payments to the *Hacienda* in monthly installments on the 17th day of each month based on the total monthly income and to some extent the profit for the immediately preceding tax year.[51] The basis for making these estimated payments is adjusted at mid-year to account for actual profitability. A final correction and payment is made when the annual return is filed on or before March 31 of the following year.

---

[47] *LISR* § 19.

[48] See discussion at Part I.F.2, *infra*.

[49] *LISR* §§ 19, 25–XVIII.

[50] *Codigo Fiscal* § 11.

[51] *LISR* §§ 10, 12.

8. Accounting Method

Generally, businesses must use the accrual method of accounting.[52]

9. Loss Carryforward[53]

Tax losses incurred in a given fiscal year may be carried forward five years. There is no loss carryback. Subject to certain rules, losses may be carried forward another five years, for a total of ten years. The amount of tax losses deducted in a fiscal year will be adjusted for inflation by the NCPI corresponding to the length of time between the last month of the year in which tax losses are deducted and the last month of the fiscal year in which the loss occurred.

10. Election to File Consolidated Returns

Mexican holding companies may file consolidated income tax returns with respect to companies in which they own more than 50 percent of the stock, directly or indirectly, provided certain other requirements are met.[54] Each company involved in the consolidation must first prepare and file a separate company return. The holding company, in preparing and filing the consolidated return, determines the consolidated tax due on the basis of the proportion of ownership held in each consolidated company.

11. Avoidance of Double Taxation at the Corporate and Shareholder Levels

Mexico employs an integrated tax system for corporations and their shareholders in the form of exempting dividend distributions from a shareholder-level tax.[55] Dividends paid by a Mexican company generally have no Mexican tax consequences to the extent they are paid from a net taxable income account known as the *CUFIN*.[56] The distribution of tax-free dividends depends upon the satisfaction of a number of factors.

---

[52] *LISR* §§ 15, 16.
[53] *LISR* § 55.
[54] See *LISR* § 57–A, –B.
[55] *LISR* § 15.
[56] *Cuenta de Utilidad Fiscal Neta.*

a. The CUFIN

This account consists of a company's cumulative annual "net taxable income" as adjusted for a number of items.[57] The beginning point is taxable income for the year after deduction for any net operating loss carryforward. The net taxable income is then decreased by income tax payments, nondeductible employee profit sharing payments for the year, and any other nondeductible expenses for the year. After this amount is determined, it is then added to the accumulated CUFIN (as adjusted for inflation) from prior years. Finally, this amount is then increased by the amount of dividends received from other companies resident in Mexico and decreased by any dividends paid in cash or in kind during the year to arrive at the CUFIN. If a dividend is not paid from this net taxable income account or is in excess of such account, the Mexican corporation must pay a 34 percent tax on the grossed up amount of such excess.

b. Transfer of CUFIN

The CUFIN balance may be transferred to another company by means of a merger or split-up. In the latter case, the balance is proportionately allocated among the surviving companies in accordance with the division of capital.[58]

12. Transfer Pricing Rules and Related Party Transactions[59]

Intercompany pricing is becoming as big an issue in Mexico as it is in more economically developed countries. The transfer price between related parties is important both for income tax and customs laws. Mexican income tax law in this area is still in the initial development stage, and it presently relies upon very broad statutory provisions which generally require that related party transactions be based upon free market terms.[60] A reallocation by the *Hacienda* can result in underpaid taxes,

---

[57] See generally *LISR* § 124.

[58] *LISR* § 124, last paragraph.

[59] For a general discussion of this issue, see Levey, Amante and Palsen, "Mexican Transfer Pricing Practice Develops Along With Foreign Trade," 5 *J. Int'l Tax'n* 69 (Feb. 1994).

[60] *LISR* §§ 64, 64–A.

surcharges, penalties, and an inflation adjustment. Generally, for customs purposes, sales to a Mexican affiliate must be at the price for which sold on the Mexican market, unless a fair market value can be established by either a sale of the same product to an unaffiliated Mexican company, or a sale of a similar product to a Mexican company by a different exporter.

D. Other Taxes

1. Payroll Related Taxes

The Mexican Constitution and its laws are extremely protective of its workers and the employer's obligation to provide monetary benefits clearly reflects such basic policy.

a. Social Security

The employer must contribute approximately 14.42 percent of its employees' salaries as premiums for health and maternity insurance, as well as for disability, old age, unemployment, and death benefits. The compensation base used for calculating the health premium cannot exceed 25 times the daily minimum wage in effect in Mexico City and the compensation used for calculating the disability premium cannot exceed ten times such daily minimum wage. The employee must also contribute 5.15 percent of his salary. As a complement to Social Security, a 2 percent contribution program was established during 1992 for employee pensions. Employers must deposit an amount equal to 2 percent of salaries (up to a maximum contribution base of 20 times the daily minimum wage in effect in Mexico City) in a bank savings account for the employee.

b. Workers Compensation and Day Care

The following insurance is paid entirely by the employer: (1) occupational risks (1.67 to 166.67 percent of the employer's payment for disability, old age, unemployment, and death quota of 5.18 percent), according to the hazardous nature of the employer's activities; and (2) day care (1 percent of normal wages).

c. INFONAVIT[61]

For the *Infonavit* program (National Workers' Housing Fund Institute), employers are required to make bimonthly contributions equal to 5 percent of their employees' salaries, up to a maximum contribution base equal to ten times the minimum wage base in effect for the area of employment. These funds may be withdrawn for specified housing benefits. Any unused amounts accumulate as a pension account for each individual.

2. Value Added Tax[62]

Mexico's value added tax ("VAT") is a noncumulative tax imposed on products for the value added at each stage of the production process. Because it is a component of the transfer price at each stage, it does not constitute an incremental cost to the sellers involved in such process. The purchaser or user of the goods or services must accept the passing on of the tax, until it reaches the ultimate consumer. The taxpayer can credit the VAT that has been passed on expressly to him and pay only the difference; if the creditable tax exceeds the tax due, the difference can be offset later only against VAT or a refund obtained. Credit against other taxes is allowed only by complying with very complex rules.

a. Taxable Transactions

The taxable transactions are:

(1) the sale or other disposition of property;

(2) the rendering of independent services in Mexico, including technical assistance and technology transfers[63] (VAT does not apply to wages);

(3) the temporary use or enjoyment of property (leasing); and

---

[61] *Aportaciones al Fondo Nacional de la Vivienda.*

[62] *Ley del Impuesto al Valor Agregado*, published in the *Diario Oficial* on Dec. 29, 1978 ("*LIVA*").

[63] *LIVA* § 14–V.

(4) the importation of goods or services (paid by the importer of record).

b. Exempt Transactions

The principal exempt transactions are sales of land, credit instruments, residential construction, banking services, medical services, certain types of public entertainment, and most activities of government agencies.

c. Tax Rate

VAT is payable at a general rate of 10 percent. A 0 percent VAT generally applies to certain agricultural goods, listed basic foodstuffs, medicines, and imports of certain goods and services. Application of a zero rate means that the seller in generally entitled to a credit of previously paid VAT even though no VAT is collected on the sale.

3. Assets Tax

Under the Assets Tax Law ("ATL"),[64] a 2 percent tax is annually assessed on the value of a taxpayer's business assets. Thus, the taxpayers are principally corporations or individuals engaging in trade or business activities. In effect, the assets tax serves as an alternative minimum tax, i.e., it is paid only if it is greater in amount than the regular income tax. As such, it serves as a minimum income measure based on a return on assets of 5.9 percent (i.e., a 5.9 percent return times the normal income tax rate of 34 percent yields a tax of 2 percent of the asset value).

a. Exempted Taxpayers

Taxpayers' exempted from payment of the tax are the following:

— any company during its preoperative period;

— any company during its first two fiscal years of operation and when being liquidated;

---

[64] *Ley del Impuesto al Activo,* published in *Diario Oficial* on Dec. 31, 1988.

— taxpayers not subject to payment of the income tax; and

— companies considered as part of the financial system.

b. Tax Base

There are a number of complex rules for determination of the taxable base. Some asset items for this purpose are financial assets,[65] fixed assets, deferred expenses and collections, realty and inventories. Additionally, the tax base is reduced by the average value of liabilities owed to taxable Mexican residents.

c. Tax Returns

The assets tax is paid by filing monthly estimated returns and an annual return.[66]

d. Creditable Income Tax

A crucial aspect of the assets tax is that upon filing the yearly income tax return the taxpayer's income tax liability is creditable against the amount of the assets tax.[67] As indicated above, any assets tax amount that exceeds the amount of income tax paid for the same year shall be the tax payable pursuant to the ATL.[68] When it is determined in a fiscal year that the income tax to be credited exceeds the initial assets tax liability calculated for that year, taxpayers may, to that extent, request a refund of the amounts they have paid as assets tax (adjusted for inflation) during any of the ten immediately preceding fiscal years, on the condition that said amounts have not been previously refunded.

---

[65] Cash is no longer regarded as an asset subject to the tax. ATL § 4–I. However, investments and deposits in institutions of the "financial system" are deemed to be financial assets. ATL Reg. Art. 13.

[66] ATL §§ 7 and 8.

[67] ATL § 9.

[68] The Internal Revenue Service of the United States ("IRS") has ruled that this interaction of the assets tax and the income tax does not affect the creditability under IRC § 901 of the Mexican income taxes paid. Rev. Rul. 91–45, 1991–2 C.B. 336. However, because the assets tax is not imposed on income, it is not a creditable tax for U.S. foreign tax credit purposes. IRC § 901(b).

e. Treaty Impact

Under the Treaty, Mexico may continue to impose the assets tax on U.S. residents, but only if and to the extent such a person either (1) maintains a permanent establishment in Mexico, (2) has real property in Mexico, or (3) leases or otherwise permits a Mexican resident to use industrial, commercial, scientific equipment or intangible property, that gives rise to royalty income.[69] With respect to real property, Mexico must grant a credit against the assets tax in an amount equal to the income tax that would be imposed on the gross income from such property in the absence of the Treaty.[70] In the case of equipment or intangibles, a credit must be granted against the assets tax in an amount equal to the Mexican withholding tax that would be imposed in the absence of the Treaty on the gross royalty income from those assets.[71] Thus, absent a permanent establishment in Mexico, the U.S. owner receiving rental or royalty income from such properties should not be subject to the assets tax because, in the absence of the Treaty, the *LISR* withholding rate on such income is 21 percent.[72]

4. Property Acquisitions Tax

An acquisitions tax is imposed on the acquisition of land and improvements thereto, or any interests therein.[73] The tax rate is 2 percent. Generally the tax base is equivalent to the transactional value of the property.

---

[69] Treaty, Protocol 3.

[70] However, the credit is available only if less than 50% of the U.S. resident's gross income from the subject property is used, directly or indirectly, to meet liabilities to nonresidents of the U.S. *Id.*

[71] The normal Mexican withholding rate on royalties is 35%, which Art. 12.2 of the Treaty reduces to 10%.

[72] *LISR* § 148.

[73] *Ley del Impuesto Sobre Adquisicion de Inmuebles,* published in the *Diario Oficial* on Dec. 31, 1979.

5. Profit Sharing

Under the Mexican Constitution, employers are required to share business profits with their employees.[74] The profit sharing amount is 10 percent of the business taxable income (adjusted by increases to remove some inflation adjustments that are deductible for income tax purposes, including dividend income exempt from income tax, and to reimburse amortization of losses).

a. Exemptions

Depending upon a company's structure, the general manager or director is not entitled to participate in such a bonus. In addition, the following companies are exempt from payment of such a bonus:

— newly organized companies during their first year of operation;

— newly organized companies whose purpose is to develop a new product during their first two years of operation; and

— newly organized extractive industries during their period of exploration.

b. Deductibility

This bonus amount is deductible for income tax purposes. However, for all practical purposes, it will yield no deduction because the deductible amount is reduced by the amount of any nontaxable fringe benefits provided to employees.

---

[74] See, *Ley Federal Del Trabajo* and the *Resolucion de La Comision Nacional Para La Participacion de los Trabajodores en las Utilidadas de las Empresas,* published in the *Diario Oficial* on Mar. 4, 1984.

E. Choice of Entity

1. Branch[75]

A branch clearly is a permanent establishment under the *LISR* and as such the business profits derived therefrom become subject to taxation in accordance with Mexican law. In addition to Mexican income tax, the Mexican Federal Labor Law requires the branch to distribute among its employees working in Mexico an amount equal to 10 percent of profits generated in Mexico during the fiscal year. The branch will also be required to withhold payroll taxes for its employees, including Social Security and the *Infonavit*. Under the *LISR*, the deductions available to the branch may be limited. For example, *LISR* § 23 provides that no deduction is allowed to a permanent establishment for payments made to its home office when such payments consist of "royalties, honoraria, or similar payments in exchange for the right to use patents or other rights . . . or for interest accrued on money transferred to the permanent establishment." As a branch, the after-tax profits can be remitted to the foreign parent corporation without the imposition of any withholding or other Mexican taxes.[76]

2. Subsidiary Corporation

Subsidiary operations can take on a number of forms as permitted by the GLCC. Historically, the corporate entity has served as the most acceptable vehicle for foreign investment in Mexico. Corporations are generally of two types:

---

[75] *Sucursal de Sociedad Extranjera.* Branches are subject to regulation under various provisions of Mexican law. The Commerce Code, *Codigo de Comercio*; the General Law of Commercial Companies, *Ley de Sociedades Mercantiles* ("GLCC"); and the Foreign Investment Law, *Ley de Inversion Extranjera* ("FIL"), contemplate their use in Mexico. The GLCC, Art. 250, acknowledges their corporate existence and their right to carry out commercial activities, while FIL § 17 requires approval from *SECOFI* prior to registration with the Public Registry of Commerce.

[76] For U.S. tax purposes, the branch's business profits also become subject to inclusion in the gross income of the U.S. "parent" corporation.

— A traditional corporation, *Sociedad Anonima*. Such a corporation may not increase or decrease its capital without amending its organizational documents and obtaining government approval.

— A corporation with variable capital, *Sociedad Anonima de Capital Variable*. Such a corporation may increase or decrease its capital without amending its organizational documents and without seeking government approval.

Regardless of the corporate form, the domestic corporation will be subject to the Mexican tax system with regard to its worldwide income.

3. Partnership

Partnerships consist of three principal forms: general partnership, *Sociedad en Nombre Colectivo ("SNC")*; the limited partnership, *Sociedad en Comandita ("SC")*; and a joint venture contract, *Asociacion en Participacion ("AP")*.

a. Liability

Although for liability purposes these entities are regarded as partnerships, they are organized under the GLCC and for many, if not most, purposes are regarded as corporations.

b. Income Taxation

Under the *LISR*, the *SNC* and the *SC* are taxed the same as corporations which domestically does not yield the potential for double taxation because payment of "dividends" by the partnership does not result in a second tax.[77] Generally, such partnerships pay the taxes on

[77] For U.S. investors, the *Sociedad de Responsibilidad Limitada* may be the entity of choice because of its potential for classification as a "partnership" for U.S. tax purposes, and at the same time offering limited liability for its members under the GLCC. The *Limitada* exhibits characteristics of both a corporation and a partnership under applicable U.S. Treasury Regulations, and therefore the organizational documents must be carefully drafted to ensure recognition as a "partnership" for U.S. income tax purposes.

their net income which can then be distributed to the partners as a dividend free of any additional income tax. However, the *AP* is treated as a pass-through entity with its partners taxed much in the same manner as under the tax laws of the United States.[78]

F. Nonbusiness Activities of Foreigners

Like many other countries, Mexico utilizes a withholding tax system for payments of income items to foreigners who are either nonresidents or do not have a permanent establishment in Mexico. The character of the income generally determines the amount to be withheld, which is subject to any applicable treaty limitations.

1. Sales of Real Property

A person purchasing Mexican real property from a foreign person must generally withhold a tax at a rate of 20 percent of the gross sales proceeds.[79] However, the nonresident may elect to pay the tax at a rate of 35 percent of the net taxable gain realized, provided the nonresident has a legal representative either residing in Mexico, or who has a permanent establishment or fixed base in Mexico, who has the obligation of calculating and paying the corresponding tax to the *Hacienda*, and the sale is publicly recorded.[80]

a. Treaty Impact

The Treaty specifically allows Mexico to tax U.S. residents on such income in accordance with Mexican laws.[81] However, it does permit the nonresident to elect for any taxable year to compute the tax on a net

---

In this regard, the Internal Revenue Service has announced the conditions under which it will consider ruling requests that relate to the U.S. tax classification of a foreign limited liability company as a partnership. Rev. Proc. 95–10, 1995–3, IRS (Jan. 17, 1995). This Revenue Procedure should be consulted as a drafting guide in the preparation of the *Limitada's* organizational documents.The IRS apparently has not issued any ruling with respect to the U.S. tax classification of a *Limitada.*

[78] *LISR* § 8.

[79] *LISR* § 150.

[80] *Id.*

[81] Treaty, Art. 13.1.

income basis as if such income were attributable to a permanent establishment in Mexico. Such an election is to be binding for the taxable year thereof and all subsequent tax years unless an exemption is granted by competent authority.

2. Stock Sales

Gains from the sale of stock or credit instruments issued by Mexican companies are taxed at a rate of 20 percent of the gross sales proceeds.[82] The nonresident may elect to pay the tax at a rate of 30 percent of the net taxable gain realized, provided the nonresident has a legal representative in Mexico who meets certain requirements.[83] Sales of securities on the Mexico Stock Exchange *(Bolsa de Valores)* generally are exempt from income taxation.[84]

a. Real Property Companies

The Treaty permits taxation of gain on the sale of shares of a real property company if at least 50 percent of the value of its assets consists of real property.[85]

b. Non-Real Property Companies

The Treaty also permits Mexico to tax the gain on the sale of equity interests of a resident company if the seller, within the 12-month period preceding the sale, had a participation, directly or indirectly, of at least 25 percent of the equity capital of the company sold.

3. Leasing of Real or Personal Property

Nonresidents are subject to a withholding tax on income derived from the leasing of real or personal property at a flat rate of 21 percent of the

---

[82] *LISR* § 151.
[83] These requirements are set out in *LISR* § 160.
[84] *LISR* §§ 77–XVI and 151.
[85] Treaty, Art. 6.

gross rents, except for the leasing of railroad cars, containers, airplanes, and ships for commercial transportation, which are taxed at 5 percent.[86]

a. Real Estate Rentals

Article 6(5) of the Treaty allows for an irrevocable election to be taxed on a net basis. Absent such election, the normal withholding taxes will apply.

b. Equipment Rentals

The Treaty limits withholding on equipment rentals to 10 percent of gross rent. As indicated herein, whenever this rate applies, the Treaty also provides that Mexico shall grant a credit against the assets tax for the hypothetical 21 percent withholding tax that would normally be imposed without the Treaty.

4. Dividends

As indicated elsewhere herein, Mexico does not currently impose a withholding tax on dividends and therefore the Treaty has no real impact on this statutory exemption. However, if Mexico were to change its laws respecting the taxation of dividend income, the Treaty would limit any withholding taxes to 5 percent for companies which own at least 10 percent of the voting stock of the payor, and in all other cases the present rate is 15 percent, which will be reduced to 10 percent in 1999.[87]

5. Interest

Generally, the withholding rate on payments of interest to foreigners depends upon the nature of the business conducted by the payee, and in some instances the purpose for the interest payment.[88] The *LISR* rates are as follows: (1) 15 percent for payments to foreign banks registered before the *Hacienda*, other financial entities registered before the *Hacienda*, and

---

[86] *LISR* §§ 148, 149. However, rental income derived with respect to residential property is subject to a 35% withholding tax. *LISR* § 148–A.

[87] Treaty, Art. 10(2)(b) and (3).

[88] *LISR* § 154.

financial leasing arrangements; and, (2) 21 percent for interest payments to foreign financial entities which have not registered before the *Hacienda*, interest paid to foreign suppliers of machinery and equipment that become part of the buyer's fixed assets, and interest payments to suppliers or lenders for the acquisition of machinery and equipment for general, commercial and industrial activities, provided such circumstances are stated in a contract and the payee has registered for such business purpose with the *Hacienda*.

a. Interim Rate

Effective as of January 1, 1994, and through December 31, 1995, Mexico reduced the 15 percent and 21 percent rates referred to above to 4.9 percent and 10 percent respectively.[89] However, these reduced rates will not apply if the effective beneficiary of the interest payments resides in a country in which the income tax rates on interest income, treating the interest income as if it were the sole source of income, is less than 70 percent of the income tax liability that would have been payable to Mexico.

b. Treaty

As a general rule, the Treaty sanctions taxation of interest by the source country.[90] The interest is regarded as having a Mexican source when the debtor is either a resident thereof, or has a permanent establishment or fixed base in Mexico. Subject to certain specific exemptions,[91] the Treaty establishes the following maximum tax rates:

(1) 10 percent on interest payments with respect to loans made by U.S. banks, insurance institutions and securities traded on a well-known stock exchange. This rate will remain in effect until January 1, 1999, and thereafter will be reduced to 4.9 percent.

---

[89] *LISR*, Transitory Art. V.

[90] See generally Treaty, Art. 11.

[91] Interest items exempt from withholding tax are: (1) interest paid to or by the U.S. or Mexican government or a political subdivision thereof; (2) interest paid to an exempt pension plan; and (3) interest paid on a loan of at least three years that is made, guaranteed or insured by a government bank. Treaty, Art. 11(4).

The 4.9 percent rate is somewhat unique, and it is extremely important for U.S. lenders because it will enable them to obtain more favorable treatment of the Mexican withholding tax for purposes of utilizing the U.S. foreign tax credit.[92]

(2) 15 percent with respect to loans granted by U.S. persons other than those described above, interest paid by Mexican banks, and interest paid by a buyer to a seller of machinery and equipment. This rate remains in effect until January 1, 1999, and thereafter will be reduced to 10 percent.

These reduced treaty rates will not apply whenever the effective beneficiary thereof performs any entrepreneurial or professional activity in the country from which the interest is paid, or where the interest is derived from certain types of public debt. In addition, both governments reserved significant rights to apply their domestic law regimes with respect to issues involving characterization of interest payments for tax purposes. Specifically, the contracting states may apply their own thin capitalization and equity characterization rules to deny interest deductions.[93]

6. Royalties

Royalty payments pose a perplexing problem under the Treaty and the *LISR* provisions.

---

[92] The allowance by the U.S. of the foreign tax credit ("FTC") is subject to a number of separate "basket" limitations. IRC § 904(d). Among these baskets are those relating to passive income, financial services income, and "high withholding tax interest," which is defined as interest subject to a withholding tax of at least 5%. Setting the Treaty rate at 4.9% is likely to increase the likelihood that the U.S. recipient of the interest will be able to use the FTC resulting from the Mexican tax because such interest can be allocated to a potentially larger basket that includes the recipient's worldwide passive taxable income (or possibly the financial services basket).

[93] Treaty, Protocol 9. This language grants explicit recognition to the U.S. earnings stripping rules and common law debt/equity principles. Moreover, it sanctions the Mexican provisions which recharacterize shareholder loans as equity. See discussion at Part I.C.3.a., *infra*.

— On the one hand, the Treaty provides that the tax may not exceed 10 percent of the gross amount.[94]

— However, Mexico has specific provisions that provide that "technical assistance" is taxed at the rate of 15 percent.[95] It is an open question whether technical assistance constitutes a royalty.

— Under the *LISR*, "technical assistance" is defined as the transfer of knowledge, scientific, commercial or technical principles that benefit the industrial or professional fields, and are related to a production process, or assistance on matters that are not commonly known, non-patentable and originate with the personal experience of the technical assistance provider.

— To avoid the 15 percent rate it can be argued that Article 12 of the Treaty, regarding royalties, controls and therefore the tax rate can be no greater than 10 percent. The Treaty does not specifically refer to "technical assistance" but paragraph 2 of Article 12 provides that the term "royalties" means payments for "information concerning industrial, commercial, or scientific experience . . . ." When this Treaty language and the *LISR* definition are read in conjunction with each other, an argument can be made that the Treaty definition of "royalty" contemplates technical assistance services.

— The argument can also be made that such services are not royalties, and even if they are "technical assistance" within the meaning of the *LISR*, under the Treaty they cannot be subject to Mexican taxation unless the service provider has a permanent establishment in Mexico. Support for this argument can be found in Protocol 11 of the Treaty which provides that the term "information concerning industrial, commercial or scientific

---

[94] Treaty, Art. 12. In addition, Protocol 3 provides that Mexico will grant a credit against the assets tax for the normal tax that would have been imposed on the royalties applying the Mexican general rates of 15% or 35%.

[95] *LISR* § 156.

experience" is to be defined in accordance with paragraph 12 of the Commentary to Article 12 of the 1977 OECD Model Convention, which indicates that "information" should be interpreted to mean "know-how," and further appears to say that payments for "technical assistance" are to be analyzed under those treaty provisions which address independent contractors and permanent establishments.

7. Independent Contractor Payments

Mexico generally imposes a graduated tax rate for income attributable to the rendering of independent personal services,[96] whereby the first *N*$36,000 is exempt, the next *N*$36,001–*N*$290,000 is taxed at 15 percent, and any excess at 30 percent. However, such income is not taxable if the period for rendering services is less than 183 days, whether or not consecutive, during any 12-month period. Article 14 of the Treaty exempts from taxation compensation paid for services of independent contractors without a fixed base in Mexico and if the independent contractor is not present in the country more than 183 days in a 12-month period. It appears that because the Mexican statutory exemption refers to "service" days and not days of a physical presence, that the current Mexican law grants a greater exemption from local taxation than that provided by the Treaty. Compensation received by persons serving as members of a board of directors should be subject to similar treatment.[97]

II. Additional U.S.–Mexico Treaty Implications

A. Permanent Establishment

1. Treaty Definition

The Treaty defines a "permanent establishment" as a fixed place of business through which the business of an enterprise is conducted, including in particular:

— a place of management, branch, office, factory, or workshop,

---

[96] *LISR* § 147.

[97] See *LISR* § 145.

— a mine, an oil or gas well, a quarry, or other place of extraction of natural resources; and

— a building or construction site or place for exploration or exploitation of natural resources, but only if lasting for more than six months.[98]

2. Preparatory Activities

The Treaty contains an exception to the "permanent establishment" definition for the maintenance of a fixed place of business merely to perform certain activities that have a preparatory or auxiliary character belonging to the U.S. enterprise.[99] Thus, for example, domestic law concepts are narrowed to exclude from the definition the maintenance of inventories for delivery to customers on behalf of the U.S. enterprise, or advertising, scientific research, and a specific protective clause is included for "preparations related to the placement of loans."

3. Agency Relationships

A "deemed permanent establishment" results when the U.S. enterprise operates through an agent that has and habitually exercises the authority to conclude contracts in the name of the enterprise. However, independent agents operating in the ordinary course of business and on arm's length terms do not create a "deemed permanent establishment."[100] Nevertheless, the carrying on of business through a controlled affiliate does not necessarily make either party a permanent establishment of the other but, in order to preserve Mexico's authority to tax U.S. parent companies of *maquila* operations, a deemed permanent establishment is created by a person that habitually processes on behalf of the U.S. parent goods or merchandise maintained in the U.S., provided that the processing uses assets furnished, directly or indirectly, by the U.S. enterprise or its affiliates.[101]

---

[98] Treaty, Art. 5(1) through (3).

[99] Treaty, Art. 5(4).

[100] Treaty, Art. 5(5) and (7).

[101] Treaty, Art. 5(5)(b). See also discussion at Part III.C., *infra*.

B. Taxation of Business Profits

1. General Concept

The Treaty provides that the "business profits" of an enterprise will generally be subject to tax only by the country of residence, unless the enterprise carries on (or has carried on) business in the other country through a permanent establishment.[102] Then, the taxation right of the source country is restricted to income "attributable" to that permanent establishment. The Treaty contains several important provisions that could limit the scope of these rules.

2. Force of Attraction Rule

The nonresident country may tax sales of goods or merchandise "of the same or similar kind as the goods or merchandise sold through" the enterprise's permanent establishment. However, this right of taxation beyond income "attributable" to the permanent establishment does not apply if the enterprise "demonstrates that such sales have been carried out for reasons other than obtaining a benefit" under the Treaty.[103]

3. Definition of Business Profits

Unlike the U.S. Model Treaty,[104] the Treaty does not contain a definition of the term "business profits." Accordingly, the term is controlled by each country's separate application of domestic law.[105] This fact is particularly significant since the Treaty permits the source country

---

[102] See generally Treaty, Art. 7.

[103] Treaty, Art. 7. In this context, to illustrate a non-tax avoidance motive, the Treasury Department provides the example of a U.S. company based in San Diego and having a permanent establishment in Mexico City. Under that fact pattern, it "may be more efficient for [the] U.S. company . . . to sell goods to Tijuana directly from San Diego, whereas that may not be the case with respect to sales to Mexico City." *Treasury Department Technical Explanation of U.S.–Mexico Income Tax Treaty* , Nov. 30, 1993.

[104] U.S. Model Treaty, Art. 7(7), defines "business profits" to include "income derived from any trade or business, including the rental of tangible personal property and the rental or licensing of cinematographic films or films or tapes used for radio or television broadcasting."

[105] Treaty, Art. 3(2).

full rights of taxation with respect to "other income" not mentioned specifically in other articles.[106] As a result, if a particular item of income does not constitute "business profits" as defined under Mexican domestic law, it would not be afforded any Treaty protection from Mexican tax.

C. Definition of Royalties

"Royalties" are broadly defined to include payments for intangible property.

1. Knowhow

Under Protocol 11 of the Treaty, the reference in the Article 12(3) definition of royalties to "information concerning industrial, commercial, or scientific experience" is to be defined in accordance with the Commentary to the OECD Model Treaty. As previously noted herein, that Commentary clarifies that these terms refer to the concept of "knowhow," which involves "special knowledge and experience which remain unrevealed to the public."[107] This distinction is significant to the extent that it protects payments for technical assistance, e.g., professional service fees, from being subject to royalty withholding rates, and potentially preserves their exemption as business profits.

2. Equipment Leasing

The definition of royalties includes payments of any kind for the right to use "industrial, commercial or scientific equipment not constituting immovable property . . . ."[108] This provision preserves the source country right to tax equipment rentals at a 10 percent gross withholding rate (rather than exempting rentals as "business profits"), but represents a significant reduction from the 21 percent rate that applies to rental payments under the *LISR*.

---

[106] Treaty, Art. 23.

[107] OECD, *Model Double Taxation Convention on Income and Capital*, Commentary on Art. 12, ¶ 12, (1977).

[108] Treaty, Art. 12(3).

D. Branch Tax

The Treaty allows the countries to impose a branch profits tax and excess interest tax. Mexico does not currently impose such a tax, but the United States does. Under the Treaty, the branch profits tax is limited to the direct investment rate of 5 percent of the "dividend equivalent amount," but could be subject to a reduction under the most-favored nation clause. The withholding tax rate for excess interest is limited to 10 percent (with the 4.9 percent rate applicable to banks and insurance companies after five years).[109]

E. Income From Real Property

The Treaty generally follows the U.S. Model Treaty with respect to income from real property, permitting full rights of taxation by the country where the real property is located.[110] In addition, the Treaty confirms that the recipient of such income can elect to be taxed on a net basis, in place of a gross basis withholding tax. Although the net basis election is already available to Mexican investors in U.S. real estate under IRC §§ 871(d) and 882(d), except for sales of real property a reciprocal election is not presently available under Mexican law. As a result, for U.S. investors in Mexican real estate, the Treaty expands the options for the method of taxation.

F. Capital Gains

1. General Rule

The Treaty generally exempts capital gains from tax outside of the country where the seller is a resident. Exceptions are provided allowing source country taxation with respect to sales of:

— assets attributable to a permanent establishment,

— "immovable property," and

---

[109] Treaty, Art. 11A.

[110] Treaty, Art. 6.

— interests in entities resident in one of the states with assets consisting of at least 50 percent, by value, of immovable property situated in that state.[111]

2. Stock Sales

The Treaty does not prohibit the imposition of Mexico's 20 percent tax on the gross sales price for sales by nonresidents of stock in a Mexican corporation,[112] but imposes a condition that the nonresident shareholder must have held at least 25 percent of the capital interests during the 12 months preceding the gain.[113] In the case of a U.S. corporation, this provision will permit the U.S. to impose a withholding tax on gains recognized by Mexican shareholders, should Congress resurrect its prior proposals to impose U.S. tax on such sales.

G. Assets Tax Effects

1. Mexican Domestic Law

As indicated above,[114] the Mexican assets tax is a 2 percent tax on the gross value of business assets used in Mexico.

2. Treaty Effects

Although the Treaty does not make the assets tax a creditable tax, it limits Mexican authority to impose the assets tax to the following cases.[115]

a. Permanent Establishment

Situations in which the U.S. resident has a permanent establishment in Mexico and is therefore subject to Mexican income tax.

---

[111] Treaty, Art. 13.

[112] See discussion at Part I.F.1, *supra*.

[113] Treaty, Art. 13(4).

[114] See Part I.D.3, *supra*.

[115] Treaty, Protocol 3.

b. Royalties

Mexico can impose the assets tax where a U.S. resident transfers property to a Mexican resident in exchange for a royalty. The "income tax" measure for purposes of comparison to the minimum assets tax, however, is deemed to be at the higher 21 percent royalty rate under domestic law.

c. U.S. Residents Owning Real Property in Mexico

The assets tax applies to U.S. owners of Mexican real estate. Similar to royalty transactions, the treaty deems the "income tax" paid to be the full 21 percent of the gross rental income, even if the U.S. resident has in fact made a net basis election. To ensure that only "real" U.S. residents use this advantageous rule, a base erosion test is applied to prohibit its use if more than 50 percent of the gross income from the property is "eroded" to non-U.S. residents.

d. Transfer Pricing Protection

If the amount of rental or royalty payments are below arm's length rates (or zero), the above assets tax rule provides a backstop to Mexican income tax revenues. For example, if an intangible is transferred for a royalty payment of zero, the assets tax would be compared to 21 percent of zero, resulting in a full application of the assets tax.

H. Limitation on Benefits

1. General Structure

Following the approach to treaty shopping in other recent U.S. treaties, the Treaty provides a series of tests that limit benefits to eligible residents.[116] These rules provide explicit protection for residents that are:

(1) individuals;

(2) the Contracting States and their subdivisions;

---

[116] Treaty, Art. 17.

(3) residents engaged in active business in the other states;

(4) residents that pass ownership and base erosion thresholds;

(5) publicly traded companies and their wholly-owned subsidiaries; and

(6) recipients of dividends, interest, and royalties owned by persons that have not received marginal treaty rate reductions by using the Treaty.

2. NAFTA Reference

The Treaty also includes references to the North American Free Trade Agreement ("NAFTA") parties in applying certain of the limitations on benefits tests.

III. Impact on *Maquiladora* Program

Mexico's *maquiladora* program involves the duty-free importation on a temporary basis of raw materials, parts, and components to be assembled, manufactured or repaired and then exported either to the country of origin or a third country. Tools, machinery, equipment, and other items necessary for production can also be imported on a temporary basis free from any duties. Such operations typically have been conducted either on a sub-contract basis through so-called "shelter" operations, or subsidiaries of the foreign suppliers of the raw products and/or production materials. Historically, U.S. companies have utilized these operations because of the significant savings attributable to labor and operational overhead costs. In addition, the program offered an entry into the Mexican market because up to 50 percent of the *maquiladora's* "increased production" could be sold in Mexico. The combined implementation of NAFTA, the FIL, and the Treaty appear to eliminate the long-term need for U.S. companies to utilize such entities.

A. NAFTA Impact

Under NAFTA all tariffs imposed by Mexico with respect to United States and Canadian goods and services are to be phased out within 15 years. In addition, restrictions on the sale of *maquiladora* products in the Mexican marketplace are to be eliminated by January 1, 2001.[117] The combination of these factors are likely to eliminate the need for this program. However, a need should remain for U.S. and Canadian companies who ship components and raw materials to Mexico which do not satisfy the NAFTA rules of origin.

B. Impact of FIL

Because the *maquiladora* operations have enjoyed a privileged position under Mexican law and because they are regulated by specific Decree,[118] the FIL is not likely to have a significant impact on this program.

C. Treaty Impact

Article 5.5(b) of the Treaty generally provides that an enterprise of one treaty country will be treated as having a permanent establishment in the other country if a person, other than an independent agent, "habitually processes in the . . . [other country] on behalf of the enterprise goods or merchandise maintained in that [other country] by that enterprise, provided that such processing is carried on using assets, furnished, directly or indirectly, by that enterprise or any associated enterprise." Undoubtedly the purpose of this provision is to allow Mexico, if it so chooses, to impose the income and assets tax on a *maquila* operation.[119] Thus, under the Treaty, every U.S. company that takes advantage of the *maquiladora* program will be treated as having a permanent establishment in Mexico. It remains to be seen whether the *Hacienda* will elect to tax

---

[117] Commencing in 1994, a maquiladora is allowed to sell products domestically in an amount equal to 55% of its prior-year's export production.

[118] *Decreto para el Fomento y Operacion de la Industria Maquiladora de Exportacion,* published in the *Diario Oficial* on Dec. 22, 1989, and amended on Dec. 24, 1993.

[119] See Joint Committee on Taxation, *Explanation of Proposed Income Tax Treaty (and Proposed Protocol) between the United States and Mexico* (JCS–16–93), Oct. 26, 1993.

such operations, and therefore it is now difficult for a U.S. company to achieve certainty with respect to its Mexican tax planning.[120]

[120] For a general discussion of this and other issues, see Levey, Gordon and Sanders, "Planning for New and Existing Operations under the U.S.-Mexico Income Tax Treaty," 80 *J. Tax'n* 368 (June 1994).

CHAPTER 10

Legal Framework for the Sale of Goods in Mexico*

Lic. Eduardo Siqueiros T.
Barrera Siqueiros y Torres Landa, S.C.

I. Preface

"U.S.-Mexico trade has undergone tremendous growth in recent years. During 1993 imports from Mexico were valued at $39.9 billion, while U.S. exporters to Mexico totaled $41.6 billion. Total United States-Mexican trade for 1993 surpassed $81 billion dollars. Mexico is the third largest trading partner of the United States, trailing only Canada and Japan."

This chapter discusses Mexican law regarding the sale of goods by a foreign seller into Mexico.[1] Discussion will include an overview of the

* This chapter previously appeared in 12 *Hous. J. Int'l Law* 291 (1990). Reprinted with permission.

[1] Both Mexico and the U.S. are parties to the United Nations Convention on Contracts for the International Sale of Goods (CISG). U.N. Doc. A/CONF. 97/18, Annex 1, reprinted in 52 Fed. Reg. 6264 (1987), and in 19 I.L.M. 668 (1980). CISG's provisions govern the buyer's and seller's rights and duties when the parties fail to make a valid choice of law in an international sales contract. If one of the parties to such a contract is a resident of Mexico, and if the other party resides or has its principal place of business in a country which has adopted CISG, CISG governs the transaction.

laws invoked upon the sale of goods to Mexico, various forms of doing business in Mexico from which a seller can choose, import and customs considerations, currency issues, standard contract provisions, and dispute resolution procedures.[2]

II. Legal Structure for Selling Goods in Mexico

A. Introduction

Trade with other countries has permitted many companies established in North America to gain extensive experience in transnational business. Nonetheless, since sales of different commodities are guided by different rules, and since different markets have unique practices, sellers should be aware of the applicable Mexican trade regulations. Specialized knowledge helps avoid the risks of being driven out of the Mexican market or of becoming involved in prolonged litigation.

B. Identifying the Buyer

Different laws and regulations apply to sales to Mexican governmental agencies, to state-owned enterprises, and to the Mexican private sector. There are a few laws that all sellers should know.

The U.S. has made a reservation by declaring that it will not be bound by Art. 1(1)(b) of CISG. Senate Treaty Doc. No. 98–9, 98th Cong., 1st Sess., App. I(B) (1983) (provides explanation of this reservation). The U.S. ratified CISG in 1986, and on Jan. 1, 1988, it became effective. Mexico ratified CISG in 1987, and enacted it in 1988. *Decreto de Promulgacíon de la Convención de las Naciones Unidas Sobre los Contratos de Compraventa Internacional de Mercaderias, Diario Oficial (D.O.),* Mar. 17, 1988; United Nations Convention on Contracts for the International Sale of Goods, Apr. 11, 1980, 52 Fed. Reg. 6262–6280 (Mar. 26, 1987). The Convention applying to Agents and Representatives was also enacted into law by Mexico in 1988. *Decreto de Promulgacíon de la Convencin Sobre Representación en la Compraventa Internacional de Marcaderías, D.O.,* Feb. 22, 1988.

[2] For a comparative analysis of Mexican law and the CISG, see J. Barrera Graf, *La Convención de Viena Sobre los Contratos de Compraventa Internacional de Mercaderías y el Derecho Mexicano* 925 (1982).

1. Sales to the Public Sector

Sales to the public sector" include not only direct sales to ministries, departments, and agencies, but also sales to state enterprises (*organismos descentralizados*) such as *Petroleós Mexicanos* (Pemex) and *Comisión Federal de Electricidad* (CFE). Public sector sales also include sales made to entities in which the state has a majority interest.

Previously, domestic suppliers were heavily favored and international sources were permitted only when local firms could not adequately supply certain goods. As a result of the North American Free Trade Agreement ("NAFTA"), significant liberalization in the area of public sector sales has been achieved.

a. NAFTA

In general, the NAFTA rules on government procurement apply to the purchase of goods, services and construction services by specified federal government entities and enterprises of the NAFTA countries provided that certain value thresholds are met.[3] Currently, the NAFTA rules on government procurement do not apply to state and provincial government entities and enterprises. However, the parties to NAFTA have agreed to conduct negotiations with their state and provincial governments with the goal of obtaining their commitments, on a voluntary and reciprocal basis, to be governed by NAFTA's rules on government procurement.[4]

In particular, NAFTA provides that, for procurements governed by its terms, the parties must accord nondiscriminatory and national treatment to the goods and services of producers of other NAFTA

---

[3] NAFTA, Art. 1001. With respect to contracts with federal government entities, the threshold for contracts for goods and services (excluding construction services) between Mexico and the U.S. is $50,000. The threshold for construction service contracts between Mexico and the U.S. is $6.5 million. Regarding contracts with government enterprises, such as PEMEX and CFE, the value threshold for contracts for goods and services (excluding contract services) between Mexico and the U.S. is $250,000 while the threshold for contract services contracts is set at $8 million. These threshold values are subject to adjustment each year according to the U.S. rate of inflation. NAFTA, Art. 1001.

[4] NAFTA, Art. 1024.

countries.[5] Thus, each party to NAFTA must treat the goods and suppliers of goods and services of any other NAFTA country no less favorably than it treats its own goods and suppliers of goods and services or those of any other NAFTA country. Moreover, in general, no party may accord less favorable treatment to a locally established supplier on the basis of (1) the supplier's degree of foreign affiliation or ownership or (2) the fact that the goods and services offered by the supplier are those of another NAFTA country.[6]

Nevertheless, each party to NAFTA has reserved the right to favor national suppliers for procurement in certain situations. For example, the NAFTA procurement rules to not apply to U.S. minority and small business set asides.[7] Similarly, while PEMEX and CFE are included on the list of government enterprises to which the NAFTA procurement rules apply, they are subject to certain phase-in rules between 1994 and 2003. During this transition period, a certain percentage of the procurements of these government enterprises may be reserved for Mexican suppliers.[8]

NAFTA also regulates the procurement process by establishing rules regarding the qualification of suppliers, the provision of notice of a proposed procurement, time periods for the receipt of tenders by suppliers, the distribution of tender documentation, the submission, receipt, and opening of tenders from suppliers, and the awarding of contracts.[9] Under NAFTA, a contract will be awarded to the supplier who:

(1) conforms to the essential requirements of the notices/tender documentation;

(2) complies with the conditions for participation;

(3) is found to be fully capable of performing the contract; and

---

[5] NAFTA, Art. 1003.

[6] *Id.*

[7] NAFTA, Annex 1001.2b.

[8] NAFTA, Annex 1001.2a.

[9] NAFTA, Arts. 1008–1015.

(4) submits the lowest-priced tender or the most advantageous tender in terms of specific published criteria.[10]

In addition, NAFTA requires that each party establish and maintain a procedure whereby a supplier may challenge any aspect of the procurement process (which begins once an entity has decided on its procurement requirements an continues through the contract award).[11]

b. Domestic Legislation

Every sale of goods or services in the federal public sector is governed by the Acquisitions and Public Works Law of 1993.[12] This law provides procedural rules for arranging a transaction. As a general rule, public bids must be solicited; only under certain conditions may contracts be awarded directly. Supervision of the bidding process is entrusted to the Ministry of the General Comptrollership of the Federation. Contracts may be terminated by the government at any time "for any reasons of public interest."[13] Other supplementary laws also govern purchases, such as the Mexican Commercial[14] or Civil Codes.[15]

Additionally, a "procurement committee" is normally required to make government purchases through a public bidding process. Each governmental entity has its own procurement committee.

2. Sales to the Private Sector

A foreign seller and a Mexican buyer may freely agree on the terms of their relationship. Likewise, their contract may contain any freely

---

[10] NAFTA, Art. 1015.

[11] NAFTA, Art. 1017.

[12] *Ley de Adquisiciones y Obra Pública, D.O.*, Dec. 30, 1993.

[13] *Id.*, Art. 40.

[14] *Código de Comercio* [hereinafter, C.Com.], 1889. Commercial legislation in Mexico is of a federal nature and derives its authority from constitutional powers granted to the federal Congress.

[15] *Código Civil Para el Distrito Federal* [hereinafter, C.C.D.F.] (applicable on federal matters and supplementary to the C.Com.).

agreed upon provisions, with limits only on provisions that are contrary to the public law of order.[16]

C. Structuring Sales to the Mexican Market

A wide range of alternatives is available to a seller of goods wishing to enter the Mexican market. A seller's decision regarding the manner in which it wishes to enter the Mexican market will depend in large part on the amount of resources that it wishes to commit to the Mexican market at that time. A foreign seller may choose from the following forms of doing business.

1. Direct Sales by a Foreign Supplier

The seller can make direct contact with a Mexican customer. This usually occurs when either the customer seeks specific goods from a foreign supplier or the supplier advertises in Mexico. In general, no restrictions exist upon advertising in Mexico by foreign manufacturers.[17] Advertising mediums include the newspapers, special interest periodicals, and direct mail.

2. Representative Office

The supplier may establish a representative office to facilitate sales to buyers in Mexico. These offices are recognized under Mexican legislation. The office's activities must be limited to the promotion of the supplier's goods or the gathering of information for the purchase of goods in Mexico. Representative offices may not make direct sales to Mexican buyers or receive income directly from Mexican buyers. However, samples may be exhibited without import duties or restrictions,[18] under the new Foreign Investment Law[19] and the 1989 Regulations to the prior

---

[16] C.Com., Art. 78. This is the principle of commercial contracts of liberty to include provisions.

[17] Suppliers should take care to meet requirements that may be imposed by specific legislation on registering with health authorities to advertise foodstuffs, medicines, and alcoholic beverages, as well as requirements imposed by consumer protection laws.

[18] See Part III, *infra*.

[19] *Ley de Inversión Extranjera, D.O.*, Dec. 27, 1993 [hereinafter "FIL"].

Foreign Investment Law (FIL Regulations).[20] The Mexican Income Tax Law (ITL)[21] and the U.S.-Mexico tax treaty ("Tax Treaty")[22] exempt the activities by these offices from Mexican taxation by providing that these activities will not create a "permanent establishment," a taxable entity, for the non-Mexican seller.[23] The opening of a representative office subjects the seller to Mexican general investment, commercial, and labor laws. Labor laws in addition to the Federal Labor Law include those on Social Security and the Low Cost Housing Fund (*Infonavit*), and other regulations depending on the particular nature of the activity.[24]

3. Branch Office

For a seller who wishes to maintain direct contact with the Mexican market, the natural step following the opening of a representative office is to establish a branch office.[25] Prior approval of the Ministry of Commerce and Industrial Development (*Secretaría de Comercio y Fomento Industrial*—"SECOFI") is required.[26] Moreover, the branch must be registered with the National Registry of Foreign Investment[27] as well as formally recognized in the Public Registry of Commerce in the city where it is established. Additionally, the applicant must acquire the

---

[20] *Reglamento de la Ley para Promover la Inversión Mexicana y Regular la Inversidn Extranjera, D.O.*, May 16, 1989 [hereinafter, FIL Regulations]; see Camil, "Mexico's 1989 Foreign Investment Regulations: The Cornerstone of a New Economic Model," 12 *Hous. J. Int'l L.* 1 (1989).

[21] *Ley del Impuesto Sobre la Renta, D.O.*, Dec. 30, 1980, Art. 3, 1 v.

[22] *Convenio entre el Gobierno de los Estados Unidos Mexicanos y el Gobierno de los Estados Unidos de América para Quitar la Doble Imposición e Impedir la Evasión Fiscal en Materia de Impuesto Sobre la Renta, D.O.*, Feb. 3, 1994.

[23] ITL, Art. 33. In the case of the Tax Treaty with the United States, goods may even be warehoused and delivered within Mexico, without such action being deemed to be a "permanent establishment." See Part III, *infra*. For a detailed discussion of Mexico's taxation, see M. Tron, *Régimen Fiscal de los Extranjeros en Mexico* (1990).

[24] *Ley Federal de Trabajo* [Federal Labor Law], *D.O.*, Apr. 1, 1970; *Ley del Instituto Mexicano del Seguro Social, D.O.*, Mar. 12, 1973 [hereinafter, Social Security Institute Law]; *Ley del Instituto del Fondo Nacional de la Vivienda para los Trabajadores, D.O.*, Apr. 24, 1972 [hereinafter, National Fund for Workmen's Housing Institute Law]. A brief analysis of Mexican labor laws can be found in Ch. 12, *infra*.

[25] *Ley General de Sociedades Mercantiles, D.O.*, Aug. 4, 1934 and Aug. 28, 1934 [hereinafter, GLCC], Art. 251.

[26] FIL, Art. 17.

[27] FIL, Art. 32.

"blessing" of the Ministry of Foreign Affairs (*Secretaria de Relaciones Exteriores*—"SRE") before setting up the branch office,[28] and the company must submit information on its legal incorporation and on the validity of the corporate resolution authorizing the branch to the MFA.[29]

4. Broker

A variation on making direct contacts between the seller and the buyer in Mexico is the use of a broker or intermediary (*corredor/mediador*).[30] The broker's purpose is to put a potential buyer in touch with the seller. The broker will receive a fee for this service. *Corredores* or *mediadores* do not act as legal representatives or employees nor do they have any power to bind the buyer or seller.[31] They merely serve as a bridge between the seller and buyer. The broker relationship may be ongoing or entered into on a case-by-case basis.

5. Sales Agent

Brokers' services may not be sufficient for a seller with inadequate knowledge of Mexican language, customs, and commercial practices. Or, the seller may simply not have the time and resources to pursue the Mexican market. In either case, the seller may seek assistance from an agent in Mexico.[32] Agents (*comisionistas*) are subject to the rules of attorneys-in-fact (*mandatarios*).[33] Although the agent may have flexibility in performing its duties, it may not act beyond the scope of authority granted by the principal.[34] Any actions undertaken in excess of

---

[28] The Ministry will require the applicant to execute the "Calvo Clause." This clause will require the applicant to deem itself to be Mexican with regard to its activities and not seek the protection of its own government. See H. Steiner & D. Vagts, *Transnational Legal Problems* 522 (1976).

[29] C.C.D.F., Arts. 2736–2738.

[30] A. Gargollo, *Contratos Mercantiles Atípicos* 132 (1985).

[31] C.Com., Arts. 51–74.

[32] A. Díaz Bravo, *Contratos Mercantiles* 217 (1983).

[33] See C.Com., ch. 1, tit. III (regulates the comisionistas activities and principal-agent relationships). For a detailed analysis of agent and distributors under Mexican law, see Siqueiros, *Agency and Distribution Agreements in Mexico, International Agency and Distribution Agreement* (1991).

[34] C.Com., Art. 286.

its authority are non-binding on the principal. However, for the protection of third parties, such actions will bind the agent.[35]

Mexican commercial law allows the agent to act in its own name or in the name of the principal. In either case, however, any action is for the benefit or detriment of the principal, with the exception of acts beyond the agent's authority. When acting within the scope of its authority, an agent may contract with the buyer.[36] The agent has a direct action against and personal liability to the buyer. Actions include those for payment of the price, and actions for liability under warranties.

The commercial agency contract is not required to contain a minimum duration; agencies may be structured for an open term or a specified period. Expiration of a specified term will free both parties and release them from any further liability, unless specific contract provisions direct otherwise. Options may extend the contract's term, or terms may provide that the contract expires if one of the parties is in default. As a general rule, an agency agreement for an open term allows the parties to terminate the agreement upon 60-days prior notice.[37] However, the Mexican Supreme Court has established that a principal may terminate the contract at any time, but in such event the principal must indemnify the agent for any damages caused by premature termination. These damages may include unreimbursed expenses incurred by the agent in pursuing the business, or its provable lost profits such as those from business deals scheduled to close in the near future.[38]

An agency contract does not have to be registered with any government office in Mexico. The United Nations Convention on Contracts for the International Sale of Goods [39] sets out rules governing authority of appointment for contracts where both the principal and buyer are domiciled in different countries, and where the agent is domiciled in a country that is a party to this Convention.

---

[35] *Id.,* Art. 289.

[36] *Id.,* Art. 285.

[37] C.C.D.F., Art. 2478 (this is applied in a supplementary manner for *tracto sucesivo* contracts).

[38] *Informe 1979, Tercera Sala,* no. 15, p. 14.

[39] See N. 1, *supra.*

6. Consignment

Under a consignment arrangement, a seller ships goods to a Mexican consignee.[40] The seller requests that the consignee sell the goods on agreed upon terms. Terms may include an obligation on the part of the consignee to return the goods to the consignor if the sale is not accomplished within a specified time. Title to goods under consignment does not pass to the consignee, and in the case of bankruptcy of the consignee, the goods will be withdrawn from the consignee's assets.[41]

7. Distribution

A foreign manufacturer or seller may not want to sell goods directly to the Mexican consumer because of the inherent risks in this type of sale. Instead, it may wish to do business only with an individual who will bear the risks of sale, service, and payment.

In this case, the manufacturer should act through a distributor.[42] The distributor purchases directly from the seller for resale in the Mexican market. The distributor is normally the only contact that the seller has in Mexico. Once the sale is perfected between the seller and the distributor, the distributor sells the goods. A buyer that purchases from a distributor has recourse only against the distributor and not against the foreign manufacturer or supplier.

Contracted terms in the distributorship agreement may include warranty requirements, service requirements, maximum or minimum price discounts, and other terms of trade. Distributors, like agents, may be

---

[40] Gargollo, N. 30, *supra,* at 61.

[41] *Ley de Quiebras y Suspension de Pagos, D.O.,* Apr. 20, 1943 [hereinafter, Bankruptcy Law], Art. 159, VI(a).

[42] Gargollo, N. 30, *supra,* at 169. See also Siqueiros, "International Agency and Distribution Agreements," (1991); Saltoun & Spudis, "International Distribution and Sales Agency Agreements: Practical Guidelines for U.S. Exporters," 38 *Bus. Law.* 883 (1983).

appointed with geographical limitations. Furthermore, exclusive distributorship arrangements are not, per se, invalid under Mexican law.[43]

Distribution contracts usually require the distributor to make a minimum number of sales within the territory. Contracts usually must provide guidelines on prices, delivery, and transfer of title. Although rare, contracts occasionally provide that the final consumer, purchasing from a distributor in Mexico, will take title and delivery of the goods at the manufacturing or warehousing facilities of the foreign manufacturer-seller.

8. Franchise

If a franchise operation is desired for the Mexican market, it is best established through a distribution contract, complemented by other contracts involving the licensing of trademarks and trade names, and involving provision of technical expertise.[44] Unless the contract contains a trademark license, it will not require registration in Mexico; if it does, then it will need to be recorded with the General Bureau of Technological Development under the penalty of unenforceability.[45]

9. Manufacturing (*Maquila*)

A foreign business may have a Mexican company assemble or fabricate goods not intended for sale in Mexico. Any materials or components utilized in the process of manufacture or assembly will be either supplied directly by the foreign supplier or purchased by the local

---

[43] The recently enacted Competition Law (*Ley Federal de Competencia Económica, D.O.*, Dec. 24, 1992) in force since June, 1993, will examine whether a relationship will create a relative (or vertical) monopolistic practice in light of the relative market and the power of the parties within such market. See Part III.P, *infra*.

[44] *Ley de Fomento y Protección de la Propiedad Industrial, D.O.*, June 29, 1991. Although such specific legislation only contains provisions governing franchise contracts from the point of view of a transfer of intellectual property, other rules that apply to the purchase sale contract and other commercial practices are admitted by reference.

[45] *Id.*, Art. 11.

manufacturer on behalf of the foreign business. This agreement constitutes a *maquila* operation. [46]

A *maquila* operation is one in which the manufacture or assembly of goods in Mexico is accomplished by using components and materials imported temporarily into Mexico on a duty-free basis. The finished goods are subsequently re-exported. Although not widely known, current regulations allow domestic sales in an amount not to exceed 55 percent of the value of exports generated within the preceding 12 months, provided that a permit for such sales is obtained from SECOFI. Moreover, under NAFTA, restrictions on sales of a *maquiladora* to the domestic market will be phased out over a seven-year period.[47] When a *maquila* operation sells goods into the Mexican market, the seller is required to pay import duties on the foreign components integrated into the finished product before it is sold to the local consumer.[48]

The importance of the *maquila* as a form of doing business in Mexico has been somewhat diminished due to the passage of NAFTA, because as a result of the trilateral agreement virtually all tariffs between the U.S. and Mexico will be eliminated over a 15-year period. As these tariff reductions take effect, the advantage of the *maquiladora*—namely, its ability to temporarily import goods into Mexico on a duty-free basis—will be lost. Essentially, under NAFTA, *maquiladoras* will be placed on equal competitive footing with other Mexican companies. Nevertheless, NAFTA's tariff reductions are subject to a phase-in period. Thus, the *maquiladora* program will retain significance in the short-run. Pursuant to NAFTA, the *maquila* program will terminate in the year 2001.[49]

10. Partnership Ventures

If the seller wants a permanent operation in Mexico, it can enter into a partnership agreement with a domestic manufacturer or seller who will

---

[46] For a description of the rules governing the maquiladora industry, see Ch. 7, *supra*.

[47] NAFTA, Annex I at I–M–34.

[48] *Decreto para el Fomento y Operación de la Industria Maquiladora de Exportación,* Art. 12, *D.O.,* Dec. 22, 1989.

[49] NAFTA, Art. 303 and Annex 303.7, § B.

manufacture or sell the foreign product in the Mexican market. Through a partnership agreement (*asociación en participación*),[50] a domestic company or individual becomes an *asociante,* who acts in its own name and need not disclose the participation of the other silent partner (*asociado*). *Asociados* transfer title to contributed goods to the *asociante.* [51] Any liability involving the goods falls on the Mexican *asociante.* Profits and losses from this transaction are shared by the *asociante* and *asociado(s).*[52] The ITL imposes a duty on the *asociante* to withhold income taxes payable by the *asociado.*[53] Normally, the *asociado* is not responsible for losses exceeding its contributions.[54]

11. Mexican Sales Corporation

If acting as a silent partner in a Mexican business is not satisfactory to the foreign seller, it can establish a sales company. This company is formed under Mexican law to make sales exclusively in the Mexican market. Under this scenario, a company is formed under Mexican law and protects the owners from liability exceeding their capital contribution. This can be done through a *sociedad de responsabilidad limitada* (SRL),[55] which is a limited liability company, or a *sociedad anónima* (SA).[56]

---

[50] GLCC, Arts. 252–259. This business organization is analogous to a limited partnership under U.S. law.

[51] If title is not actually transferred, but instead only certain benefits are transferred, this fact must be recorded in the Public Registry of Commerce of the *asociante's* domicile; otherwise, the goods may be deemed owned by the *asociante*. GLCC, Art. 257.

[52] Absent agreement to the contrary, sharing is on a pro rata basis in proportion to each party's contributions.

[53] ITL, Art. 9.

[54] GLCC, Art. 258.

[55] See GLCC, ch. V. This organization is intended mainly for close-ended corporations.

[56] A *sociedad anónima* is regulated under ch. V of the GLCC. Its structure allows for public trading. Traditionally, SA's were preferred over all other companies (including SRL's) not only due to limited liability, but mainly because they could issue bearer shares. However, since 1983, SA's may only issue nominative shares. In certain foreign jurisdictions (perhaps even in the U.S.), the SRL may be treated as a "partnership" for tax purposes, because of its characteristics of limited transferability of interest and life.

Different rules apply to formation and operations depending on the selected type of company. In the SA, stock is issued and is transferable by a simple endorsement. Corporate resolutions are governed by the principle of a simple majority vote. In contrast, the SRL does not issue stock. Instead, partners participate in proportion to their capital contributions. Decisions in an SRL are normally adopted by qualified majorities. Participation in this sales entity may be in either a minority or majority position.[57]

a. Majority Shareholding

In order to control decisions or ensure distribution of profits, a foreign seller may desire to hold a majority or all of the shares of a Mexican company. While the FIL reserves certain activities to the Mexican government or to Mexican investors, and imposes certain percentage limitations on foreign investment in other sectors, majority participation by foreign investors is currently possible in all except for this limited number of activities without seeking governmental approval. Further, whereas governmental approval was once required when a foreign investor purchased more than 25 percent of the capital of *an existing company*, the FIL now provides that the Federal Investment Commission (FIC) approval will be required only in the event that the degree of foreign participation in the existing entity is to exceed 49 percent and the total value of the assets of the acquired company exceeds the amount set annually by the FIC.[58] That amount is currently set at N$85 million (approximately US $28 million).[59] Such companies must be registered with the National Registry of Foreign Investment.[60]

b. Minority Shareholding

Under Mexican law, it is possible to include certain provisions for the protection of minority shareholders in a company's charter documents

---

[57] Any foreign investment above 49% is legally deemed to be a majority interest and is subject to establishment and growth limitations and controls. FIL Regulations, *D.O.*, May 16, 1989.

[58] FIL, Art. 9. This is normally referred to as a "demexicanization" of an existing company.

[59] FIL, Art. 9 and Tenth Transitory Article.

[60] FIL, Art. 32.

which essentially create quasi-veto rights for the minority shareholders. Under such provisions, where a company's bylaws require a qualifying vote for a decision, the participation of the foreign investor would be required in order for the decision to be adopted.[61]

Minority shareholders can assure themselves of return by pyramiding the investment (where permitted under the FIL),[62] or providing different series of stock with different distribution rights.[63] As previously mentioned, any company with foreign shareholders must register with the National Registry of Foreign Investment.[64]

To achieve a sales organization that meets the needs of the foreign supplier, a Mexican sales company can be combined with a distributorship, an agency, a license for trademarks, or a *maquila*. The final decision regarding establishing a Mexican company with the seller's participation in the capital must be analyzed under the tax regulations of Mexico and the seller's country. This is necessary because any profit transferred from the seller to the Mexican sales company will inevitably be taxed under the Mexican ITL.

III. Import, Customs, and Other Considerations

A. Introduction

Like any sales transaction inside or outside the borders of a country, sales to Mexico may be made with provisions for delivery *ex works* at the manufacturer's facilities, free on board (FOB) at a port of the seller's territory, or FOB at either the manufacturer's facilities, the seller's

---

[61] For an analysis of protection of minority rights, see E. Siqueiros, *El Llamado Veto de las Minorías en la Sociedad Anónima* (1979).

[62] "Pyramiding" is accomplished by a holding company owning "Mexican" shares representing 51% of the ownership. The foreign shareholder has 49% of the capital stock in this holding company. Therefore, the net foreign participation is effectively 73.99%. Additional holding companies can be established and tiers of ownership can be formed.

[63] Under the GLCC, Art. 16, the shareholders may provide in the by-laws of a corporation for the distribution of earnings in a proportion different than equity participation, such as, for example, allotting 40% of earnings to a class of stock representing 25% of capital stock.

[64] FIL Regulations, II, tit. VII, Arts. 42–79. Annual reports are also required.

facilities, or those of a transportation agent. Sales may be made cost, insurance and freight (CIF) invoiced by a seller within its borders, or as free alongside (FAS) for transportation by vessel to a Mexican port or other ports.[65] In the case of delivery of goods within its own borders, the seller will not be confronted with any customs requirements. However, it may need to obtain an authorization for the export of goods from its government if any restrictions are in effect.[66]

B. Delivery of Goods

When delivery is to be made within Mexico, the seller has two options.

1. Sales With Delivery Inside Mexico

A seller may agree with the buyer or its local agent or representative to deliver goods inside Mexico. This may involve delivering them at a port of entry without clearing customs. Examples of such deliveries include delivering goods at a Mexican seaport, airport, or a Mexican border station. In these cases, the seller will be exempted from complying with any customs requirements under Mexican law. If the seller delivers goods elsewhere inside Mexico, the seller will face all of the legal requirements for importation of goods and payment of duties.

Delivery within Mexico will mean that the seller shall be deemed to have a permanent establishment, and therefore will be subject to Mexican income tax on profit earned on the sale. However, the U.S.-Mexico tax treaty now allows delivery to be made locally without triggering the concept of a permanent establishment.[67]

---

[65] For a precise description of these and other standard terms for delivery of goods, see International Chamber of Commerce, *International Rules for the Interpretation of Trade Terms: Incoterms* (1990) (I.C.C. Pub. No. 350).

[66] See, in the case of U.S. residents, Export Administration Act, 50 U.S.C. § 2401–2420 (1988); Trading with the Enemy Act, 50 U.S.C. § 1–44 (1988); Arms Export Control Act, 22 U.S.C. § 2751–2796d (1988); International Emergency Powers Act, 50 U.S.C. § 2405 (1988).

[67] See Art. 5, U.S.-Mexico Tax Treaty.

2. Sales With Delivery at Bonded Warehouses

Goods can be delivered closer to the facilities of the customer by delivering goods to one of many bonded warehouses. These warehouses, referred to as *Almacenes Generales de Deposito,*[68] are found in most Mexican cities. The warehouses will take delivery without requiring payment of import duties and taxes until the buyer actually withdraws the delivered products from the warehouse. A customer may withdraw the shipment of goods in whole or in part. This allows the customer to avoid paying his duties in a single payment, which could strain its cash flow. Goods may remain in the warehouse for a one year period, with a one year renewal option. In these cases, the import duty shall be determined prior to the deposit of the goods.

C. Imports

1. Definite Imports

In addition to import duties specified by NAFTA and/or the Import Duties Law,[69] as applicable, other taxes must also be paid.

The value added tax[70] (VAT) is imposed on most goods at a normal rate of ten percent. Medicines and processed food are taxed at a rate of six percent. However, medicines will be taxed at a "zero" tax rate during 1994.[71] basic foodstuffs are taxed at a "zero" percent rate, in order to allow crediting of taxes paid by seller.

If a seller agrees to deliver goods CIF at a Mexican customer's facilities within the territory, for example, in Mexico City, the seller must consider payment of the value added tax in addition to the costs of the product, insurance, and transportation. In addition to the VAT, a customs

---

[68] *Ley General de Organizaciones y Actividades Auxiliares de Crédito, D.O.*, Jan. 14, 1985, Arts. 11–23.

[69] *Ley del Impuesto General de Importación, D.O.*, Feb. 12, 1988 [hereinafter, Import Duties Law].

[70] *Ley del Impuesto al Valor Agregado*, ch. V, *D.O.*, Dec. 29, 1978 (deals with value added tax on imported goods).

[71] *Ley de Ingresos de la Federación, D.O.*, Dec. 27, 1993, Art. 16.

processing fee of eight-tenths of one percent is also assessed.[72] Under NAFTA, this customs processing fee may not be increased with respect to goods originating from countries that are a party to NAFTA and must be eliminated with respect to such goods by June 30, 1999.[73] The importation of samples does not result in import duties.[74]

2. Temporary Imports

A Mexican buyer may wish to import the products temporarily in order to integrate them into a final product. Companies with a *maquila* program are allowed to import into Mexico the materials, components, and equipment needed to manufacture their products without paying import duties. Mexican companies without a *maquila* program that only temporarily import such goods on a case by case basis may receive authorization for the importation of such products for up to two years.

Under another program, a company may obtain registration for the temporary importation of goods for further export. These programs are also known as PITEX[75] and ALTEX.[76] Each program requires the importer to submit a performance bond granted by a local authorized company. The bond guarantees payment of import duties and penalties if the goods are not withdrawn from the country prior to the duration specified in the temporary import permit.

---

[72] *Ley Federal de Derechos, D.O.,* Dec. 31, 1981, as amended Dec. 28, 1989, Art. 49 (assesses fee for customs processing).

[73] NAFTA, Art. 310, Annex 310.1, § A.

[74] Import Duties Law, n. 70, Art. II, Rule 7 (d). Under NAFTA, commercial samples of negligible value may be imported duty-free when imported on a temporary basis. NAFTA, Art. 305.

[75] *Decreto que Establece Programas de Importación Temporal para Producir Artículos de Exportación, D.O.,* May 9, 1985, amended by *Decreto que Modifica el que Establece Programas de Importación Temporal para Producir Artfculos de Exportación, D.O.,* Sept. 23,1988.

[76] This program requires exports of at least $3 million or 40% of annual sales. *Oficio por el que se Hace del Conocimiento de las Dependencias y Entidades de la Administración Pública Federal, la Relación de Empresas Altamente Exportadoras, D.O.,* Dec. 4, 1987, amended by *Oficio por el que se Actualiza la Relación de Empresas Altamente Exportadoras Publicada el 4 de Diciembre de 1987, D.O.,* July 15, 1988.

Under NAFTA, these performance-based duty waiver programs are prohibited, and all such existing programs will terminate by the year 2001.[77]

With regard to temporary imports not subject to these special programs, the importer is allowed to deposit the amount of the import duty in a special bank account, referred to as *cuenta aduanera.*[78] When the goods are exported, the importer will be allowed to recover the deposit, plus the interest earned. The foregoing is not applicable to the VAT, which must be paid in full.

In addition, NAFTA mandates that each party allow duty-free entry of certain goods imported on a temporary basis, including professional equipment, press equipment, equipment for sound or television broadcasting, cinematographic equipment, sports equipment, goods intended for display or demonstration, and commercial samples and advertising films.[79]

D. Import Restrictions

The Mexican government eliminated in the late 1980's most of the prior import restrictions that were a part of the very protectionist policies relating to the Mexican manufacturing industry base. Further, under NAFTA, quantitative prohibitions and restrictions on imports, such as quotas and licensing requirements, are prohibited. However, Mexico has excepted certain sensitive products from this prohibition. For example, firearms, certain pharmaceuticals, endangered species, and used computers, printers, and peripherals have been excepted. In addition, certain Mexican import restrictions will be phased out over a ten-year period, such as those on automobiles.[80] Existing indirect restrictions include registration requirements. For example, importers must be registered with the "Importers Registry" operated by the Ministry of Finance and Public Credit.[81]

---

[77] NAFTA, Art. 303 and Annex 303.7, § B.

[78] *Ley Aduanera,* Art. 58A and 58B [hereinafter, Customs Law].

[79] NAFTA, Art. 305.

[80] NAFTA, Art. 309 and Annex 301.3, § B.

[81] This registry is the *Padrón de Importadores.*

E. Harmonized Import Classification

A great step towards advancing Mexico's international trade was Mexico's adoption of the Harmonized Import Classification on July 1, 1988.[82] Under this program, imports are covered under the same classification number code that is in force in the exporter's country. Previously, products subject to classification for export purposes did not necessarily correspond to the same classification for import purposes under Mexican law. Disparities frequently arose among customs officials and importers over import classifications and the import duty. The Harmonized System of tariff classification has taken on added importance with the passage of NAFTA since the rules of origin, which determine whether goods are eligible for preferential tariff treatment under NAFTA, are keyed to changes in tariff classifications for goods incorporating non-NAFTA components.[83]

F. Exchange Controls

Mexico abandoned several years back its exchange control systems for payment of imports. Today, currency is widely available for settling transactions. If an obligation is to be paid in Mexico, a daily published rate will apply for conversion into Pesos.

G. Transfer Pricing

Effective as of January 1, 1993, Mexico introduced a new system for the valuation of goods before customs (consistent with the GATT Code), the purpose of which is to simplify the determination of the basis for imposition of import duties. This system must be used by importers of goods in order to establish the taxable basis upon which the import duty (*Ad Valorem*) will be applied.

---

[82] *Ley del Impuesto General de Importación* [General Import Tax Law], *D.O.*, Feb. 12, 1988; *Reglas Generales y Complementarias para la Aplicación e Interpretacion de la Tarifa del Impuesto General de Importadores* [General and Complementary Rules for the Application and Construction of the General Import Tax Tariff], *D.O.*, May 20–31, 1988 (explanatory notes).

[83] NAFTA, Art. 401.

The concept of "linkage degree" (*grado de vinculación*), previously applicable under Mexican law, has been eliminated from the customs legislation. Notwithstanding the above, the existence of a relationship between seller and importer makes the Mexican tax authorities presume that the agreed upon price may not necessarily correspond to the free market, although proof to the contrary may be presented.[84]

H. Sanitary Registration

Food products, medicines, personal care products, or alcoholic beverages must be registered with the Mexican Ministry of Health prior to their commercial importation into Mexico.[85] Additionally, these products will be required to have a "counter-label" (*contraetiqueta*) attached before they are sold. This counter-label must provide information about the product, the seller, and the Mexican importer.[86]

After Mexico joined the GATT and opened its economy to foreign manufactured products without requiring import licenses, many abuses occurred with products bearing Mexican trademarks that were purchased abroad.[87] The abuses arose when sellers marketed these products in Mexico without obtaining authorization from the trademark holder.[88]

I. Unfair Trade Practices

The GATT restricts the "dumping" of goods into the markets of a member country.[89] Dumping occurs when a seller sells goods on a

---

[84] Customs Law, *D.O.*, July 26, 1993, Art. 52–A.

[85] *Ley General de Salud, D.O.*, Feb. 7, 1984 [hereinafter, Health Law], Art. 204 (dealing with the importation of goods).

[86] The counter-label requirement has been extended to all imported goods except those to be consumed by the importer, i.e., those that will not be traded. Decree of the Ministry of Commerce and Industrial Promotion, *D.O.*, July 12, 1988. See also Ns. 107–108 and accompanying text.

[87] On the question of intellectual property and the license of trademarks in Mexico, see H. Rangel Ortiz, *"La Licencia de Uso de Marca como Sustitución del Propietario de la Marca,"* UNAM (1986).

[88] Most of the products bear labels belonging to multinational companies.

[89] See Antidumping Code and Regulations against Unfair International Trade Practices.

commercial basis at a price lower than its normal domestic market price with the intention of eliminating competition in the market. To constitute dumping in Mexico, injury to at least 25 percent of the production must occur in the Mexican manufacturing sector. In recent years, Mexico has been acting swiftly on claims alleging unfair trade practices by foreign suppliers, and has been imposing countervailing duties for sellers found to be performing such practices. In some cases, even though there have been instances of "dumping," no injury to the local producer has been found, and no duty was levied.[90]

Investigations of dumping activities commence in accordance with the Foreign Trade Law[91] and its Regulations. While the investigation is proceeding, a temporary countervailing duty may be imposed. Thereafter, if dumping is found to exist, the duty is confirmed or adjusted. If no unfair practice or injury is found, the duty will be dropped. Contrary to the internal legislation of other GATT members, Mexico's law does not impose countervailing duties in a retroactive manner since this would violate constitutional prohibitions on the retroactivity of legislation in administrative actions.[92]

Under NAFTA, each party reserves the right to apply its own antidumping and countervailing duty laws to goods imported from another party.[93] However, NAFTA does provide for the creation of binational review panels that will act as a substitute for judicial review of the final administrative decision of a party involving goods imported from another party.[94]

---

[90] One example of this is a claim submitted by a local subsidiary of a U.S. alkaline battery manufacturer against another U.S. competitor for dumping. The decision rendered indicated that the claimant did not foresee a decline in sales but rather an increase in sales in a growing market.

[91] See N. 89, *supra*.

[92] *Constitución Política de los Estados Unidos Mexicanos* [Const.], Art. 14 (the first paragraph states that "no law shall be given retroactive effects in detriment of any person.").

[93] NAFTA, Art. 1902.

[94] NAFTA, Art. 1904.

J. Tax

A seller of goods who is domiciled outside of Mexico will rarely need to be concerned with the assessment of income taxes by Mexican authorities.[95] But, in the following cases, provisions of the ITL will subject the foreign seller to Mexican income taxes.

1. Source of Income Concept

The Mexican ITL is based primarily on the concept of the source of income: when the source of profit is found within Mexico, it is taxed. A non-resident seller is subject to income taxes only when the activity developed in Mexico, for example, delivery of goods within the territory, has triggered the concept of a permanent establishment. As an exception, the U.S.-Mexico Tax Treaty allows U.S. residents to deliver goods within Mexico without triggering the concept of a permanent establishment.

2. Permanent Establishment

Under the Tax Treaty, a non-resident seller will be deemed to have a "permanent establishment" for purposes of the ITL when it has a "fixed place of business through which the business of [the] enterprise is wholly or partly carried on."[96] Thus, for example, a "permanent establishment" includes a place of management, a branch, an office, a factory or a workshop.[97] In addition, where the non-resident seller has a representative in Mexico who is empowered to conduct business on its behalf, and the representative either acts on behalf of the seller in executing sales contracts or habitually processes goods or merchandise of the seller in Mexico, he will be deemed to have a "permanent establishment." [98] The effect will be to tax any income arising from these transactions as income received by a Mexican corporation; such income is subject to a tax of 34 percent on realized profits" [99]

---

95 See Tron, N. 23, *supra,* at 165.

96 See U.S.-Mexico Tax Treaty, Art. 5.

97 *Id.*

98 *Id.*

99 ITL, Arts. 2, 3.

3. Branch or Domestic Sales Company

A seller acting through a branch or a Mexican company will pay income taxes on profit, which is calculated from income less allowable deductions. The tax rate will be 34 percent.

K. Currency of Payment

If a seller receives payment outside of Mexico (normally at its main offices abroad), it usually will not encounter any exchange control restrictions on non-Mexican currency. In these cases, Mexican law allows such payments precisely as required under the contract. If payment is to be made within Mexico, the buyer can pay the equivalent in pesos at the rate published on a daily basis by the Central Bank.[100]

L. Consumer Protection

The Consumer Protection Law[101] applies to foreign sellers that deliver in Mexico. If a product is found defective or unfit for the ordinary purpose for which it is used, this law provides that the consumer may elect to rescind the contract or pay a reduced purchase price.[102] It also requires payment for any actual damages caused by the product.[103] All warranties must be provided in writing and must state the scope of the coverage provided under the warranty; the duration and terms of the warranty; the procedure for making the warranty effective; the address to which claims may be sent; and the location of repair centers.[104] The warranty provided on a product may not be less than that required by any applicable governmental order.[105] A consumer may look to either the producer, importer or distributor of a product for performance under the warranty.[106]

---

[100] See *Ley Monetaria*, Art. 8. The rate is published on business days, and reflects the prior business days' market rate (hereinafter, Monetary Law).

[101] *Ley Federal de Protección al Consumidor* [CPL], *D.O.*, Dec. 24, 1992.

[102] CPL, Art. 82.

[103] *Id.*

[104] CPL, Art. 78.

[105] CPL, Art. 79.

[106] *Id.*

M. Labeling

Aside from the rules set forth in the Consumer Protection Law and other statutes like the General Health Law, several other rules have been published by SECOFI in regard to labeling through Mexican Official Standards (*Normas Oficiales Mexicanas*—"NOM'S").[107]

Labeling must appear in Spanish; however there is no prohibition against product information also appearing in another language.[108] Product information must be accurate and verifiable.[109] In addition, products imported into Mexico must disclose their place of origin, the names and domiciles of the Mexican importer and the foreign manufacturer, the location of repair centers, instructions regarding product use and maintenance, and information regarding warranties.[110] As for food and beverage products, they must comply with rules regarding the net content legend in their labels.[111] Likewise, various NOM's require legends disclosing additional information if textiles or leather articles are imported.[112] If a seller is found to have engaged in misleading product information or advertising, the Consumer Protection Law requires that the seller comply with the terms of its offer to the consumer. If the seller is unable to do so, the consumer may recover its actual expenses as well as damages from the seller.[113]

---

[107] NOM–050–SCFI–94 and NOM–050–SCFE–94, dealing with product labeling in general, and labeling for food or non-alcoholic beverage products, respectively, have been published but are still subject to comments from the public and expected to be in full force shortly.

[108] CPL, Art. 34.

[109] CPL, Art. 32.

[110] CPL, Art. 33.

[111] NOM–030–SCFI–93 published in *D.O.,* on Oct. 29, 1993.

[112] NOM—004–SCFI–94 and NOM–020–SCFI–94, respectively.

[113] CPL, Art. 37.

Imported products subject to NOM's must comply with the guidelines in order to be sold in Mexico.[114] Noncompliance will subject the seller to fines and a prohibition on the sale of the product in question.

N. Immigration

Most business persons entering into Mexico will be subject to a non-immigrant visa (*no-inmigrante*), which will allow the holder to enter the country on multiple occasions within a period of up to one year, with the possibility of four extensions. An FM–3 will be issued.

Under NAFTA, the following four categories of persons will be granted admission to Mexico on a temporary basis for the purpose of facilitating the pursuit of business activities.

1. Business Visitors

U.S. citizens engaging in certain international business activities such as attending a trade convention, taking sales orders, and negotiating contracts for goods or services[115] upon presentation of:

(1) proof of U.S. citizenship;

(2) documentation demonstrating that the business person will be engaged in an international business activity and describing the purpose of entry; and

(3) evidence demonstrating that the business person's principal place of business, actual place of accrual of profits and primary source of remuneration are outside of Mexico.[116]

---

[114] *Acuerdo que Identifica las Fracciones Arancelarias de las Tarifas de la Ley del Impuesto General de Importación y de Exportación que Clasifican las Mercancias sujetas al Cumplimiento de las Normas Oficiales Mexicanas* (Decree Identifying the Tariff Classification of Products, according to the Law of Importation and Exportation Duties, which are subject to NOM's for Importation and Exportation Purposes). Published in *D.O.* on Mar. 7, 1994.

[115] See NAFTA, App. 1603.A.1 for a complete list of activities in which business visitors may engage.

[116] NAFTA, Ch. 16 and Annex 1603, § A.

2. Traders and Investors

U.S. citizens seeking to (1) carry on substantial trade in goods or services principally between the U.S. and Mexico, or (2) provide advice or key technical services to the operation of an investment to which the business person or the business person's enterprise has committed, or is in the process of committing, a substantial amount of capital, in a capacity that is supervisory, executive, or involves essential skills.[117]

3. Intra-Company Transferees

U.S. citizens providing managerial, executive or specialized services for the enterprise by which they are employed or a subsidiary or affiliate thereof. However, Mexico may require that such business person has been continuously employed by the enterprise for one year within the three years immediately preceding the application for admission to Mexico.[118]

4. Professionals

U.S. citizens engaging in certain professional business activities, such as lawyers, accountants, architects and engineers,[119] upon presentation of: (1) proof of U.S. citizenship; (2) documentation demonstrating that the person will be engaged in a professional business activity and describing the purpose of entry.[120]

O. Corrupt Practices

Mexican law contains provisions similar to those of the United States' Foreign Corrupt Practices Act (FCPA).[121] The FCPA restricts payments to government officials, political parties, or candidates when those

---

[117] NAFTA, Ch. 16 and Annex 1603, § B.

[118] NAFTA, Ch. 16 and Annex 1603, § C.

[119] See NAFTA, App. 1603.D.1 for a complete list of qualifying professions.

[120] In general, preclearance procedures and labor certification tests may not be imposed as a condition to temporary entry under NAFTA. However, Mexico may require persons requesting temporary entry to obtain a visa prior to admission.

[121] The text for the Federal Corrupt Practices Act can be found in 15 U.S.C.A. § 78a note, 78m, 78dd–1, 78dd–2, 78ff (1988).

payments are made to influence any act or decision, to obtain or retain business, or are made to third parties when it is known or should be known that the payment would be passed on to officials. The Mexican Criminal Code also outlaws payments to officials for the purposes of retaining or procuring business. Under some interpretations, the FCPA allows for "facilitating" or "grease" payments to government officials in order to accelerate performance of their duties. A traditional example of this is paying a customs official in order to allow for swift processing of documents. Mexican law does not recognize such an exemption, and therefore, even facilitating payments will be penalized.[122]

P. Antitrust

On June 24, 1993, Mexico's new antitrust law, the Federal Law of Economic Competition (the "FLEC") took effect. The adoption of the FLEC marks an important change in Mexico's attitude toward monopolies. Even though Mexico has had laws and regulations pertaining to monopolies for decades,[123] these provisions were applied only sporadically. While the policy for enforcement of the new law is still uncertain, a number of its provisions virtually guarantee that it will have a marked impact on the country's economic life. If nothing more, these provisions will require investors contemplating certain mergers and acquisitions to provide prior notice to the government. Failure to provide the requisite notice can give rise to administrative penalties and, in certain cases, the nullification of the transaction.

Generally speaking, the FLEC applies to all "economic agents," whether individuals or corporate entities, associations or trusts, and regardless of whether they are Mexican or foreign. It grants powers to the Executive to fix maximum prices on goods and services, and addresses three practices that may be illegal: absolute restraints (horizontal agreements among competitors), relative restraints (vertical agreements

---

[122] Criminal Code for the Federal District [hereinafter, C.P.D.F.], Art. 22. This provides for a maximum of fourteen years' imprisonment in addition to a fine of a maximum of 500 times the salary for the Federal District (currently this is approximately $4.00 per day), depending on the amount involved. *Id.*

[123] The Monopolies Law (*Ley Reglamentaria del Artículo 28 Constitucional en Materia de Monopolios*) of 1934.

among a manufacturer and a distributor, or among other economic agents in the chain of sale and distribution of goods and services, and certain unilateral actions) and concentrations. The enforcement of the FLEC's provisions is delegated to a Federal Competition Commission (the "Commission").

1. Absolute Restraints

Absolute restraints (also known as horizontal restrictions on trade) are agreements between economic agents who are competitors, and have the purpose or effect of:

(1) fixing prices;

(2) allocating markets, whether with regard to suppliers, territories or periods of time;

(3) assigning production quotas; or

(4) the rigging of public bids.

These agreements are deemed illegal per se.

Persons engaging in absolute restraints may be sentenced to fines and even prison terms.[124] Finally, all agreements between competitors which constitute absolute restraints will be deemed null and void, and produce no legal effect whatsoever.

2. Relative Restraints

Relative restraints consist primarily of limitations found in vertical agreements (such as agreements between suppliers and distributors, or between wholesalers and retailers), and, to a lesser extent, certain restrictions that are unilaterally created by an economic agent. A relative

---

[124] A term in prison of up to nine years is provided for in the Criminal Code for the Federal District. The Commission also has the discretion to impose an additional fine in serious cases of up to 10% of the value of the defendant's assets or 10% of the amount of the defendant's sales for the preceding fiscal year.

restraint will exist only if it has the purpose or effect of imposing restrictions on competition or free trade in the production, process, distribution or marketing of the goods and services which are the subject of such vertical agreement.

The following are examples of agreements that may constitute relative restraints under the FLEC:

— exclusive distribution agreements, for goods or services, which contain geographic, temporary, or product limitations, or that require a party to the agreement not to manufacture or supply goods and services;

— the imposition of a mandatory resale price or conditions of resale for goods or services (i.e., resale price maintenance); and

— "tying" arrangements, which condition the sale of a good or service on the purchase or sale of a separate good or service, or upon a refusal to deal with third parties.

Relative restraints are not illegal per se and will be declared unlawful only if they cause substantial economic displacement or harm. This requires that the actor has substantial power in the relevant market, and that the restraint occurs in the relevant market. Thus, many common contractual arrangements, such as exclusive distributorships, are likely to continue to be lawful.

3. Concentrations

The FLEC prohibits any concentration, merger or acquisition of control ("concentration") which may have the purpose or effect of restricting competition and free trade of goods and services within the relevant market. Contrary to monopolistic practices, the law makes no distinctions between horizontal concentrations (among competitors) and vertical concentrations (e.g., between suppliers and distributors). Concentrations, like relative restraints, will not be deemed illegal per se; rather, it shall be necessary to examine the relevant market and to determine the power wielded by the entity resulting from the concentration. An important element of this analysis will be the degree of concentration in the market if the concentration were allowed to occur.

The FLEC contains a list of indicators that a concentration is illegal, including when it provides the resulting entity with the power to fix prices or to substantially restrict the supply of goods and services in the relevant market (without provoking an effective response by competitors); if it may unduly displace or impede the access of other agents to the relevant market; or if it may substantially facilitate monopolistic practices, whether absolute or relative.

In an attempt to control concentrations before they become a *fait accompli,* the FLEC requires that the Commission be given prior notice of certain concentrations which exceed in value or size of participants amounts set forth in the FLEC.[125]

The penalty for failing to notify the Commission of a proposed concentration meeting the requisite thresholds is a fine, and possibly an order for the partial or total break-up of the resulting entity or entities.

IV. Standard Provisions of a Sales Contract

The structure and specifics of sales contracts will naturally differ with the practices of each seller. However, certain provisions will, by the nature of a sales contract, be included in all contracts in order to clearly define the intentions and obligations of the parties. Mexican law merely requires the identification of the material object of the contract (the goods to be sold), the determination of the price or basis for its determination, and an agreement between the parties.[126] Other aspects of the relationship between the seller and the buyer, such as time for transfer of title,

---

[125] The amounts as of Sept. 1994 are close to US$50 million, although if the combined size of the participants exceeds US$220 million, then the trigger may be reduced to approximately US$20 million.

[126] C.C.D.F., Art. 2249. The use of foreign currency will be considered a sale and not a barter (*permuta*). *Ley Monetaria, D.O.,* July 27, 1931, Art. 8.

delivery of goods, or payment of the price are governed in a supplementary manner by the commercial and civil regulations.[127]

A. Obligations of the Seller

Under a sales contract, a seller has two basic obligations. These are the obligations to transfer title and to deliver the goods.

1. Transfer of Title

Determination of the time when title to the goods passes from seller to buyer is of key importance in both Mexican and United States law. Title determines who suffers the risk of loss during transportation prior to the purchaser's receipt of physical or legal possession of the goods. Mexican law provides that if the seller and buyer have failed to agree on the particular time when the property will be transferred, ownership will pass upon execution of the contract where the goods are identified.[128]

When goods are unidentifiable (such as bales of cotton or grain, title does not transfer until the quantities or types of goods are specifically designated. For goods that are deposited at a bonded warehouse (*almacén general de depósito*), title passes by mere endorsement of the certificate of deposit issued by the warehouse.[129]

Where the price of the goods is not paid immediately, the seller and buyer may agree that the goods will be delivered to the buyer, but, the buyer will not obtain title until final payment is made. Mexican law

---

[127] For rules on Mexican contractual law, see A. Gargollo, N. 30, *supra*, Diaz Bravo, N. 33, *supra*. See also *Rojina Villegas, Derecho Civil Mexicano,* vols. VI and VII (1986), and R. Sanchez Medal, *De Los Contratos Civiles* (1986). For a more international perspective, see Sanders, "Trade Agreements: Selected Issues for Negotiating Terms: Including Issues of Payment, Countertrade, and the Use and Application of the International Sales of Goods Convention," *Negotiating and Drafting International Commercial Agreements* (1986).

[128] See *Codiso de Comercio*, Arts. 2014, 2015.

[129] Rules on transfer of *certificados de depósito* are the same as those applicable to other negotiable instruments. *Ley General de Titulos y Operaciones de Crédito* [General Law on Negotiable Instruments and Credit Operations], *D.O.,* Aug. 27, 1932 [hereinafter, LGTOC], Arts. 229–251. Bearer endorsements are not permitted. *Id.*

recognizes these transactions as installment sales with a reservation of ownership (*ventas con reserva de dominio*).[130] However, in order for the ownership provision to be enforceable, the contract must be recorded in the Public Registry of Commerce in the domicile of the buyer.[131] Furthermore, as part of this duty to record the contract, the seller must issue to the buyer an invoice or other documentation evidencing the transfer.

2. Delivery of Goods

The delivery of the goods sold includes four delivery requirements or obligations on behalf of the seller. These are the obligations to deliver at the correct time, at the correct place, in the correct quantity, and in the correct quality.

Failure of the parties to agree on the time of delivery will impose an obligation on the seller to place the goods at the disposal of the buyer within 24 hours after execution of the contract.[132] Failure to agree on a place of delivery allows the seller to deliver the goods at the place they are located at the time of the sale or at the seller's domicile.[133] Failure to deliver the goods in full quantity allows the buyer to object to partial delivery; however, if the goods are accepted, the price is reduced pro rata.[134] If the agreement does not specify the quality of the product, the seller should consider the purpose for which the goods are intended. If the purpose is not known, the seller can provide goods of average quality.[135]

---

[130] C.C.D.F., Art. 2312.

[131] The transfer is accomplished for income and value-added tax purposes from the date of execution, and taxes are payable as of such date. Federal Fiscal Code, Art. 14.

[132] C.Com., Art. 379.

[133] C.C.D.F., Arts. 2082, 2291.

[134] C.Com., Art. 375.

[135] *Id.*, Art. 87.

Failure by the seller to meet the delivery requirements allows the buyer to rescind the contract, reject the goods, return them to the seller, and demand payment of damages and lost profits.[136]

B. Obligations of the Buyer

The buyer also has two obligations: to pay the price and to take delivery of the purchased goods.

1. Payment of the Price

Customarily, the price for foreign goods sold into Mexico is denominated in a foreign currency. Usually, the price is stated in United States dollars or in the seller's own currency. As indicated above,[137] it is of the utmost importance, from the seller's point of view, that the contract clearly state that the price is to be paid precisely in the agreed upon currency. If this is a foreign currency, the contract should state that the payment will be made outside of Mexico.

Methods for payment include cash, letters of credit, or an open account.[138] If there is no agreement regarding payment, Mexican law provides for payment in cash with immediately available funds.[139]

a. Cash in Advance or Against Delivery

Payment in cash includes payment by means of a check, money order, cashier's check, and any other method of providing the seller with immediately available funds. If an instrument is not honored due to a lack of funds, the General Law on Negotiable Instruments and Credit Operations stipulates that payment is made subject to collection of the instrument.[140]

---

[136] *Id.*, Art. 375; C.C.D.F., Art. 1949. The parties may stipulate at the time the contract is made to liquidated damages (*pena convencional*) in lieu of any other compensation. *Id.*, Art. 1840.

[137] See Part III.K, *supra.*

[138] For an excellent and clear discussion, see Clasen, *Foreign Trade and Investment: A Legal Guide* (1987).

[139] C.Com., Art. 380.

[140] LGTOC, Art. 7, *Salvo buen cobro.*

b. Letter of Credit

When payment is made under a letter of credit, the payor bank makes the funds available to the seller upon the seller's presentation of certain documents. These documents will usually include a bill of lading, an invoice, and other documents chosen by the parties, such as an insurance policy or export permit. These documents will prove shipment of the goods at the stipulated time, to the specified place of delivery, and in the requested quantity. Unless required documentation attests to the quality of the product delivered, the payor bank will not verify, nor will it be obligated to verify, the quality of the products shipped or delivered.

Mexican laws contain few provisions governing letters of credit. For international trade, most commercial letters of credit incorporate the International Chamber of Commerce's Uniform Customs and Practices for Documentary Credits.[141] A letter of credit might be irrevocable if payor banks may not cancel credit for a stated term. It may be confirmed by a financial institution in the domicile of the seller. Of course, the most secure method of payment for the seller is an irrevocable letter of credit confirmed by a domestic institution. Mexican banks can provide letters of credit and certain Mexican banking institutions have representative offices or agencies in the United States.

c. Credit to the Buyer

When the buyer is unable to pay in cash and has no credit available, or when a seller is promoting its goods, the vendor may grant the buyer an open account for payment of the price. In this case, the seller undertakes the risk that the buyer cannot pay for the goods. Although this risk may be minimized, it cannot be eliminated.

Methods of evidencing the debt, aside from drawing the invoice issued by the seller, include execution of a contract providing for deferred payment (*venta con reserva de dominio*).[142] However, the simplest document that can prove acknowledgment and obligation to pay is a negotiable instrument such as a *letra de cambio* or a promissory note

---

[141] I.C.C. No. 400 (1983).

[142] See N. 140, *supra*, and accompanying text.

(*pagaré*). Whereas a *letra de cambio* may not provide for interest,[143] a promissory note permits both ordinary and penalty interest.[144] Failure to provide interest allows for penalty interest at a rate of only 6 percent.[145]

The seller may also find a more secure means of securing the buyer's obligation to pay the price in addition to selling with *reserva de dominio*. Common ways of guarantying obligations which are recognized in Mexican law include mortgages, chattel mortgages on movable goods, performance or surety bonds, joint obligations with a third party, or pledges on stock. A mortgage and a chattel mortgage will require registration at the Public Registry of Commerce for the region where the goods are located or at the domicile of the grantor.[146]

Unsecured credit subjects the seller to the normal risks of collection.[147] A simple invoice serves as a method of evidencing the debt. However, a negotiable instrument allows swift collection and simple transferability of the debt by means of an endorsement.[148]

2. Take Delivery of Goods

Just as it is important for the buyer to have the seller deliver the goods, it is equally important to the seller for the buyer to take delivery of the goods. In a contract for delivery of goods *ex works*[149] the seller's plant, the seller is burdened if the buyer does not clear the goods within a certain time. Not only do undelivered goods take up space needed for other goods, they may subject the seller to certain costs of conservation

---

[143] LGTOC, Art. 78

[144] *Id.*, Art. 78.

[145] C.Com., Art. 362.

[146] C.C.D.F., Arts. 2312, 3069 (contains regulations to the Public Registry of Property).

[147] Under the Bankruptcy Laws, unsecured creditors for commercial trade will take priority over unsecured civil creditors, but will be subordinate to secured creditors and tax and labor obligations. *Ley de Quiebras y Suspensión de Pagos, D.O.*, Apr. 20, 1943, Art. 261.

[148] A negotiable instrument will be subject to an executive judgment (acción ejecutiva). This presumes the prima facie validity of the debt and allows goods to be secured through attachment at the time process is served.

[149] For this and other terms of international trade, see Guide to INCOTERMS, International Chamber of Commerce, Pub. No. 354 (1990).

and risks of destruction, loss, or spoilage. Failure of the buyer to take delivery of the goods releases the seller from its obligation to indemnify the buyer in case the goods are lost at the seller's facilities. However, the seller's obligation is not released if the loss is due to the seller's negligence, in which case the seller is considered a simple depository.[150]

C. Termination and Rescission of the Contract

1. Expiration

A requirements contract will terminate upon expiration of the stipulated term unless it provides for automatic extensions. Extensions may result from action or inaction of one of the parties.

2. Unilateral Termination

Even if a contract has a certain fixed duration, Mexican law allows the seller to terminate the contract at any time by paying the actual damages suffered by the agent. These damages provide protection for both parties, such as in agency contracts, where the agent does not have an action for strict performance but may recover his damages.[151]

3. Rescission by Default

A breach of contract allows the innocent party to rescind the agreement in certain cases, regardless of whether it is a distribution, agency, or a simple sales contract. Mexican law and courts recognize the right of the innocent party to rescind a contract without prior court action if this right is explicitly provided for in the contract.[152] In cases where the contract is silent on the subject, Mexican courts have not accepted the right of the aggrieved party to unilaterally terminate the contract. Instead, they have required that the party demand, through the courts, the termination of the contract and payment of damages and lost profits.

---

[150] C.Com., Art. 377.

[151] See N. 37, *supra*, and accompanying text. The principle also applies to other contracts involving similar fiduciary relationships.

[152] C.C.D.F., Art. 1949. This clause is known as *pacto comisorio expreso*.

Mexican law only recognizes actual provable damages suffered and actual lost profits as grounds for compensation claims.[153] "Moral" damage to a victim's reputation or his standing in the community may also be compensated.[154] Penalty damages are not recognized or accepted. However, in the contract, the parties may freely stipulate an amount of liquidated damages in the event of default.[155] The only limitation on a liquidated damages provision is that it may not exceed the value of the principal obligation.

D. Substantive Law Applying to the Contract

Mexican law provides principles of conflict of laws dealing with contracts.[156] In a contract for the sale of goods, Mexican law recognizes a valid choice of law made by the parties, provided the selected forum has a nexus with the seller, the buyer, or another term of the contract such as the place of delivery or manufacture.[157]

Failure to specify a choice of law in the agreement will probably create a conflict. If both parties reside and carry on business in countries which have adopted the Convention on Contracts for the International Sale of Goods, its rules will apply. If the Convention is inapplicable, Mexican law will be applied to substantive issues if the obligation contemplated in the contract is to be performed in Mexico.[158]

E. Settlement of Disputes

If a conflict arises between the parties under a contract, a Mexican court may hear the dispute. However, the parties can clearly specify in advance their desire for a different jurisdiction in case of a dispute. Although the applicable rules depend on the particulars of the contract

---

[153] *Id.*, Arts. 2108–2110. Damages and lost profits are recognized only when they are a direct and immediate consequence of the default.

[154] *Id.*, Art. 1916.

[155] *Id.*, Art. 1840.

[156] See Bayitch & Siqueiros, *Conflicts of Laws: Mexico and the United States* (1968).

[157] Civ. Code, Arts. 12, 13.

[158] *Id.* The laws of the domicile apply to the issue of legal capacity to execute a contract. The form of the contract depends on the state where the contract was executed.

and its applicable law,[159] it is always advisable for the parties to state in the contract the jurisdiction upon which they have agreed. Settlement of the disputes may involve litigation or arbitration.

1. Adjudication of Disputes

If Mexican courts adjudicate the dispute, a judgment is binding on the parties despite the seller's residence abroad. However, if the parties specify that a court outside of Mexico has jurisdiction over the case, Mexican law still governs the enforcement of a judgment rendered by foreign courts. This foreign judgment is enforceable as long as the request for enforcement meets the following requirements:[160]

(1) A letter rogatory from the foreign court requesting the enforcement of the judgment is provided.

(2) The judgment was not rendered as a consequence of a claim based on a "real" right (such as ownership of real estate).

(3) The court issuing the judgment is competent to take cognizance of and adjudicate the matter.

(4) The defendant was duly notified in person in order to assure it the right to appear before the court and exercise its rights. This can be accomplished through personal service of process.

(5) The judgment is a final judgment without a right to appeal.

(6) The action giving rise to the judgment is not the subject of another lawsuit pending between the same parties in Mexican courts.

---

[159] See Vazquez Pando, "Mexican Law on Judicial Competence in International Sphere," 12 *Hous. J. Int'l L.* 337 (1990).

[160] Code of Civil Procedure for the Federal District, ch. 7, Title VII, Arts. 604–608. This Code was recently amended in order to clearly set forth requirements for enforcement. See Siqueiros, "Enforcement of Foreign Civil and Commercial Judgments in the Mexican Republic," 2 *Hous. J. Int'l L.* 375 (1980). See also, Siqueiros, *"La Cooperación Procesal Internacional,"* 19 *Jurídica* 3 (1988–89).

(7) The obligation on which the claim was based is not contrary to the public order of Mexico.

(8) A certified copy of the judgment is issued by the foreign court.

(9) Documentation or certificates evidencing that the conditions mentioned under subsections (4) and (5) above are provided.

(10) The documents are translated into Spanish by a duly authorized local translator.

(11) The person requesting the execution has indicated a domicile in Mexico for the receipt of notices.

2. Arbitration

The parties may use arbitration to settle disputes if they desire:

(1) to appoint an impartial individual or panel of experts in the field;

(2) to appoint an impartial individual or panel to decide the conflict in a short period of time; or

(3) to avoid the high cost and exposures of litigation.

Naturally, selection of arbitration may be made at the time the contract is executed by an arbitration clause (*cláusula compromisoria*) or thereafter by means of an arbitration agreement.

The arbitrator(s) may be appointed to act in accordance with recently updated Mexican arbitration legislation.[161] Alternatively, the rules of procedure for the arbitration may be those of an international body, such as the International Chamber of Commerce, or the Inter-American

---

[161] The arbitration process and enforcement of commercial awards is regulated by C. Com., Arts. 1415–1437, as amended, *Decreto por el que se Reforma, Adiciona y Deroga Diversas Disposiciones del Código de Comercio, D.O.*, Jan. 4, 1989, as amended, *D.O.*, July 22, 1993.

Arbitration Commission. The rules of the American Arbitration Association may also be used.

The arbitration award is enforceable in Mexico under the terms of the New York Convention on the Recognition and Enforcement of Foreign Arbitral Awards. Mexico subscribed to this Convention in April 1971 and enacted it shortly thereafter.[162] Mexico and the United States are parties to the Inter-American Convention on International Commercial Arbitration of 1975.[163] Requirements for enforcement are similar to those for the enforcement of judgments rendered by foreign courts.[164]

---

[162] *Decreto por el que se Promulga la Convencíon Sobre el Reconocimiento y la Ejecución de Sentencias Arbitrales Extranjeras* [Publication Decree of the Convention on the Recognition and Enforcement of Foreign Arbitral Awards], *D.O.*, June 22, 1971.

[163] *Decreto de Promulgacíon de la Convencíon Interamericana Sobre Arbitraje Comercial Internacional* [Publication Decree of the Convention on International Commercial Arbitration], *D.O.*, Apr. 27, 1978.

[164] Mexican federal courts allow personal service to be made according to the terms of an arbitration clause, by agreement, or by the rules of the selected arbitration body. Therefore, formal process through the Mexican court system may be unnecessary.

CHAPTER 11

Mexico's Industrial Property Law*

Alan L. Hyde**
Thompson, Hine and Flory

Supplemented by
Scott S. Havlick
Holland & Hart

I. Introduction

On December 1, 1990, President Carlos Salinas de Gortari sent to the Mexican Senate a draft of the Law on the Promotion and Protection of Industrial Property *(Ley de Promoción y Protección de la Propiedad Industrial)*. Following careful study, the Law was enacted with minor changes in June, 1991. The *Official Daily of the Federation (Diario Oficial de la Federación)* published the Law on June 27, 1991, and it took effect the following day.[1]

As stated in the presidential message that accompanied the draft law to the Senate, the proposed legislation sought to offer in Mexico a

---

 This chapter previously appeared in 4 *International Quarterly* 118 (1992).

[**] The author formerly served as Honorary Mexican Consul, Cleveland, Ohio, 1969–1974.

[1] *Ley de Promoción y Protección de la Propiedad Industrial, Diario Oficial (D.O.)* (June 27, 1991) [hereinafter cited as IPL].

framework of promotion and legal certainty for industrial property that was equal or superior to that existing in other countries against which Mexico competes on a worldwide plane.[2]

The Law on the Promotion and Protection of Industrial Property (IPL) contains provisions which repeal both the 1976 Law of Inventions and Trademarks *(Ley de Invenciones y Marcas)* (LIT)[3] and the 1982 Law on the Control and Registration of the Transfer of Technology and the Use and Exploitation of Patents and Trademarks *(Ley Sobre el Control y Registro de la Transferencia de Tecnología y el Uso y Explotación de Patentes y Marcas)* (TTL).[4]

The LIT, the TTL's predecessor 1972 law[5] and the 1973 Law to Promote Mexican Investment and Regulate Foreign Investment *(Ley para Promover la Inversión Mexicana y Regular la Inversión Extranjera)* (FIL)[6] were three pieces of complementary antiforeign business legislation enacted during the populist and leftist presidential administration of Luis Echeverría from 1970 to 1976 that have been collectively dubbed the "Echeverrian Wall."[7] The TTL and its predecessor required governmental screening and approval of all licensing and other arrangements under which technology was transferred to Mexico and enabled the government to disapprove of the transfer or, as a condition to its approval, impose royalty or other compensation rates lower than those negotiated by the parties, limit the term of the arrangement and any confidentiality requirements, and generally to disapprove or require alteration of other contractual provisions agreed to

---

[2] C. Salinas de Gortari, Message from the President to the Mexican Senate (Dec. 1, 1990).

[3] *Ley de Invenciones y Marcas, D.O.*, Feb. 10, 1976 [hereinafter cited as LIT].

[4] *Ley Sobre el Control y Registro de la Transferencia de Tecnologiá y el Uso y Explotacióon de Patentes y Marcas, D.O.*, Jan. 11, 1982 [hereinafter cited as TTL].

[5] *Ley Sobre el Registro de la Transferencia de Tecnologiá y el Uso y Explotación de Patentes Y Marcas, D.O.*, Dec. 30, 1972.

[6] *Ley para Promover la Inversión Mexicana y Regular la Inversión Extranjera, D.O.*, May 9, 1973.

[7] The term was coined by Ewell E. Murphy, Jr. See Murphy, "The Echeverrian Wall: Two Perspectives on Foreign Investment and Licensing in Mexico," 17 *Tex. J. Int'l L.* 135 (1982).

by the parties.[8] The LIT also introduced a number of restrictions on patentability into Mexican industrial property legislation, imposed harsh "working" requirements for patents, reduced the term of patent and trademark protection, contained broad compulsory licensing requirements, and was generally regarded as hostile to intellectual property protection by the international intellectual property community.[9]

The enactment of the IPL, which President Salinas initiated, constitutes the third significant step in dismantling the Echeverrian Wall. President Salinas was deeply committed to an opening and internationalization of the Mexican economy. The first step was the publication of liberalized regulations under the FIL on May 16, 1989.[10] The second was the publication of new regulations under the TTL on January 9, 1990,[11] which contain provisions for the grant of administrative exemptions based upon public policy. These provisions essentially emasculated the TTL.[12]

The IPL is a comprehensive statute, containing 227 articles and 14 transitory articles. This paper does not purport to be a complete summary of the IPL, but rather attempts to identify and briefly discuss the principal innovations in Mexican industrial property law introduced by the IPL.

II. Types of Industrial Property Protected and Protection Provided

A. Patents

The IPL expands the area of patentable subject matter to include:

---

[8] See Hyde and Ramírez de la Corte, "Mexico's New Transfer of Technology and Foreign Investment Laws—To What Extent Have the Rules Changed?," 10 *Int'l Law.* 231 (1976). See also Hyde, "1981 Mexican Transfer of Technology Law," 15 *Law. Am.* 37 (1983).

[9] See Hyde and Ramírez de la Corte, "Mexico's 1976 Law of Inventions and Trademarks," 12 *Case W. Res. J. Int'l L.* 469 (1980).

[10] *Reglamento de la Ley para Promover la Inversión Mexicana y Regular la Inversión Extranjera, D.O.*, May 16, 1989.

[11] *Reglamento de la Ley Sobre el Control y Registro de la Transferencia de Tecnología y el Uso y Explotación de Patentes y Marcas, D.O.*, Jan. 9, 1990.

[12] *Id.*, Art. 53.

(1) alloys;

(2) chemical products in general;

(3) pharmaceutical products in general, drugs, food, and drink for animal consumption, fertilizers, plaguicides, herbicides, fungicides, and products that involve biological activity; and

(4) biotechnological processes for obtaining the productions referred to in (3).[13]

The IPL grants a 12-month grace period following disclosure of the invention or its exhibition at a national or international exposition for filing a patent application.[14] When filed, the patent application must be accompanied by supporting documentation demonstrating that the grace period is applicable.[15] Standards for this documentary support will be specified in the regulations to be issued under the IPL.

The IPL increases the term of a patent to 20 years, measured from the date of filing of the application, from 14 years, measured from the date of issuance.[16] As an incentive to Mexico's indigenous pharmaceutical industry, the term is increased to 23 years if the patent relates to pharmochemical or pharmaceutical products or the processes for obtaining them and the patent is licensed upon specified terms to a corporation with majority Mexican capital.[17]

---

[13] Art. 16 of the IPL defines the term "invention" as "[e]very human creation that permits the transformation of matter or energy existing in nature for use by man through the immediate satisfaction of a concrete need," and expressly includes processes or products of industrial application within the concept of inventions. Art. 19 lists a number of specific exclusions from the definition. Art. 20 specifies those inventions relating to living material that are and are not patentable.

[14] IPL, Art. 18.

[15] IPL, Art. 18.

[16] IPL, Art. 23. Under the LIT as it was originally enacted, the term was ten years, measured from the date of issuance. LIT, Art. 40, *D.O.*, Feb. 10, 1976. By a decree amending the LIT, the term was increased to 14 years in 1987. *D.O.*, Jan. 16, 1987.

[17] IPL, Art. 23.

The IPL incorporates the "first to file" principle, which states that when various inventors have conceived the same invention independently of each other, the right to a patent shall belong to the first to file or to the one with the earliest date of recognized priority, as the case may be.[18] Mexico is a party to the Paris Convention for the Protection of Industrial Property.[19] Consequently, the date of filing a patent application in another member country of the Paris Union is treated as the date of filing in Mexico for purposes of establishing priority (so long as filing in Mexico occurs within 12 months following the first filing in a member country and certain other specified requirements are satisfied).[20]

The LIT provided that the grant of a patent implied the obligation to exploit it in Mexico within three years from the date of issuance.[21] Importation of the patented product or of the product manufactured with the patented process did not constitute exploitation.[22] The LIT provided two sanctions for nonexploitation or insufficient exploitation of a patent. The first was lapse of the patent, which ensued automatically if exploitation was not undertaken within the required three-year period and one additional year passed during which no one applied for a compulsory license.[23] The second was compulsory licensing.[24]

The IPL contains no express obligation to exploit a patent, nor does it provide that a patent shall lapse if it is not exploited. It does provide that anyone may apply to the Ministry of Commerce and Industrial Development (the Ministry) for the grant of a compulsory license if the patent is not exploited within the longer of three years following issuance of the patent application or four years following filing of the application, unless justified technical causes for failure to commence exploitation within the time period exist.[25] Exploitation by the licensee under a license registered with the Mexican Patent and Trademark Office (MPTO)

---

[18] IPL, Art. 42.

[19] *Decreto por el que se promulga El Convenio de París para la Protección de la Propiedad Industrial, adoptado en Estocolmo el 14 de julio de 1967, D.O.*, July 27, 1976.

[20] IPL, Arts. 40, 41.

[21] LIT, Art. 41.

[22] LIT, Art. 43.

[23] LIT, Art. 48.

[24] LIT, Arts. 41, 50.

[25] IPL, Art. 70.

will be considered as though carried out by the patent owner.[26] The grant of a compulsory license will not be in order when the patent owner or the holder of a contractual license has been importing the patented product or the product obtained through the use of the patented process.[27] Furthermore, an applicant for a compulsory license must have the technical and financial capacity to carry out an efficient exploitation of the patented invention.[28] One would assume that it is not anticipated that many compulsory licenses will be granted for nonexploitation of patents.

Governmental screening and approval of patent licenses and patent assignments under TTL provisions are no longer required due to the repeal of the TTL.[29] Under IPL provisions, patents may be transferred in whole or in part upon the terms and in accordance with the formalities established by general legislation.[30] Patent licenses may be granted by written agreement.[31] Patent assignments and licenses, however, must be registered with the MPTO in order to be effective against third parties.[32]

B. Utility Models

The IPL introduces utility models as a new form of industrial property subject to protection. "Utility models" are defined as "[o]bjects, utensils, apparatus or tools that, as a result of their arrangement, configuration, structure or form, perform a different function with respect to the parts of which they are comprised or advantages with respect to their usefulness."[33] Protection is obtained through registration with the MPTO and is granted for a nonrenewable term of ten years, measured from the date of filing of the registration application.[34]

---

[26] IPL, Art. 69.
[27] IPL, Art. 70.
[28] IPL, Art. 71.
[29] IPL, Second Transitory Article.
[30] IPL, Art. 62.
[31] IPL, Art. 63.
[32] IPL, Arts. 62, 63.
[33] IPL, Art. 28.
[34] IPL, Art. 29.

C. Industrial Designs

The IPL continues the availability of protection for industrial designs, which may take the form of either industrial drawings or industrial models.[35] Protection is obtained through registration with the MPTO and is granted for a nonrenewable term of 15 years, measured from the date of filing of the registration application,[36] as contrasted with a term of seven years from the date of registration provided under the predecessor LIT.[37]

D. Industrial Secrets

The IPL is also Mexico's first industrial property legislation expressly affording protection to industrial secrets. An "industrial secret" is defined as

> "[any] information of industrial application treated by a natural or legal person as of a confidential nature that enables it to obtain or maintain a competitive or economic advantage over third parties in economic activities and as to which adequate means or systems have been adopted to preserve its confidentiality and to restrict access to the same.... The information of an industrial secret necessarily must relate to the nature, characteristics or uses of products, to production methods or processes, or to the means or forms of distribution or marketing of products or the rendition of services."[38]

---

[35] IPL, Art. 32. The term "industrial drawing" is defined as "any combination of drawings, lines or colors that are incorporated into an industrial product for purposes of ornamentation and that give it a special and unique appearance." IPL, Art. 32. The term "industrial model" is defined as "any three-dimensional form ... that serve[s] as a prototype or guide for the production of an industrial product ... that give[s] it a special appearance and do[es] not involve technical aspects." IPL, Art. 32

[36] IPL, Art. 36.

[37] LIT, Art. 81.

[38] IPL, Art. 82. Information that is in the public domain, that is obvious to a technician in the field, or that is required to be disclosed by law or by judicial order shall not be considered an industrial secret. Information that is furnished to any authority by a person who possesses it as an industrial secret, when he furnishes it for purposes of obtaining licenses, permits, authorizations, registrations, or any other official acts, shall not be considered as entering the public domain or as being disclosed by judicial order. IPL, Art. 82.

Information entitled to protection as an industrial secret may be set forth in documents, electronic or magnetic media, optical discs, microfilms, films, or other similar instruments.[39] The person who is entrusted with an industrial secret may transfer it to or authorize its use by a third party, in which event the obligation extends to the authorized user.[40]

The IPL expressly provides that confidentiality provisions to protect industrial secrets may be included in agreements for the transfer of technical information, technical assistance, or the supply of basic or detailed engineering.[41] Once included, these provisions must specifically set forth those confidential aspects.[42] This IPL provision should be contrasted with the provisions of the now-repealed TTL that called for disapproval and denial of registration of technology transfer agreements which contain provisions obligating the transferee to treat the technical information supplied thereunder as confidential for a period longer than the term of the agreement.[43]

The IPL subjects any natural or legal person that hires a former employee of or adviser to a trade secret owner for the purpose of obtaining the trade secret to liability for damages resulting from the disclosure of the trade secret.[44] Liability for damages is also imposed on any natural or legal person that obtains information constituting an industrial secret by any illegal means.[45]

E. Trademarks

While the IPL introduced a number of detailed changes in Mexican trademark law, of most general interest is the extension of the term of a trademark registration to ten years, measured from the date of filing of the registration application with the MPTO.[46] Trademark registrations

---

39 IPL, Art. 83.
40 IPL, Art. 84.
41 IPL Art. 84.
42 IPL, Art. 84.
43 TTL, Art. 15(XI).
44 IPL, Art. 86.
45 IPL, Art. 86.
46 IPL, Art. 95.

may be renewed for successive ten-year periods.[47] Under the LIT, the term of a trademark registration was five years, and the registration was renewable for successive five-year periods.[48]

With the repeal of the TTL, governmental screening and approval of trademark license agreements are no longer necessary. Such agreements, however, must be registered with the MPTO to be effective against third parties.[49] Similarly, trademark assignments no longer require governmental screening and approval and are to be carried out upon the terms and with the formalities set forth in general legislation.[50] Trademark assignments, however, must be registered with the MPTO to be effective against third parties.[51] The provisions of the IPL relating to the licensing and transfer of trademarks are equally applicable to the registration of a franchise.[52]

F. Collective Trademarks

Collective trademarks are another innovation under the IPL. Lawfully constituted associations of producers, manufacturers, businesspeople or service providers may apply for the registration of a collective trademark to distinguish, in the marketplace, the products or services of their members from the products or services of nonmembers.[53] A list of the members of the association and the rules for use of the trademark must be filed with the registration application.[54] The MPTO must be advised of changes in association membership occurring after registration.[55]

---

[47] IPL, Art. 95.

[48] LIT, Art. 112.

[49] IPL, Art. 136.

[50] IPL, Art. 143.

[51] IPL, Art. 143.

[52] IPL, Art. 142. A franchise shall exist when a license for use of a trademark is accompanied by the transfer of technical knowledge or the provision of technical assistance, so that the person to whom it is granted may produce or sell goods or render services in a uniform manner and with the operating, marketing and administrative methods established by the owner of the trademark, designed to maintain the quality, prestige, and image of the products or services that the trademark distinguishes.

[53] IPL, Art. 96.

[54] IPL, Art. 97.

[55] IPL, Art. 97.

A collective trademark cannot be transferred to a third party; its use is reserved to the members of the association.[56]

G. Commercial Notices

For purposes of the IPL, "commercial notices" are "[p]hrases or expressions that have the purpose of announcing commercial, industrial or service establishments or businesses to the public, to easily distinguish them from others of their kind."[57] The exclusive right to use a commercial notice is obtained by registration with the MPTO.[58] Registrations of commercial notices have a term of ten years, measured from the date of filing of the registration application, and may be renewed for successive ten-year periods.[59]

H. Trade Names

The trade name of an industrial, commercial, or service business establishment and the right to its exclusive use is protected without the necessity of registration.[60] The user may, however, apply to the MPTO for publication of the trade name in the Gazette.[61] Publication has the effect of establishing a presumption of good faith in the adoption and use of the trade name.[62] The protection of a trade name encompasses the geographic zone of the effective clientele of the business or establishment to which it applies and extends to the entire Mexican Republic if there is a massive and constant diffusion of the same to the national level.[63]

---

[56] IPL, Art. 98.

[57] IPL, Art. 100. The Spanish term *avisos comerciales* may also be translated as "commercial advertisements" or "commercial slogans."

[58] IPL, Art. 98.

[59] IPL, Art. 103.

[60] IPL, Art. 105.

[61] IPL, Art. 106. The Ministry of Commerce and Industrial Development is to publish the Gazette at least quarterly, containing the publications to which the IPL refers and other information of interest about industrial property. IPL, Art. 8.

[62] IPL, Art. 106.

[63] IPL, Art. 105.

The effects of publication of a trade name continue for ten years from the date of application for publication and may be renewed for the same period by republication.[64]

I. Appellations of Origin

The IPL defines the term "appellation of origin" to mean "the name of a geographic region of Mexico that serves to designate a product that originates from the same, and whose quality or characteristic stems exclusively from the geographic sphere, including both natural and human factors."[65] Presently, the only Mexican appellation of origin is "tequila."

The IPL seeks to give extraterritorial effect to Mexican appellations of origin by providing that the MPTO, in ruling on the authorization of protection, may, in effect, require foreign distributors of the product to which the appellation of origin is applied to use the appellation only as authorized and to meet any standards applicable to the protected product.[66]

III. Powers of Attorney

A troublesome detail for American industrial property owners and their lawyers and patent agents in filing patent and trademark registration applications and other documents with the MPTO has been compliance with the formal requirements of Mexican law for the grant of a power of attorney to a Mexican lawyer or other agent to act in their behalf. The IPL provides significant relief for this problem by providing that an agent's capacity may be evidenced by a power of attorney granted in conformity with the legislation applicable in the place where it is granted, or in accordance with an international treaty, agreement or convention to which Mexico is a party if the grantor of the power is a foreign legal person.[67] Furthermore, when the power attests to the existence of the legal person in whose name it is granted, as well as the authority of the

---

[64] IPL, Art. 110.

[65] IPL, Art. 156.

[66] IPL, Arts. 164, 165.

[67] IPL, Art. 181.

signer to grant it, the power of attorney will be presumed valid in the absence of proof to the contrary.[68]

IV. Enforcement

The IPL incorporates a number of technical changes in the procedures for inspection visits, which are authorized for purposes of determining whether violations exist.[69]

In addition, the IPL criminalizes the misappropriation or unauthorized use of an industrial secret, if the purpose is to obtain a financial benefit or to damage the person who maintains the secret of his authorized user.[70]

V. Conclusion

The IPL, despite a number of relatively minor imperfections, achieves significant advances in the protection afforded to industrial property under Mexican law. Most important are the expansion of the area of patentable inventions and the protection afforded for the first time to industrial secrets.

One area that is left untouched, however, is the enforcement of protected industrial property rights through private civil litigation. Historically, the plaintiffs in patent and trademark infringement actions in the Mexican courts have been notably unsuccessful. Furthermore, the Mexican Codes of Civil Procedure do not generally contemplate the grant of injunctive relief to prevent the unlawful disclosure of an industrial secret.

It is unclear when and how these remaining deficiencies in Mexican industrial property protection will be remedied.

---

[68] IPL, Art. 181.

[69] IPL, Arts. 203–12.

[70] IPL, Art. 223.

VI. Supplement: NAFTA's Enforcement Provisions

The North American Free Trade Agreement ("NAFTA") contains a wide array of provisions governing the enforcement of intellectual property rights. These provisions apply to all "intellectual property rights," which, by definition, include trade secrets, as well as patent, trademark, and copyrights. This is somewhat of a deviation from U.S. law, which currently has no federal trade secret statutes. Most states, however, have adopted some version of the Uniform Trade Secrets Act, which provides for enforcement mechanisms akin to those mandated by NAFTA.

NAFTA's enforcement provisions include a series of procedural safeguards that are consistent with the fundamental aspects of current U.S. intellectual property protection laws. For example, NAFTA provides for basic due process rights (the right to be heard reasonably promptly, to a written and reasoned decision, and to an appeal), discovery rights (the right to obtain discovery protective orders to preserve confidences), injunctive relief (including temporary restraining orders preliminary and permanent injunctions), security bonds for temporary and preliminary injunctions, and immediate post-seizure hearings in the case of *ex parte* seizures.

The substantive aspects of NAFTA's enforcement provisions offer the holders of intellectual property rights protections that are, with a few exceptions, equivalent to those offered under U.S. law. For example, NAFTA Section 1715(3) provides for injunctive relief against persons who infringe upon the intellectual property rights of others. The right to injunctive relief under NAFTA is somewhat narrower than that available under U.S. law because Section 1715(3) does not require the member countries to provide for injunctive relief against innocent infringers, until "that person knew or has reasonable grounds to know that dealing in [the infringing product] would entail infringement of an intellectual property right." As a practical matter, this difference may prove to be insignificant because it is extremely uncommon under U.S. law for an injunction to be entered (except perhaps the rare *ex parte* temporary restraining order) without a full hearing during which every enjoined party obtains express knowledge that its activities entail infringement.

A potentially greater difference between the right to injunctive relief under NAFTA and under equivalent U.S. law is that NAFTA does not require that the governmental authority hearing the request for injunctive relief balance the irreparable injury that may be suffered if injunctive relief is not granted against the hardship an injunction would place on the defendant. Presumably, those negotiating NAFTA felt that NAFTA's requirement that the plaintiff post a security bond would adequately protect the defendant, but this may not be so in all cases.

As under U.S. law, NAFTA also permits the award of damages against those who infringe the intellectual property rights of others. NAFTA's damage provisions, however, fail to measure up to those of U.S. law in a least one significant respect. Under U.S. patent, trademark, copyright, and even trade secret laws, the property owner is entitled to damages (usually lost profits, wrongfully obtained profits, or a reasonable royalty) regardless of the defendant's intent. Under U.S. law, innocent infringement is no defense to plaintiff's entitlement to damages and is only sporadically considered in quantifying damages. Intentional infringement justifies an enhanced damage award and often trebling of actual damages.

In contrast, NAFTA Section 1715(2)(d) provides for the recovery of actual damages only "where the infringer *knew or had reasonable grounds to know* that it was engaged in an infringing activity." This significant limitation on the right to recover damages does not apply to the infringement of copyrighted works and sound recordings.

The fact that NAFTA permits member countries to require proof of knowing infringement as a prerequisite to an award of damages means that U.S. companies must carefully plan their intellectual property protection programs, *before* selling or producing protected products in Mexico. Under NAFTA's approach, advance measures, such as the careful use of copyright, patent, and trademark notices, insistence on agreements acknowledging the existence of intellectual property rights, and others, will become critically important to recovering damages for intellectual property infringement.

Finally, NAFTA provides the holders of intellectual property rights with the ability to demand that a member country detain shipments of infringing goods at the country's border. The provisions governing this right are quite extensive and are generally consistent with U.S. patent, copyright, and trademark laws.

Mexico has up to three years to bring its laws into compliance with NAFTA's intellectual property enforcement provisions. Until this process of legal revision is completed, the extent of the differences between Mexico's and the U.S.'s intellectual property protections will not be fully known.

CHAPTER 12

Labor Relations in Mexico

Lic. Luis Ruiz Gutierrez
Barrera, Siqueiros y Torres Landa, S.C.

William E. Mooz, Jr.
Holland & Hart

I. Introduction

One of the most important issues for a company locating in Mexico will be labor relations. Many people in the United States, as evidenced by some of the more heated rhetoric during the debate over the North American Free Trade Agreement ("NAFTA"), hold the view that workers in Mexico are poorly paid and devoid of any legal protection. The business that takes this perspective into Mexico is in for a rude awakening. While salaries at the minimum wage level in Mexico are well below those in the United States, they escalate quickly with the employee's level of skill, and for certain positions can easily reach U.S. levels. Moreover, the legal protection and benefits afforded to employees under Mexico's Federal Labor Law go well beyond what employers in the United States are used to, and commonly amount to 30 to 40 percent of basic payroll costs.

II. Nature and Formality of the Labor Relationship

All work relationships in Mexico are governed by the Federal Labor Law. The Labor Law is of constitutional origin, and its application cannot be waived or bargained away.

The Labor Law requires that all employment contracts be in writing. This requirement can be satisfied by either a single collective bargaining agreement that covers all unionized workers or individual agreements between each worker and the employer.

Employment agreements can be for a specific task, a defined period of time, or for an indefinite period. Contracts for a limited duration are permissible only when work conditions so require or for the purpose of obtaining coverage for a worker who is temporarily absent. Even where permissible, contracts for a defined period of time may be deemed to extend beyond their fixed duration if the underlying conditions that gave rise to the need to retain the worker continue to exist.

III. Compensation

The minimum wage in Mexico depends upon the zone in which the company is located. The daily minimum wage for zone A, which includes the Mexico City metropolitan area, the border zone and portions of the oil patch, is 15.27 new pesos (about USD $4.80) for 1994. Zone B includes the metropolitan areas of Guadalajara and Monterrey, and parts of Sonora, Tamaulipas, and Veracruz, and carries a daily minimum wage of 14.19 new pesos (about USD $4.15) during 1994. Zone C encompasses the remainder of the country and has a daily minimum wage of 12.89 new pesos (about USD $4.05) for 1994. This represents approximately a 7 percent increase over the minimum wage for 1993.

Companies must be prepared, however, to pay higher rates for more skilled workers. For example, a typical factory worker in the Mexico City area is likely to earn a daily salary of approximately 30.00 new pesos (about USD $9.40). Where a collective bargaining agreement is in place, the Labor Law permits the union to insist on renegotiating wages one time each year and benefits once every two years.

The salaries that must be paid to managers and technical people will be considerably higher.[1] A mid-level manager or technician is likely to

---

[1] A salary survey published by the American Chamber of Commerce in 1993 found that, on average, the following annual salaries prevailed: finance director, $83,934; marketing manager, $51,519; accountant, $16,834; data processor, $7,030; and bilingual

command a salary that may be somewhat lower than his or her U.S. counterpart. The high-level executive, however, will probably command a compensation package that is as high, or even higher, than what is usually paid in the U.S. Demand for bilingual, high-level executives is quite high, and the pool of such people is comparatively limited. Consequently, it is not uncommon for key people to be the target of frequent offers. Expatriate employees typically receive compensation packages that are comparable to what it will take to retain a key Mexican executive.

IV. Legally-Mandated Benefits

The benefits mandated by law are quite extensive and often amount to a large portion of an employee's total compensation. The more significant of these benefits are listed below.

A. Christmas Bonus

Employees who have worked with a company for the entire year are entitled to a Christmas bonus of at least 15 days of salary. Employees who have worked for the company for less than a year are entitled to a partial bonus. This bonus must be paid before December 20 of each year. Most companies give their employees more than the minimum bonus and the average bonus typically is around 25 days of salary.

B. Vacations

Employees are entitled to the following amounts of paid vacation: six days for the first year of service; eight days for the second; ten days for the third; and twelve days for the fourth. From the fifth year on, the employee is entitled to an additional two days for every additional five years of service. For example, an employee with seven years of service would have the right to twelve days of paid vacation and an employee with nine years would be entitled to fourteen days. While on vacation employees are legally entitled to receive their normal salary, plus a

---

executive secretary, $17,272. American Chamber of Commerce, *Guide to Mexico for Business* 20 (1993). These figures are in U.S. dollars and represent before-tax compensation. Benefits and perquisites will add to these figures substantially.

vacation bonus of an additional 25 percent. Most union contracts, however, call for an even higher vacation bonus, which averages around 40 percent of the vacationing worker's normal salary for that time period.

C. Sunday Bonus

Employees whose normal work week includes Sunday are entitled to a bonus of 25 percent of their salary for that day. Most collective bargaining agreements call for a higher bonus of 30 to 40 percent of the base daily salary for work on Sundays.

D. Days Off and Holidays

Employees are entitled to one day off for every six working days. If the employee works on his or her day off, the employer must pay the normal daily wage plus a premium of two extra days of salary. If the employee works less than a full day, he or she is entitled to a proportionate amount of the daily wage and the premium.

In addition to weekly days off, employees are entitled to receive a minimum of seven prescribed holidays per year, plus the day on which the federal government changes administrations every sixth year. Most businesses in Mexico grant their employees more holidays than the minimum number required by law. Employees who are required to work on a designated holiday are entitled to receive the same premium that applies when an employee works on his or her weekly day off.

E. INFONAVIT

Employers must contribute to the Low Income Housing Fund ("INFONAVIT") in the amount of 5 percent of the "qualifying compensation"[2] paid to their workers.

---

[2] As a general rule, qualifying compensation is limited to 25 times the minimum wage in effect for the Federal District of Mexico. For certain programs, such as INFONAVIT and disability, death, and retirement insurance, the ceiling is ten times the minimum wage in effect for the Federal District.

F. IMSS (Social Security)

The Mexican Social Security System ("IMSS") operates as an insurance program which provides workers with a wide variety of benefits. Employers and employees contribute varying amounts to each aspect of the program. Some of the more significant benefits provided through IMSS are as follows:

1. Day Care

The employer must pay a premium equal to 1 percent of its employees' qualifying compensation for day care.

2. Work Risk Insurance

Employers must pay a premium toward work risk insurance, which is akin to the worker's compensation insurance that prevails in the United States. The amount of the premium will be determined by the nature of the employer's activities and its safety record. Typical premiums can range from a low of 0.34 percent of the employees' qualifying compensation to a high of 10.035 percent.

3. Sickness and Maternity Insurance

The employer and the employee each pay premiums toward this insurance. The employer's share is 8.75 percent of the employee's qualifying compensation, and the employee's share is 3.125 percent.

4. Disability, Retirement, and Death Insurance

The premiums for this insurance will cost the employer 5.67 percent of the employee's qualifying compensation, and the employee 2.025 percent.[3]

---

[3] The contributions required for this portion of the fund are scheduled to change in 1995 and again in 1996. The contributions required for all other aspects of IMSS do not change from year to year.

5. Retirement Savings Fund

In 1992, the government established a new retirement system in Mexico. Employers now must deposit a tax-deductible 2 percent of each employee's salary into an individual retirement account. Such accounts may be managed by commercial banks, brokerage houses, and insurance companies. The employees determine how their pension funds will be invested, with the permissible choices including government bonds and mutual funds.

For 1994, the employer's total cost for IMSS's programs will be 17.42 percent of its employees' qualifying compensation, plus the applicable charge for work risk insurance.

V. Profit Sharing

Although technically a legally-mandated benefit that could be discussed in conjunction with all others, the employees' right to profit sharing is so significant that it warrants separate treatment. By law, 10 percent of the employer's gross profits must be shared with workers. Half of this fund is apportioned on the basis of salary and the other half is apportioned on the basis of the number of days that each employee worked during the year. Every employee other than the director general of the company is entitled to participate in the profit sharing fund.

The profit sharing obligation applies to all companies that have employees in Mexico. Thus, if a U.S. company opens a Mexican branch, the branch's income is subject to the profit sharing obligation.

The profit sharing obligation is sufficiently significant that many companies limit their operations in Mexico to a company that provides the capital (including machinery, equipment, facilities and the like) necessary to carry out the relevant business, which then contracts with another company to provide a work force. Since the first company has no employees other than a director general, it will not be subject to the profit sharing obligation. These types of arrangements, however, are subject to being scrutinized as sham transactions, particularly where the capital company and the company providing the labor are under common control.

VI. Optional Benefits

It is common for employers to grant their employees additional benefits such as qualified savings plans, food assistance, and more.

Qualified Savings Plans. Mexico's Income Tax Law permits the employer to establish a qualified savings plan for its workers. Contributions must be made by the employer and the employee in equal amounts and are capped at 13 percent of that portion of the worker's salary which does not exceed ten times the applicable minimum wage. These funds are distributed annually and may be borrowed against during the year.

Food Assistance. Many employers grant their employees food stamps.

Others. Other common benefits include life insurance, medical insurance, scholarships, and marital and birth bonuses.

VII. Retention, Promotion, and Termination of Employees

A. Hiring Employees

In principle, the employer has the right to hire whomever it wishes. The Labor Law, however, establishes a mandatory preferential hiring scheme that can curtail this freedom sharply. The scheme of preferences will not apply when the company has executed a collective bargaining agreement that requires the company to hire any of the workers it needs from the union. Where the union is a reasonable one, such an arrangement can give the employer the freedom to hire whomever it chooses.

B. Promotions

Article 159 of the Labor Law requires that promotion be based exclusively on seniority. The employer may, however, enter into a collective bargaining agreement which provides for merit-based promotion so long as the employer also agrees to provide training to its workers.

C. Termination and Severance Pay

The Labor Law permits an employer to terminate employees only upon the occurrence of the following specified events:

(1) mutual consent of the parties;

(2) death of the worker;

(3) completion of the work project or expiration of the defined time period for which the worker was hired;

(4) physical or mental disability that prevents the worker from performing the job;

(5) *force majeure*;

(6) manifest cost inefficiency of the operation;

(7) bankruptcy of the employer declared by a competent authority;

(8) installation of new machinery; and

(9) the worker's commission of certain specified acts, i.e., cause.

The employer will be obligated to give the worker severance pay unless the termination is by mutual consent or for cause. Cause is defined by the Labor Law as:

(1) The worker obtains his or her position through false documents or by misrepresenting his or her credentials. This cause for termination expires 30 days after the worker begins rendering services to the employer.

(2) The worker engages in acts of dishonesty or disruptive or violent behavior on the job.

(3) The worker engages in similar acts outside the workplace if such acts are serious enough to render the work relationship an impossible one.

(4) The worker intentionally damages the workplace.

(5) The worker negligently causes serious damage to the workplace.

(6) The worker's behavior constitutes a safety risk.

(7) The worker commits immoral acts at the workplace.

(8) The worker reveals manufacturing secrets or confidential matters to the detriment of the employer.

(9) The worker is absent more than three times in a period of 30 days, without permission of the employer or without justified cause.

(10) The worker disobeys work-related orders without justified cause.

(11) The worker refuses to follow the prescribed health and safety procedures.

(12) The worker comes to work drunk or under the influence of any narcotics or nonprescribed drugs. Before starting work, a worker taking prescribed medication must notify the employer and present a prescription signed by a medical doctor.

(13) The worker is unable to perform his or her duties because he or she has been sentenced to jail.

(14) Causes similar to those described above if they are of a sufficiently serious nature.

Whenever the employer terminates a worker for cause, it must give the worker written notice of the date and cause of the termination. If the worker refuses to accept such notice, the employer must give notice to the appropriate Labor Court within five days of the termination, along with the terminated worker's address, and request that notification thereof be given to the worker. Failure to provide the requisite notice to the worker or the Labor Court is sufficient reason to consider the dismissal unjustified.

Employees are free to resign at any time. As a general rule, workers who resign are not entitled to severance pay unless the resignation is coerced by the employer. (The worker who resigns will have the burden of proving that the employer coerced his or her resignation through pressure or threats.) Workers having more than 15 years of service with the employer are entitled to a seniority premium of 12 days of salary for each year of service upon resignation.[4]

The employee also has the right to rescind his or her work contract if the employer fails to live up to its obligations, for example, by failing to provide hygienic conditions, a safe work place, make payments, etc. In such a case, the employee may be deemed to have been constructively discharged and entitled to severance pay.

Because of the limited right of termination, it is quite common for employers to negotiate for the resignation of employees who they wish to terminate. Under such an arrangement, the parties typically agree to a "severance bonus" amounting to two to three months pay plus a seniority premium. The Labor Law requires that any agreement of termination be made in writing and ratified by the Arbitration and Conciliation Board.

The amount of severance pay that a worker is entitled to will depend upon the reason for his or her termination or resignation. It can range from nothing where termination is for cause, to four months' salary plus 20 days pay per year of service if he or she is terminated because the installation of new machinery renders his or her services unnecessary. This amount is in addition to the mandatory seniority premium discussed above, and, unlike the seniority premium, is not subject to any ceilings.

---

[4] This premium will be calculated based upon the worker's actual wage up to a ceiling of 200% of the minimum wage.

VIII. Work Shifts

The Labor Law sets a standard six-day, 48-hour work week. Work shifts vary depending on whether they are day shifts (8 hours), mixed shifts (7.5 hours), or night shifts (7 hours). For overtime, workers must be paid twice their normal rate, and three times the normal rate for all overtime in excess of nine hours per week.

IX. Unions

A. Right to Unionize

Workers in Mexico have an absolute right to unionize. As soon as two or more employees affiliate with a union, the employer must enter into a collective bargaining agreement if the workers so demand.

B. Types of Unions

There are two types of union: company unions and industrial unions. Company unions represent only the workers of a single company. In keeping with the company-specific nature of this union, it cannot be formed unless at least 20 of the company's workers serve as its founders.

The Secretary General of a company union must be a worker of the company. The worker chosen typically has no union experience, and in many cases, his acts will be motivated by personal whim or the constant pressure of peers. Company unions can be autonomous from the government and the policies that they follow tend to be somewhat unpredictable.

Industrial unions are those that are formed by workers who render services to two or more companies in the same industry. Industrial unions, such as the well known CTM, CROC, CROM, COR, and CTC, are far more prevalent than company unions.

Labor relations typically are handled on behalf of an industrial union by a single person who is well versed in both the industry and labor matters. As an outside professional, this person tends to be insulated from the frictions which may arise in daily dealings on the job site and usually looks for a pragmatic solution to any problems that may exist. Furthermore, industrial unions often have close relationships with the government and have supported the government's desire for stable labor relations.

C. Scope of Union Representation

All employees other than those "in a position of confidence" have the right to belong to a union. Positions of confidence include those of management, inspection, auditing, and finance. Whether an employee occupies a position of confidence will be determined by his or her duties, and not his or her title.

The number of workers in positions of confidence, and thus who can be excluded from affiliating with a union, is quite limited. Nonetheless, in practice most unions traditionally have limited their membership to blue-collar workers. Employees such as doctors, nurses, lawyers, managers, supervisors, and administrative staff rarely belong to a union.

D. Right to Change Unions

A company may only sign a collective bargaining agreement with a single union, and that contract will apply to all of the company's workers. However, the workers can, at any time, attempt to replace the current union with another one by filing a special lawsuit before the Arbitration and Conciliation Board. During this proceeding, the authorities will attempt to determine which union is favored by a majority of the workers. The most important element of this determination will be the so-called "count" procedure (*recuento*), in which all unionized workers vote for the union to which they wish to belong.

At the conclusion of the count, the Board will determine which union holds majority support. That union will be awarded the right to represent the workers, and will become a party to the existing collective bargaining agreement. This agreement will remain in place until it expires, but the prevailing union will have the right to administer its provisions. Since these provisions by law include the right to renegotiate salaries annually and benefits every two years, this right is a significant one.

Workers who support the vanquished union are not likely to fare very well in this process. While, in theory, a company can employ workers who do not belong to the union that is party to the collective bargaining agreement, in practice this rarely occurs. Collective bargaining agreements commonly have an exclusion clause which requires the company not to employ workers affiliated with other unions. A union that gets wind of a possible challenge to its position is likely to use this clause to demand that the employer fire employees who support the dissident union. If this is not enough to quell the challenge, the vanquishing union, whichever it may be, is likely to make similar demands. These demands may be hard to resist, and often result in the employer being obligated to provide severance pay and other benefits to the workers who are fired.

E. Impact of Unionization

From the employer's perspective, there are a number of advantages and disadvantages to having its workers affiliate with a union. The more significant ones are set forth below.

Advantages of Not Having a Union. Where the company is not unionized the employer retains the freedom to hire its own personnel and fix the salaries it deems appropriate. The employer must, of course, respect the minimum wages established by the Labor Law, but will not be forced to revise salaries under the threat of a strike. Most importantly, the employer will not be subject to the obligation, which appears in many collective bargaining agreements, to allow the union to propose and select any new hires to perform work covered by the union contract.

These advantages may prove to be short lived. As mentioned above, Mexican law provides workers with an absolute right to unionize. When as few as two workers affiliate with a union, that union can demand that the employer execute a collective bargaining agreement with it. The employer may find this demand difficult to resist, even if the union chosen is not to its liking, since the law permits workers to go on strike to enforce such a demand.

Advantages of Unionization. The employer does not lose its powers over the direction and administration of the company simply because its workers belong to a union and a collective bargaining agreement has been signed. Workers not belonging to a union have the same rights under the Labor Law as unionized workers.

By entering into a collective bargaining agreement with a mainstream union, the employer may well be able to increase its abilities to control the workplace and labor relations. As mentioned above, Mexico's industrial unions tend to be professional and committed to maintaining healthy labor relations. Having such a union in place can provide the employer with immediate and accurate reports of labor's grievances as well as a reasonable counterpart with whom to negotiate a solution.

Furthermore, the Labor Law permits certain of its mandatory schemes, such as those for hiring and promotion, to be overridden only by a collective bargaining agreement. Similarly, a collective bargaining agreement can serve as a concrete mechanism for guaranteeing that the employer has complied with some of the Labor Law's more opaque obligations, such as those of "providing training" and "filling vacancies."

F. Power of Organized Labor

The strength of organized labor in Mexico has been on the wane over the past decade, particularly during the economic crisis of 1982-1987. The country's large labor unions generally have supported the government's economic restructuring program, in part because real wages in most sectors of the economy have begun to rise again. To the dismay of organized labor in the U.S. and Canada, Mexico's big unions also supported NAFTA.

In May 1992, the government, employers, and employees agreed to a non-binding National Accord for raising productivity. This voluntary pact commits the government and employers to increase investments to strengthen workers' skills. For their part, the workers agreed to negotiate agreements with their companies aimed at increasing productivity. This accord was reiterated in the Pact for Stability, Competitiveness, and Employment (PECE) for 1994. (The PECE is an annual consensus on economic policy reached by various sectors of Mexico's governmental, labor and business communities.)

The 1994 PECE recommended that the minimum wage for 1994 be increased by the amount of inflation anticipated for 1994, or 5 percent. In fact, the minimum wage was increased by 7 percent. The 1994 PECE also suggested that during the annual renegotiations of wages required by law where a collective bargaining agreement exists, bonuses or other incentive payments based upon productivity and quality be used in place of general wage hikes. The PECE is not binding on employers and it remains to be seen how this directive will be implemented.

CHAPTER 13

Environmental Regulation of Business in Mexico*

Douglas W. Alexander
Brown McCarroll & Oaks Hartline

L. Roberto Fernandez R.

I. Introduction

Developing countries, such as Mexico, usually have growth and development as a number one priority, sometimes at a high environmental cost.

Mexico, coincident with the important growth in its industrial sector in the past ten years, has responded to the inherent environmental problems by enacting an omnibus environmental law—the General Law on Ecological Balance and Environmental Protection, "the Environmental Law"—and a series of rules and regulations which together represent a comprehensive effort to restore and preserve Mexico's ecosystems.

* This chapter was edited and supplemented by William E. Mooz, Jr. The authors gratefully acknowledge the assistance of R. Keith Hopson, Elizabeth Rose, and Lic. Maria Teresa Fuentes E.

With regard to foreign companies doing business in Mexico, the body of law lays out the clear principle that "Mexico does not want to be the dumping ground of other countries." This principle is reiterated in the North American Free Trade Agreement ("NAFTA"), which expressly prohibits the member countries from lowering environmental standards to attract investment, and in the North American Agreement on Environmental Cooperation.

II. Mexico's Environmental Laws and Regulations

A. List of Environmental Laws and Regulations

Mexico's principal environmental provisions are as follows:

(1) The Environmental Law:

The General Law on Ecological Balance and Protection of the Environment, published in the Federal Official Gazette on January 28, 1988, effective March 1, 1988.

(2) Regulations:

(a) Regulations for the Prevention and Control of Water Pollution, published in the Federal Official Gazette on March 29, 1973, effective May 29, 1973, "the Water Regulations."

(b) Regulations of the General Law on Ecological Balance and Protection of the Environment, regarding Environmental Impact, published in the Federal Official Gazette on June 7, 1988, effective June 8, 1988, "the Environmental Impact Regulations."

(c) Regulations of the General Law on Ecological Balance and Protection of the Environment, regarding Prevention and Control of Atmospheric Pollution, published in the Federal Official Gazette on November 25, 1988, effective November 26, 1988, "the Atmospheric Pollution Regulations."

(d) Regulations of the General Law on Ecological Balance and Protection of the Environment, regarding Hazardous Waste, published in the Federal Official Gazette on November 25, 1988, effective November 26, 1988, "the Hazardous Waste Regulations."

(e) Regulations for the Protection of the Environment Against Pollution Originated by Noise, published in the Federal Official Gazette on December 6, 1982, effective December 7, 1982, "the Noise Regulations."

(3) Decrees:

Decree pertaining to the importation or exportation of hazardous materials or waste that due to their nature may cause harm to the environment or to property or constitute a risk to the public health and well-being, published in the Federal Official Gazette on January 19, 1987, effective January 20, 1987.

(4) Ecological Technical Standards:

These are the heart of most environmental provisions. Ecological technical standards, ("Technical Standards") are rules issued by the *Secretaria de Desarrollo Social* (Ministry of Social Development), "SEDESOL,"[1] which is the agency of the Executive Branch entrusted with the administration of the Environmental Law and its regulations. The Technical Standards are defined by Article 36 of the Environmental Law, as "a series of scientific or technical rules issued by the Department of Urban Development and Ecology, which set forth the requirements, specifications, conditions, procedures, parameters, and permissible limits that must be observed in the performance of activities or in the use of goods, which cause or may cause ecological imbalance or harm to the environment,

---

[1] Until relatively recently, the enforcement and administration of Mexico's environmental laws came within the purview of the *Secretaria de Desarrollo Urbano y Ecologia* (Ministry of Urban Development and Ecology), "SEDUE." SEDUE has since been assimilated by SEDESOL.

rules which also permit uniform principles, criteria, policies and strategies in relation to the subject."

On October 18, 1993 and October 20, 1993 SEDESOL published a complete new set of Technical Standards that superseded the preexisting set of Technical Standards. It is anticipated that in 1994 SEDESOL will publish a significant number of additional Technical Standards, providing very specific situational guidance. In keeping with the directives in NAFTA regarding harmonization of environmental and other laws, it is likely that Mexico will develop a body of Technical Standards comparable in scope to those promulgated by the U.S. Environmental Protection Agency. This process is well under way and, even though Mexico often adopts Technical Standards that differ from its U.S. counterpart, it is clear that SEDESOL has reviewed and considered the U.S. standard before deciding on what the Mexican standard will be.

B. Division of Authority Among Federal, State, and Local Agencies

The Mexican political structure is similar to that of the United States. The Government is divided into three branches: the Executive, the Legislative, and the Judiciary.[2] Mexico has 31 States and one Federal District. The governments of the States are also divided into the same three branches. SEDESOL is the agency of the Federal Executive entrusted with the administration and enforcement of the Environmental Law, which is a federal statute.

Title I, Chapter II of the Environmental Law divides jurisdiction over environmental affairs among federal, state and local agencies pertaining to environmental affairs.

States and local governments may legislate in the area of ecology and environmental protection, except as to matters specifically reserved to the

---

[2] Art. 49 of the *Constitucion Politica de los Estados Unidos Mexicanos* (Mexican Political Constitution).

Federal Government, for example management of hazardous waste.[3] The Environmental Law lays the groundwork for the states and local governments to promulgate environmental laws and ordinances applicable in their respective jurisdictions. However, such laws and ordinances may not, in any instance, be inconsistent with the Environmental Law. A large number of states have enacted environmental laws. As a practical matter, this means that businesses contemplating commercial operations in particular locations in Mexico should ascertain whether any state or local environmental provisions exist in addition to the federal requirements.

C. Environmental Impact Evaluation

Under Article 28 of the Environmental Law certain commercial activities cannot be carried out without preparation of an environmental impact statement and prior authorization from the corresponding federal, state, or local environmental agencies. These commercial activities include all works and actions undertaken either by the public or private sector that may:

(1) cause ecological imbalance; or

(2) exceed the limits and conditions set forth in the environmental regulations and in the technical standards issued by the Federal Government for the protection of the environment.

The corresponding authority may grant authorization to perform the works or activities as requested. It may also condition authorization on the undertaking of measures aimed at diminishing or reducing the environmental impact, if any, as the authority sees fit.

Specific projects that SEDESOL is responsible for evaluating prior to implementation include the following: construction of hydraulic works, road works, and oil and gas pipelines; manufacture of chemicals, petrochemicals, paper, sugar, beverages, cement, and automobiles; generation and transmission of electricity; certain mineral and non-mineral extraction and refining activities; establishment of installations for

---

3 Environmental Law, Art. 5, § XIX; see also Art. 139.

treatment, refining or disposal of hazardous wastes; and certain forestry activities in environmentally sensitive areas.[4]

Additionally, all individuals or corporations, either public or private, that intend to engage in activities that may generate or entail the handling of hazardous waste, must obtain proper authorization.[5]

The environmental impact statement itself is a document in questionnaire form. There are three types.[6] All parties required to prepare a statement must initially submit the so-called "General" version. If the reviewing authority determines that additional information is required for proper evaluation of the project, it may require submission of one or both of the more exacting versions—the so-called "Intermediate" and "Specific" versions.[7]

The environmental impact statement must be accompanied by a "Risk Study" (*Estudio de Riesgo*). The Risk Study must set forth the environmental risks of the project, as well as the measures planned to prevent or diminish the adverse impact on the environment during the proposed work itself, during normal operations, and in case of accident.[8]

An environmental impact statement must be supported by an environmental impact study, which may only be performed by persons duly authorized by SEDESOL.[9] SEDESOL is responsible for maintaining a registry listing such authorized persons.[10] Once the environmental impact statement has been evaluated, the reviewing authority is responsible for rendering a decision permitting the proposed project on the terms requested, denying it, or, as already stated, making it conditional upon compliance with certain modifications.[11]

---

4 Environmental Law, Art. 29.

5 Hazardous Waste Regulations, Art. 7.

6 Environmental Impact Regulations, Art. 9.

7 *Id.*

8 Environmental Law, Art. 32.

9 *Id.*

10 Environmental Impact Regulations, Art. 4, § VI.

11 Environmental Law, Art. 34.

SEDESOL's practice has been to require the submission of environmental impact statements only by newly formed enterprises, or by existing private or public entities that expand or modify their operations in such a manner that a statement is called for.[12]

D. Creation of Protected Natural Areas

Title II of the Environmental Law concerns protected natural areas. It contemplates certain areas in the Republic being set aside for special environmental protection. The areas are to be designated primarily by the Federal Government, although some are to be designated by state and local authorities.[13] The Environmental Law sets forth specific restrictions on activities depending on the character of the protected area in question. These restrictions obviously have practical consequences for those contemplating operations in such areas. The various protected areas described in the Environmental Law are addressed separately below.

1. Biosphere and Special Reserves

These reserves are to be established in areas described as being "biogeographically" representative of the country, and containing one or more ecosystems not altered significantly by the action of man; containing at least one zone not altered by man; and containing native plant or animal species considered threatened or in danger of extinction.[14] In such areas, the only permitted activities are those deemed productive to the native flora and fauna and those of an educational, recreational, or investigative nature. The Environmental Law specifically prohibits the authorization of new population centers in such areas.[15]

2. National Parks

National parks are to be established in forested territories considered outstanding for their scenic beauty, scientific, educational, recreational,

---

[12] As discussed *infra*, a party may wish to voluntarily prepare an impact statement when it believes that it may be in violation of the applicable laws and norms.

[13] Environmental Law, Art. 46.

[14] Environmental Law, Arts. 48, 49.

[15] Environmental Law, Art. 48.

or historical value, or for their potential for tourism development. In such areas, only activities consistent with the protection of the environment, including touristic activities, would be permitted. Forestry activities would be banned, except as permitted by SEDESOL.[16]

3. Natural Monuments

These consist of sites and natural objects of national concern due to their unique or exceptional character. In such areas, the only activities permitted are those related to preservation of the monuments, as well as activities of a scientific, investigative, recreational, or educational nature.[17]

4. National Marine Parks

These consist of designated territorial waters, and may include the contiguous beaches and lands in the federal maritime zone. In marine parks, the only activities permitted are those consistent with preservation of the aquatic ecosystems, as well as authorized exploitation of natural resources.[18]

5. Areas for Protection of Natural Resources

These are areas designated for the preservation and restoration of forestry zones, and for the preservation of soils and waters.[19]

6. Areas for Protection of Flora and Fauna

Exploitation of natural resources in these designated areas must comply with technical ecological standards and soil use regulations.[20]

---

16 Environmental Law, Art. 50.
17 Environmental Law, Art. 51.
18 Environmental Law, Art. 52.
19 Environmental Law, Art. 53.
20 Environmental Law, Art. 54.

7. Urban Parks

These are areas created by states and municipal governments for the preservation of the environment in urban industrial areas.[21]

8. Zones Subject to Ecological Preservation

These are created by states and municipal governments in zones adjoining population centers, where one or more ecosystems in a good state of conservation can be found.[22]

The protected areas outlined above, with the exception of the last two, fall exclusively within federal jurisdiction.[23] SEDESOL is responsible for proposing to the Federal Executive the creation of the protected areas.[24] The Declarations creating the areas are to set forth the precise delimitation of the areas, a description of activities permitted therein, and specifics concerning any expropriation of land.[25] The Declarations themselves are to be published in the Federal Official Gazette, with prior notice given to owners and occupants of affected properties.[26] For the protection of those acquiring property rights within protected areas, as well as for the protection of the areas themselves, every act, agreement, or contract concerning property located within a protected area, must contain a reference to the corresponding Declaration creating the area. Public Notaries and other government officials may only authorize public deeds, acts, agreements, and contracts that comply with this requirement.[27] All the various protected areas are to be incorporated into a so-called national system of protected areas. SEDESOL is responsible for recording the protected natural areas that form part of the national system in the corresponding Property Recordation Offices.

---

[21] Environmental Law, Art. 55.
[22] Environmental Law, Art. 56.
[23] Environmental Law, Art. 57.
[24] Environmental Law, Art. 59.
[25] Environmental Law, Art. 60.
[26] Environmental Law, Art. 61.
[27] Environmental Law, Art. 75.

The establishment of this system of protected natural areas will obviously have practical consequences for companies considering commercial operations in affected zones. Any activities undertaken in such areas would have to comply with applicable restrictions and technical standards. Accordingly, companies contemplating the acquisition of property rights within Mexico or the undertaking of commercial activities in particular regions should, as part of any feasibility or title search study, determine whether the territory in question falls within a protected natural area or within an area proposed to be so included.

E. Rational Use of Natural Elements and Resources

Title III of the Environmental Law contains a series of provisions aimed at regulating the rational use of the natural elements and resources. The following subject areas are addressed under this Title:

— the rational use of water and aquatic ecosystems;

— the rational use of the soil and its resources; and

— the effects of the exploration and exploitation of non-renewable resources on the ecological balance.

Each of these areas is discussed separately below.

1. The Rational Use of Water and Aquatic Ecosystems

The Environmental Law sets forth the following guiding principle: "The use of natural resources, including aquatic ecosystems, must be done in a manner such as to avoid adversely affecting the ecological balance."[28] The Environmental Law outlines numerous criteria to accomplish this broad end, including the formulation of a so-called National Hydraulic Program; the granting of concessions and permits for activities which affect or which are capable of affecting the aquatic environment; the establishment of prohibitions on the use of subsurface waters; the suspension of works and activities that are harmful to the nation's water

---

[28] Environmental Law, Art. 88, § II.

resources; and, the creation and administration of fishery protective zones and programs for the protection of certain aquatic species.[29]

SEDESOL, in coordination with other ministries, may issue Technical Standards aimed at the creation and administration of protected areas for rivers, springs and reservoirs, and, in general, sources of water supply for human consumption and for industrial use. SEDESOL is also responsible for seeking the establishment of water reserves for human consumption.[30]

2. The Rational Use of Soil and Its Resources

The Environmental Law sets forth the following general criteria concerning the protection and use of soils.

(1) Use of the soil must be compatible with its natural calling and must not alter the balance of the ecosystems.

(2) Use of the soil must be such as allows it to maintain its physical integrity and productive capacity.

(3) Productive uses of the soil must avoid activities that encourage erosion, degradation or modification of the topographic characteristics, with adverse ecological consequences.

(4) In steep slope areas that present soil erosion and degradation problems, suitable crops and appropriate technologies must be adopted.

(5) The performance of public or private works that may cause severe deterioration of the soils must include programs aimed at restoration.[31]

For areas that present serious ecological imbalances (not the same as zones subject to ecological preservation, see Part II.D.8, *supra*), the Federal Executive may, upon proposal by SEDESOL in coordination with

---

[29] Environmental Law, Art. 89.
[30] Environmental Law, Art. 90.
[31] Environmental Law, Art. 98.

other competent agencies, issue Declarations for the purpose of regulating land use. This is similar to the zoning ordinance system in the United States. A proper title search should suffice to ascertain whether a given area is subject to a Declaration of the Federal Executive, since such Declarations, in order to be binding and effective upon third parties, must be recorded with the corresponding Property Recordation Office.

3. Effects of the Exploration and Exploitation of Non-Renewable Resources on the Ecological Balance

SEDESOL is vested with authority to issue Technical Standards aimed at preventing and controlling the adverse effects of the exploration and exploitation of natural nonrenewable resources. Specifically, such Technical Standards must encourage:

(1) protection of waters utilized in such activities, so as to render the waters useable in other activities;

(2) protection of soils and terrestrial flora and fauna, in a manner so that the topographic changes generated by such activities may be timely and duly restored; and

(3) proper location and forms of exploitation of ore, ore sweepings, mines, slags, and minerals.

Notably, the government agency generally in charge of issuing permits and authorizations regarding nonrenewable resources is the Ministry of Agricultural and Hydraulic Resources and, as regards mining, the Ministry of Energy, Mining and State Industry. SEDESOL participates with these two ministries as necessary to protect the environment.

F. Restrictions on Activities Capable of Causing Pollution

Numerous provisions of the Environmental Law and its regulations are directed at the prevention and control of environmental pollution. The law itself addresses three principal areas: air pollution, water pollution, and soil pollution. Regarding air pollution, the Environmental Law is supported by the Atmospheric Pollution Regulations, issued in

November 1988. As already stated, there is one set of regulations which deals specifically with water pollution, the Waste Water Regulations. It is anticipated that new regulations pertaining to waste water will soon be replacing the regulations currently in effect. Provisions regarding the prevention and control of soil pollution are contained in Chapter III of Title IV of the Environmental Law, and related provisions are spread throughout the text of the Hazardous Waste Regulations. These three principal areas are addressed below.

1. Air Pollution

Air pollution is regulated by three different sets of provisions:

(1) Environmental Law, Title IV, Chapter I;

(2) Atmospheric Pollution Regulations; and

(3) Technical Standards regarding the prevention and control of air pollution.

Under Articles 18 and 19 of the Atmospheric Pollution Regulations, all "fixed sources of air emissions," e.g., facilities constructed for industrial, commercial, or service activities which generate or may generate polluting emissions to the atmosphere,[32] must apply for an operational license issued by SEDESOL. Common practice and SEDESOL's criteria dictate that all new industries file for the operational license. Under Article 19 of the Atmospheric Pollutions Regulations the applicant must provide specific information to obtain the license. SEDESOL has issued special questionnaires to assist in fulfilling this obligation, requesting information including the following:

(1) general data concerning the applicant;

(2) location of the facility;

(3) description of the process;

---

[32] The definition of fixed source of air emissions is contained in the fourth full paragraph of Art. 6 of the Atmospheric Pollution Regulations.

(4) distribution within the facility of machinery and equipment;

(5) raw materials or fuels utilized in the production process and a description of the storage of same;

(6) description of the transportation of the raw materials or fuels to the production area;

(7) description of the production process that the raw materials or fuels undergo;

(8) products, by-products, and waste generated;

(9) description of the warehousing, transportation, and distribution of the products and by-products;

(10) amount and nature of the expected pollutants to the atmosphere;

(11) description of equipment for the control of atmosphere pollution to be installed; and

(12) contingency plan outlining the measures and steps to be taken in event of adverse meteorologic conditions, or in the event odors, gases, or solid and liquid uncontrolled particulates occur.[33]

Article 110, Section I of the Environmental Law mandates satisfactory air quality in all population centers. Accordingly, SEDESOL is empowered, when conditions warrant, to require those performing polluting activities within metropolitan areas, located in two or more states or within areas of federal jurisdiction, to install air pollution control equipment.[34] Additionally, state legislatures may empower state and local environmental protection agencies to require those engaged in activities that generate air emissions to install control equipment or adopt other preventive measures.

---

[33] Environmental Law, Art. 3, § II.

[34] Atmospheric Pollution Regulations, Art. 19.

Parties responsible for the operation of so-called fixed sources of air emissions[35] in areas falling under federal jurisdiction must satisfy certain specific requirements. Furthermore, those responsible for fixed sources of air emissions located within state and local jurisdictions may face additional requirements imposed by state and local governments. Under the specific requirements of the federal scheme, affected facilities must:

(1) utilize systems and equipment designed to maintain contaminating air emissions at a level below maximum allowable limits;

(2) prepare an inventory of contaminating air emissions, on the form provided by SEDESOL;

(3) install testing and sampling apparatus;

(4) measure contaminating emissions, register the results on the form provided by SEDESOL, and provide the results to SEDESOL upon request;

(5) Perform peripheral monitoring of polluting air emissions when the source is located within urban or suburban areas, or when the source abuts protected natural areas, or when in SEDESOL's opinion, due to the nature and characteristics of the operation, severe damage may be inflicted upon ecosystems;

(6) maintain a logbook to record the operation and maintenance of process and control equipment;

(7) provide prior notice to SEDESOL of any renewed startup of operations in the event of a scheduled shut-down, or in the event of an unforeseen shut-down provide notice immediately following a renewed startup, if pollution may be generated thereby; and

---

[35] See note 32, above.

(8) provide immediate notice to SEDESOL in case of any failure of control equipment, if such failure may generate pollution.[36]

2. Water Pollution

The Environmental Law sets forth the general principle that the use of water in productive activities susceptible of causing pollution carries with it the responsibility of treating the water discharges.[37]

Any individual or business entity that as a result of its activities will discharge waste water containing hazardous materials or waste must obtain prior authorization from SEDESOL.[38] In any event, all discharges of waste water, regardless of the location of discharge, must meet the discharge conditions and maximum permissible limits set forth by the applicable technical standards.

Pursuant to Article 7 of the Waste Water Regulations all water discharges, except domestic ones, must be registered. SEDESOL has issued a form for the registration of such discharges, which must be filed regardless of whether hazardous wastes are contained in the waste water. This form calls for a laboratory analysis yielding the following basic information:

(1) sedimentable solids;

(2) oils and greases;

(3) floating material;

(4) temperature; and

(5) P.H.

---

[36] Atmospheric Pollution Regulations, Art. 17.

[37] Environmental Law, Art. 117, ¶ 3.

[38] Environmental Law, Art. 123, ¶ 2.

If there is reason to believe that metal residues may be found in the waste water, it is also necessary to perform an analysis to identify the metals present and their concentrations in the water discharges.

SEDESOL has issued Technical Standards setting forth permissible limits of hazardous waste in water discharges, applicable to specific industries, such as the tire industry, soft drink industry, cement industry, etc. The Water Regulations also contain several schedules that provide permissible limits for water discharges from various sources.

Under the Environmental Law, SEDESOL is to take certain additional actions to prevent water pollution including: issuing Technical Standards for the storage, use, and discharge of waste water; promoting the incorporation of systems to separate waste water of domestic origin from water of industrial origin; issuing opinions concerning placing conditions on the construction of new industries capable of producing polluting discharges; and outlining works and facilities that can be established for purifying industrial waste water.[39]

Under the Environmental Law, it falls to states and municipalities to take steps to control the discharge of waste water into local drainage and sewage systems. Notably, the Environmental Law requires those who generate discharges into these systems and who do not comply with the required Technical Standards to install their own treatment systems.[40]

Significantly, the Environmental Law provides that when waste water affects or is capable of affecting sources of water supply, SEDESOL will communicate with the Secretary of Health and seek the denial of the permit or authorization for the proposed activity, or, in appropriate cases, the suspension of activities.[41] The issuance of authorizations or permits for the use of water for economic purposes capable of polluting will be conditioned on treatment of the waste water produced.[42] SEDESOL is

---

[39] Environmental Law, Art. 119.
[40] *Id.*
[41] Environmental Law, Art. 124.
[42] Environmental Law, Art. 129.

responsible for ruling on applications and permits for discharges of waste water.[43]

G. Restrictions on Hazardous Activities and Hazardous Wastes

1. Hazardous Activities

The regulation of all activities—commercial, industrial, or services—that have been identified by the applicable laws as hazardous, is preempted by the Environmental Law, and falls under federal jurisdiction. Chapter IV of Title IV of the Environmental Law is devoted to the regulation of these hazardous activities. The provisions contained in this Chapter are significant to the industrial sector because they carry potential land use implications. More particularly, SEDESOL is authorized to promote the designation of certain areas dedicated to the establishment of industries, businesses and services considered hazardous, due to the serious impact which they can have on the environment.[44] In designating such areas, factors to be considered include topographic and climatological conditions; proximity to population centers; the impact which an accident could have on population centers and natural resources; and the existing and necessary infrastructure for dealing with environmental emergencies.[45] The Federal Government is to determine and publish in the Federal Official Gazette the list of activities considered highly hazardous for purposes of these provisions.[46] Undertaking operations listed as hazardous is a matter of federal jurisdiction. Accordingly, those who do engage in such activities, regardless of location, must comply with all federal requirements. Such establishments may be required, among other things, to install special equipment and to develop and submit for approval programs for the prevention of environmental accidents.[47]

---

43 Environmental Law, Art. 130.
44 Environmental Law, Art. 145.
45 *Id.*
46 Environmental Law, Art. 146.
47 Environmental Law, Art. 147.

2. Hazardous Waste and Materials

The regulation of hazardous waste and materials in governed by Chapter V of Title IV of the Environmental Law, the Hazardous Waste Regulations, and several Technical Standards.

The initial task of any manufacturer is to determine whether any waste it generates is in fact hazardous. The Environmental Law, in Article 3 Section XXVII, sets forth a broad definition of the term "hazardous waste." Technical Standards specifically list those wastes considered hazardous. In determining whether any waste is hazardous, sometimes it is necessary to perform tests and laboratory analysis in accordance with the procedure set forth in this Technical Standard.[48]

The installation and operation of systems and facilities for the handling of hazardous wastes requires prior authorization from SEDESOL.[49] The term "handling" includes storage, collection, transportation, warehousing, re-use, treatment, recycling, incineration, and final disposal.[50]

General guidelines concerning the import and export of wastes are set forth in Article 153 of the Environmental Law. The guidelines are more specifically developed in the Hazardous Waste Regulations. The significant provisions of Article 153 are as follows:

(1) SEDESOL controls and oversees the import and export of hazardous materials.

(2) Authorization for importing hazardous materials or waste for treatment, recycling, or re-use may only be granted if the use thereof complies with applicable laws and regulations.

(3) Importation of hazardous materials and/or waste may not be authorized for the purpose of final disposal, storage, or confinement in Mexico.

---

48 Ecological Technical Standard No. NTE CRP-001/88.

49 Environmental Law, Art. 151 and Hazardous Waste Regulations, Art. 10.

50 Hazardous Waste Regulations, Art. 9.

(4) Authorization to export hazardous wastes or materials for the sole purpose of final confinement shall be subject to the express consent of the recipient country.

(5) Hazardous wastes and materials generated from raw materials imported on a temporary basis under the maquiladora program must be returned to the country of origin, generally within six months.

(6) Authorization to import hazardous wastes and materials may be subject to the posting of a bond to guarantee due compliance with applicable terms and provisions.

(7) In certain circumstances, SEDESOL may revoke any authorization for the importation of hazardous wastes and materials.

Under Article 7 of the Hazardous Waste Regulations, persons contemplating operations involving the generation or handling of hazardous wastes must prepare an environmental impact statement and secure prior authorization from the Federal Government.

Under Article 8 of the Hazardous Waste Regulations, a hazardous waste generator is required to do the following:

(1) Register as a generator in the registry maintained by SEDESOL. To register, the generator must describe the chemical composition of each waste stream it generates; the frequency of generation; and, the corresponding treatment or disposal of each waste stream generated. There is a special SEDESOL form for complying with this requirement.

(2) Maintain a monthly logbook recording the generation of hazardous waste.

(3) Handle all hazardous wastes in compliance with the Hazardous Waste Regulations and the corresponding Technical Standards.

(4) Separately handle incompatible wastes.

(5) Properly containerize all hazardous wastes.

(6) Properly label all hazardous wastes.

(7) Properly store all hazardous wastes.

(8) Transport hazardous wastes exclusively in vehicles complying with standards of the Department of Communications and Transportation (equivalent to the U.S. Department of Transportation), and in compliance with the requirements of the Hazardous Waste Regulations and the applicable Technical Standards.

(9) Properly treat hazardous wastes.

(10) Dispose of hazardous wastes as required by the applicable Technical Standards.

(11) Submit to SEDESOL a semiannual report (form published on May 3, 1989) reporting movements of all hazardous wastes during such period.

Generators may handle their own hazardous wastes. Alternatively, they may contract a specialized company to perform some of the handling services, such as transportation.

3. Requirements for the Transportation of Hazardous Waste

To transport hazardous waste, the transporter must:

(1) be an authorized transporter;

(2) obtain a *Guia Ecológica* (Ecological Waybill);

(3) have necessary equipment, as required by SEDESOL;

(4) have emergency equipment to handle any contingency that may arise, e.g., salvage drums;

(5) obtain the corresponding "*Manifiesto*" from the hazardous waste generator;

(6) verify that the hazardous wastes being released by the generator are adequately packaged, labeled, and marked;

(7) secure all necessary information concerning the chemical composition of the wastes;

(8) be registered before the Mexican Transportation Department and comply with the requirements set forth by such Department;

(9) inform the personnel involved in the operation of any potential hazards to their health;

(10) have an appropriate bond to guarantee the payment of any damage that may be caused during the handling of the hazardous wastes; and

(11) equip the personnel involved in the operation with necessary protection devices.

4. Requirements for Storage of Hazardous Wastes

Hazardous Wastes may be stored on-site or at special storage facilities. Both types of storage sites must meet the requirements set forth in the Hazardous Waste Regulations. Technical Standards for storage may impose more specific guidelines as well.

Generally, all hazardous wastes must be safely stored in specified areas; packaged in appropriate containers; segregated from incompatible wastes; and properly labeled, including the names and characteristics of the wastes. Specific requirements concerning designated storage areas are set forth in Article 15 of the Hazardous Waste Regulations, which requires that such areas meet the following minimum conditions:

(1) be segregated from production and office areas, and from storage areas for raw materials and finished products;

(2) be located in areas of reduced risk in the event of accidental emissions, leaks, fires, explosions, or floods;

(3) have retaining walls and retention pits for capturing wastes or leaches;

(4) have floors containing drainage channels for conducting any spillage into retention pits with sufficient capacity to retain at least one-fifth of what is stored;

(5) have passageways wide enough to allow the movement of mechanical, electronic, or manual fork-lifts, as well as the movement of safety groups and firefighters in the event of emergency;

(6) have available fire extinguishing systems meeting certain minimum requirements; and

(7) have appropriate signs available to provide notice of danger.

In addition to the above requirements, Article 16 sets forth the following conditions for storage in closed areas:

(1) There must be no connection to floor drains, drainage valves, expansion joints, sewers, or any other type of opening that may allow liquids to escape the protected area.

(2) Walls must be built with nonflammable materials.

(3) The areas must be equipped with natural or artificial ventilation. In the case of artificial ventilation, there must be a minimum reception capacity of six air changes per hour.

(4) The areas must be covered and protected from the weather, have sufficient ventilation to avoid the accumulation of hazardous vapors, and be equipped with explosion proof lighting.

Open storage areas, under Article 17 of the Hazardous Waste Regulations, must meet the following additional conditions:

(1) not be located in places below the highest water level reached by the worst storm recorded in the area, plus a security factor of 1.5;

(2) have floors that are smooth and of impermeable material in the area where wastes are kept, and passageways of nonskid materials that are resistant to the hazardous wastes stored;

(3) have lightning rods in place; and

(4) have detectors for hazardous vapors or gases with audible alarms, when volatile wastes are stored.

The Hazardous Waste Regulations, Article 19, expressly forbid storing hazardous wastes that are incompatible, which exceed the capacity of the storage facilities, or are placed in areas not complying with the storage conditions outlined above.

H. Enforcement

The Environmental Law contains enforcement provisions permitting on-site inspections and the imposition of significant sanctions for violations.

1. Inspections

Under the Environmental Law, states and municipalities are empowered to conduct inspections to verify compliance, even in areas and matters of federal jurisdiction. Inspection activities are to be coordinated among federal, state and municipal authorities."[51] In every inspection visit, the inspectors are to prepare an inspection report detailing any acts and omissions discovered during the inspection.[52] The party being inspected is then provided an opportunity, at the conclusion of the inspection, to make any statement concerning the findings set forth in the inspection report.[53]

---

[51] Environmental Law, Art. 161.

[52] Environmental Law, Art. 164.

[53] *Id.*

The inspected party must permit access of authorized personnel to all places specified in the official document to be presented by the inspector prior to commencing the inspection.[54] The inspected party is also required to make available all information relating to compliance with the Environmental Law and regulations, except such matters comprising industrial property rights deemed confidential under the law.[55] Information provided to the inspector is to be maintained in confidence, if the inspected party so requests.[56] When the inspected party opposes or impedes the inspection, the authorized inspecting authority may request the assistance of public force.[57]

2. Required Corrective Measures

Upon receipt of the inspection report, the regulating authority notifies the inspected party and requires it to immediately adopt corrective measures. The inspected party then has ten days, from the date of receipt of notification, to make an appropriate response and offer of proof concerning the acts and omissions set forth in the inspection report.[58] Once the inspected party has been heard from by the regulating authority, or if the inspected party makes no response within the time allowed, the regulating authority issues an administrative decision within 30 days.[59] The decision sets forth the measures to be taken to correct the deficiencies and irregularities observed, the time limit to satisfy them, and any sanctions to be applied in the event of noncompliance. Within five days following the deadline for taking corrective measures, the inspected party must communicate with the regulating authority, in writing, detailing the measures taken to comply with the order. If additional visits are made to verify compliance, and a report is made stating that the corrective measures have not been complied with, the competent authority may impose sanctions, as described below.[60] In appropriate cases, the office of the Attorney General (*Agencia del Ministerio Publico*), may be

---

[54] Environmental Law, Arts. 165 and 162.

[55] Environmental Law, Art. 165.

[56] *Id.*

[57] Environmental Law, Art. 166.

[58] Environmental Law, Art. 167.

[59] Environmental Law, Art. 169.

[60] *Id.*

notified of the inspected party's acts or omissions that may constitute criminal offenses.[61]

3. Safety Measures

The Environmental Law provides that when an imminent risk of ecological imbalance or dangerous pollution exists, SEDESOL may, as a safety measure, order the confiscation of polluting materials or substances, and the temporary closure of the source of pollution. SEDESOL may also order additional safety measures.[62]

4. Administrative Sanctions

The Environmental Law outlines significant sanctions for environmental violations. Specifically, it provides that any violations of its provisions or of its corresponding regulations may give rise to the imposition of administrative sanctions to be determined by SEDESOL or by state or municipal authorities. One or more of the following sanctions may be imposed:

(1) a fine equivalent to 20 to 20 thousand times the daily minimum wage in force in Mexico City at the time the sanctions are imposed;

(2) temporary or permanent, partial, or total closure of the violating establishment; or

(3) administrative arrest for up to 36 hours.[63]

In addition to these sanctions, once the time limit for correcting any violations has expired and the infractions continue to exist, fines may be imposed for every day that elapses without compliance. However, the total fines may not exceed the maximum set forth above. In the event of reoccurrence of the violation, the amount of the fine may be up to two times that originally imposed, and permanent closure of the establishment

---

[61] *Id.*

[62] Environmental Law, Art. 170.

[63] Environmental Law, Art. 171.

may be ordered.[64] The Environmental Law further provides that when the seriousness of the violation so warrants, additional sanctions may be imposed. These include the suspension, revocation or cancellation of permits or authorizations for the operation of commercial, industrial or service activities, or the exploitation of natural resources giving rise to the infraction.[65] Additionally, SEDESOL may seek the limitation or suspension of the installation or operation of industries, businesses, services, urban developments, and any other activity affecting or capable of affecting the environment or causing ecological imbalances.[66]

5. Administrative Appeal

The Environmental Law provides a mechanism for contesting agency decisions, by means of an "administrative appeal." Specifically, any decisions applying the Environmental Law or its corresponding regulations may be appealed by the interested party within 15 days following the date of notification.[67] The appeal must be in writing and presented to the administrative agency responsible for rendering the decision.[68] The appeal must comply with specific requirements set forth in the Environmental Law.[69] If the appeal is timely filed, the administrative agency may suspend the sanctions previously ordered, and entertain proof during a period not exceeding 15 days.[70] Upon expiration of the time for presenting proof, the agency renders a decision confirming, modifying, or revoking the previous decision.[71]

6. Federal Offenses

In certain circumstances, violations of the Environmental Law can give rise to serious criminal sanctions. The Environmental Law itself outlines the specific violations considered to constitute criminal conduct, as well as the corresponding sanctions. Conduct considered criminal

---

[64] *Id.*
[65] Environmental Law, Art. 172.
[66] Environmental Law, Art. 175.
[67] Environmental Law, Art. 176.
[68] Environmental Law, Art. 177.
[69] Environmental Law, Art. 178.
[70] Environmental Law, Art. 179.
[71] Environmental Law, Art. 181.

includes, among other things, mishandling hazardous waste and materials through such acts as unauthorized transportation and disposal.[72] Notably, criminal sanctions, depending on the seriousness of the violation, can range up to a fine equivalent to 20 thousand times the daily minimum wage in Mexico City as well as imprisonment for up to nine years.[73]

7. Negotiated Settlements and Retroactivity

Mexico has adopted an enforcement policy of attempting to encourage private remediation efforts. This policy stems not only from the obvious desire to deploy enforcement resources efficiently, but also from uncertainty surrounding SEDESOL's ability to require a party to clean up contamination that occurred prior to the adoption of the current environmental laws in 1988.

Article 14 of Mexico's constitution prohibits the retroactive enforcement of legislation. This prohibition has been interpreted very strictly by Mexico's courts and arguably prevents SEDESOL from requiring a party to clean up contaminants that were legally released before 1988. The countervailing position is that environmental contamination is a continuing wrong, and, therefore, the clean up of past spills can be mandated under the new law. This is an issue that ultimately will have to be resolved by Mexico's Supreme Court.

SEDESOL is very cognizant of this potential limitation on its authority, and has attempted to sidestep the issue wherever possible. The typical way in which this occurs is that if SEDESOL discovers both a current and a past violation, it will attempt to use its ability to sanction the company for the current violation (by fines or closure) to get the company to agree to a negotiated settlement whereby the company voluntarily cleans up all past and present contamination in exchange for leniency on the current violation. SEDESOL's leverage in such situations is particularly strong, not only because of the stiffness of the sanctions that can be imposed, but also because the company bears the difficult burden of proving that the contamination at issue occurred prior to 1988.

---

[72] Environmental Law, Art. 184.

[73] Environmental Law, Art. 183.

8. Environmental Audits

Mexico has taken the policy of encouraging voluntary compliance to what many observers consider to be laudable levels. If a company believes that it may be in violation of the applicable environmental standards, it may come forward voluntarily to SEDESOL and agree to perform an environmental audit. The audit must be performed by a consultant on SEDESOL's approved list, and the company must commit to entering into a plan for remediating and restricting the contamination. This plan will be negotiated between the company and SEDESOL based upon the consultant's report. In exchange for coming forward voluntarily and making this commitment, SEDESOL tacitly agrees to waive its right to sanction the company and gives it a reasonable amount of time to carry out the remediation plan.[74] Numerous companies have taken advantage of this policy, enabling SEDESOL to focus its limited resources in a more efficient manner. The environmental audit policy currently is an unofficial, unwritten one, but many in the environmental community expect it to be the subject of a formal regulation to be released in the near future.

9. Enforcement Trends

Mexico has been taken to task for having strong environmental laws but weak enforcement efforts. All indications are that the laxness in Mexico's enforcement efforts rapidly is becoming a thing of the past. During the latter half of his administration, President Salinas increased the budget for environmental enforcement steadily and significantly. This increase in funding translated into a similar increase in the numbers of inspections and plant closures by SEDESOL.

The passage of NAFTA and the North American Agreement on Environmental Cooperation provide further reasons to believe that Mexico will continue to increase the aggressiveness with which it enforces its environmental laws. The North American Agreement on Environmental Cooperation expressly requires all of the parties to "effectively enforce its

[74] SEDESOL is constitutionally prohibited from expressly waiving its right to sanction a company that pollutes.

environmental laws and regulation."[75] A "persistent pattern of failure by [a Party] to effectively enforce its environmental law" can result in the imposition of monetary sanctions by a multinational panel, and/or bring multinational supervision of a plan to bring enforcement efforts up to par.[76] In addition, Mexico has committed to providing its citizens with the right to enforce its environmental laws in private actions.[77] While the manner in which these provisions will be implemented, and their ultimate effect, remain unclear, their mere presence ensure that environmental enforcement will remain in the public limelight for the foreseeable future.

III. Hazardous Wastes and the Maquiladora Industry

In the past several years, the maquiladora industry in Mexico has experienced explosive growth.[78] Environmental regulation, to the extent it existed at all, did not keep pace with that growth. However, more recently, particularly with the enactment of the Environmental Law and its Regulations, Mexico has set in place a regulatory framework that specifically addresses the unique aspects of this industry. These Mexican laws and regulations are complemented by agreements between the United States and Mexico that properly recognize the environmental problems of the maquiladora industry as bi-national ones.

Maquiladoras, even where 100 percent foreign-owned, as is typically the case, are considered Mexican companies. They are therefore not immune from any of the environmental laws and regulations applicable to enterprises operating in Mexico. Furthermore, specifically in the area of hazardous waste, maquiladoras must also comply with U.S.

---

[75] NAFTA, Art. 5.

[76] NAFTA, Art. 34.

[77] NAFTA, Art. 6.

[78] The maquiladora program allows companies to import machinery and raw materials into Mexico duty-free for use in manufacturing finished products that will be exported. The importance of the program is likely to decrease as NAFTA takes effect, and Mexico's tariffs on U.S. and Canadian goods are phased out. The need for this program will still exist to the extent that the goods imported do not meet NAFTA's rules of origin, or are not subject to a complete tariff reduction. The environmental issues associated with foreign-owned, export-oriented companies will continue to exist whether or not these companies operate strictly as maquiladoras.

environmental laws and regulations where wastes are returned to the United States for disposal.

This bi-national regulation arises from the current lack of infrastructure in Mexico. Although Mexico has opened its doors to the maquiladora industry, it is not presently equipped to properly dispose of the hazardous wastes generated by the influx of these assembly and manufacturing operations. The interweaving of Mexican laws, U.S. laws and U.S./Mexico agreements concerning hazardous waste disposal can best be understood when seen against this infrastructure backdrop.

Reduced to their most basic common denominators, the myriad of rules governing waste generated by the maquiladora industry may be summed up in three basic principles:

(1) Non-hazardous waste generated by the maquiladora industry may generally be disposed of in Mexico with a minimum of regulatory involvement because Mexico is equipped to properly dispose of such waste.

(2) Hazardous waste generated by the maquiladora industry may not be finally disposed of in Mexico because Mexico is not equipped to properly dispose of it. Such wastes must be returned to the country of origin of the raw materials, where such waste can be disposed of properly.

(3) It appears that hazardous waste capable of being recycled may be recycled in Mexico by third parties or by maquiladoras themselves when proper authorizations are secured.

To set forth the hazardous waste problems of maquiladoras in Mexico as three simple principles is not to suggest that it is a simple problem. There is a substantial difference, for example, between understanding that hazardous wastes generated by U.S. maquiladoras in Mexico must be disposed of in the United States, and understanding how to navigate the regulatory gauntlet to comply with that plain requirement. This explains at least in part why the best evidence seems to suggest there is currently a significant gap between the number of maquiladoras generating hazardous waste required to be returned to the United States and the number that are actually doing so. The other explanation, of course, is one of simple expense. Recent developments in Mexico suggest that those who fail or refuse to comply with these environmental regulations, or gamble on their not being enforced, do so at considerable risk.

These environmental regulations should not be of mere academic interest to those contemplating or engaging in maquiladora operations. A significant percentage of maquiladoras actually produce hazardous wastes as a part of the production process. For example, operations such as electronics assembly and metal finishing, that have been given priority by the Mexican government and that are considered relatively "clean" compared with traditional heavy industries, nevertheless consume raw materials which typically generate a hazardous waste stream. By both international agreement and under Mexican law, Mexico flatly prohibits the disposal of such wastes in Mexico, and unambiguously requires that such wastes be returned to their country of origin for final disposal.

A. Disposal of Non-Hazardous Wastes Generated by Maquiladoras

The maquiladora industry is regulated first and foremost by the 1983 Decree for Promotion of the Maquiladora Industry (the "Maquiladora Decree"). Generally speaking, under the Maquiladora Decree, all raw materials imported into Mexico temporarily for manufacture or assembly must be re-exported upon completion of the production process. Under Article 10 of the Decree, wastage refers to the residue materials left after the production process is complete.

Article 10 carefully controls the disposition of wastage generated by maquiladoras. It sets forth four alternative dispositions:

(1) destruction;

(2) donation to educational or non-profit institutions;

(3) exportation; or

(4) permanent importation.

Article 10 also provides that where a maquiladora desires to sell the wastage of its production process in the domestic market, it must apply for authorization with Mexican custom authorities.

The Maquiladora Decree, then, makes available to the maquiladora industry various avenues for disposal of waste in Mexico, although certain legal requirements must be met. There are no flat prohibitions as such on maquiladoras disposing of non-hazardous wastes in Mexico under the Maquiladora Decree, other laws regulating the environment, or the Customs Law and its Regulations. Accordingly, maquiladoras may properly dispose of non-hazardous wastes in Mexico, upon compliance with applicable rules and regulations.

B. Disposal of Hazardous Wastes Generated by the Maquiladora Industry

As a general matter, wastes generated by maquiladoras that constitute hazardous wastes may not be finally disposed of in Mexico. Rather, the waste must be returned to the country of origin of the raw materials for disposal. In the case of maquiladoras which import their raw materials from the United States, this means, of course, that the hazardous wastes must be returned to the U.S. Accordingly, such maquiladoras must, as a general rule, comply with both Mexican and U.S. laws and regulations relating to packaging, transportation, and disposal of hazardous wastes. Discussed below are, first, the Mexican side of this bi-national regulatory scheme and, second, the U.S. side.

1. Mexican Regulatory Scheme

In 1983, an international agreement was signed between the United States and Mexico regarding protection and improvement of the environment in the border area.[79] The so-called La Paz Agreement provided in general terms that the two countries would cooperate in protecting the border area environment and would enter into future

[79] Agreement Between the United States of America and the United Mexican States on Cooperation for the Protection and Improvement of the Environment in the Border Area, Aug. 14, 1983, T.I.A.S. No. 10827.

agreements adopting specific measures toward that end.[80] The Agreement further designated a national coordinator in each country to implement the Agreement, in the case of the United States, the Environmental Protection Agency ("EPA"), and in the case of Mexico, SEDESOL.[81]

In 1986, the United States and Mexico adopted Annex III to the La Paz Agreement.[82] This Annex specifically addresses the transboundary shipment of hazardous wastes. It provides in Article XI that hazardous wastes generated from raw materials admitted inbound into Mexico from the United States shall be readmitted by the U.S. for disposal in accordance with applicable laws and regulations.

The provisions of Annex III are complemented by Mexican laws and regulations. On January 19, 1987, Mexico promulgated a decree relating to imports and exports of hazardous materials and waste.[83] The provisions of this Decree regarding hazardous waste were abrogated by the Regulations of The Environmental Law published November 25, 1988. These Regulations retain the provisions of the Decree which banned the importation of hazardous waste into Mexico for the sole purpose of final disposal. The Hazardous Waste Regulations also retain the provision in the Decree requiring that hazardous waste generated by the maquiladora industry be returned to the country of origin. The Environmental Law, enacted in 1988, contains similar provisions. It flatly prohibits the importation of hazardous wastes or materials for final disposal.[84] It also requires that hazardous wastes generated by maquiladoras be timely returned to their country of origin.[85]

---

[80] *Id.* at Art. 1.

[81] *Id.* at Art. 8.

[82] Agreement on the Transboundary Shipment of Hazardous Wastes and Hazardous Substances, United States-United Mexican States, Nov. 12, 1986, 26 I.L.M. 25 (1987).

[83] Decree Relating to Import or Export of Hazardous Materials that by their nature May Cause Damage to the Environment or to Property or Constitute a Risk to Public Health or Welfare. *Diario Oficial*, Jan. 19, 1987.

[84] Environmental Law, Art. 153.

[85] *Id.*

2. U.S. Regulatory Scheme

The United States has a number of specific provisions relating to the importation of hazardous wastes into the United States for final disposal.

a. Definition of Hazardous Waste

The first step in approaching U.S. environmental regulations is to determine whether the product being imported qualifies as hazardous waste under federal and/or state law. For those who suspect, but are not sure, that the maquiladora operation is generating wastes which would qualify as hazardous wastes under U.S. law, a convenient flow diagram may be found in Title 40 of the Code of Federal Regulations, Part 260, Appendix 1. The criteria for identifying hazardous wastes and a list of wastes automatically deemed to be hazardous are contained in Part 261. As with many federal regulations, the federal program sets out minimum standards. States can choose to be more strict or have additional requirements. In California, for example, more wastes are considered hazardous than those listed under the federal rules. In Texas, manifests (documents which must accompany the waste shipment for tracking purposes) are required for some non-hazardous wastes. Maquiladora operators should check the statutes and regulations of the state(s) to or through which their hazardous wastes will be transported to confirm that all wastes are properly managed.

b. Standards Applicable to Generators of Hazardous Wastes

Maquiladora operators who wish to import hazardous wastes to the United States must comply with EPA's standards for hazardous waste generators. These standards are listed at Title 40 of the Code of Federal Regulations, Part 262.

Under the federal requirements, would-be importers of hazardous wastes must first determine, by testing or knowledge of the process, whether the waste is hazardous. If it is, the generator must obtain an EPA identification number. Individual states to which the wastes are consigned for disposal also may require generators to obtain a state identification number.

In addition to any federal notification requirements, some states may require generators to provide notification in advance of importing foreign hazardous wastes into that state regardless of whether the generator already has EPA and state identification numbers.

3. Hazardous Wastes Manifest

A maquiladora operator who plans to transport hazardous wastes for off-site treatment, storage or disposal within the United States must prepare a manifest. A manifest is a shipping document specifically used to track hazardous waste from its generation to its final disposal. It must originate with the generator and accompany the hazardous waste from the time it leaves the generator's facility. Each time the wastes change hands the manifest must be signed. Thus, a complete manifest which has tracked a specific shipment of hazardous wastes from cradle to grave will include the signatures of the generator, transporter(s), and treatment, storage or disposal facility operator. For wastes being imported into the United States, the name and address of both the foreign generator and the importer must appear on the form in addition to the importer's EPA identification number.

Under federal recordkeeping requirements, hazardous waste generators must keep copies of all manifests for three years or until a signed copy of the manifest is received from the designated facility which received the waste. Biennial reports must be submitted to EPA by March 1 of each even-numbered year by all generators who ship hazardous wastes off-site to a treatment, storage, or disposal facility within the United States.

4. Packaging, Labeling, Marking, and Placarding

Hazardous wastes imported from Mexico into the United States must be properly packaged in accordance with applicable Department of Transportation ("DOT") regulations. To import wastes, most generators of hazardous waste must comply with the requirements contained in Title 49 of the Code of Federal Regulations, Parts 171 through 173, 178, and 179.

The DOT packaging regulations correspond with the types of hazard a waste potentially presents once it is offered for transportation. Since it is the hazardous class of the waste which actually determines the packaging required for shipment, it is essential that each waste be properly named and classed according to DOT requirements. Wastes may, for example, be classed as poisonous, inflammable or corrosive.

General waste classifications, hazardous materials tables, special provisions and communication regulations appear in 49 C.F.R., Parts 171 and 172. Part 173 details the general requirements for shipment packaging. Specifications for shipping a variety of containers, from cylinders and drums to bags, can be found in Part 178, while Part 179 details tank car specifications.

All hazardous wastes must be correctly identified and labeled. Individual containers must also be marked with a warning that it is hazardous waste, the EPA or local authorities who should be notified if the wastes are found, and must provide the generator's name and address. The transport vehicle must also be properly posted according to DOT regulations found in Part 172.

5. U.S. Customs

The U.S. Customs Service has no additional requirements beyond those required by the EPA and DOT regarding hazardous waste manifests, packaging, labeling, marking, and placarding. Enforcement checklists are provided to customs agents by the EPA and agents are trained by the EPA in hazardous waste enforcement. Agents have the right to inspect waste shipments and may refuse to admit shipments not in compliance with EPA or DOT regulations. Customs agents have the right to seize shipments in violation of regulations for enforcement action.

6. U.S. Sanctions

Violations of U.S. regulations concerning transportation and disposal of hazardous wastes carry significant penalties. Serious violations can subject a company to fines of up to $25,000 per day per violation. Criminal violators may face fines and imprisonment. Therefore, when in doubt concerning any U.S. regulations, it is best to seek professional advice and to comply with the law.

C. Potential Recycling of Hazardous Wastes Within Mexico

Under existing Mexican law, it appears that maquiladoras may legitimately recycle recyclable hazardous wastes in Mexico. The advantage of such an alternative, where available, is that it avoids having the hazardous wastes enter United States territory, and thereby also avoids the application of U.S. laws and regulations. The Mexican laws which appear to make this alternative available are outlined below.

The Environmental Law and its regulations flatly prohibit the import into Mexico of hazardous wastes for final disposal.[86] The Environmental Law does not, however, prohibit the importation of hazardous wastes for purposes of recycling. In fact, the Environmental Law specifically permits importation for recycling under certain circumstances. More specifically, it provides that SEDESOL may authorize the importation of hazardous wastes for treatment, recycling, or reuse when in accordance with Mexican laws and regulations.[87]

While the Environmental Law requires that maquiladoras export their hazardous wastes to the country of origin, there appears to be room for harmonizing that provision with the provision permitting importation of hazardous wastes for recycling in Mexico. A procedure which would seem to harmonize these provisions would involve the maquiladora "exporting" its hazardous wastes in accordance with Mexican customs law and then a third party "importing" the same wastes to Mexico under Mexican customs laws without the hazardous wastes ever actually entering U.S. territory. As discussed below, while such a procedure might sound like an unusual artifice, there does not appear to be any reason that it should do violence to either Mexican or U.S. law.

From the standpoint of U.S. law, U.S. authorities would acquire no jurisdiction over hazardous wastes not actually entering the United States. Nor should U.S. authorities harbor any significant concern about maquiladoras having wastes recycled in Mexico, where the maquiladoras are otherwise required to seek approval of Mexican authorities and strictly comply with Mexican laws and regulations concerning proper recycling.

---

[86] Environmental Law, Art. 153, ¶ 153.

[87] Environmental Law, Art. 153, ¶ 2.

Such a procedure would also seem to be satisfactory from the standpoint of Mexican authorities. Once again, Mexican laws and regulations can best be understood against the backdrop of the country's infrastructure. Mexico currently perceives itself as not being sufficiently capable of finally disposing of hazardous wastes. It does, however, perceive itself as capable of recycling hazardous wastes. Accordingly, a procedure that would permit maquiladoras to transfer their hazardous wastes to third parties in Mexico under an export/import arrangement would not seem to be at variance with Mexican law expressly permitting the import of hazardous wastes from other countries for recycling. It would also, as a practical matter, conform to Mexico's perception of its ability to recycle those wastes.

There is some recent precedent for such an arrangement in Mexico. However, it should be cautioned that this is still a relatively new area. Additionally, there have been various reports of "sham" recyclers in Mexico. Any maquiladora operator considering having hazardous wastes recycled by third parties should take steps to verify that the Mexican recycler has obtained all necessary authorizations from SEDESOL. As an additional precautionary measure, professional advice should be sought to assure that the specific arrangement would meet with the approval of Mexican authorities. Finally, it also would be advisable to obtain written confirmation that the proposed action is acceptable to Mexican regulators.

Another recycling option seemingly available is in-house recycling by maquiladoras themselves as part of the production process. However, any maquiladora contemplating in-house recycling should secure a revised permit describing the recycling as part of the maquiladora process.

It is critically important to bear in mind that not all hazardous wastes are recyclable, nor are Mexican recyclers presently capable of recycling all the types of wastes that are recyclable in the United States. Maquiladora operators do themselves no favors by blindly turning over their hazardous wastes to third parties claiming to be legitimate recyclers. Maquiladora operators should verify that the recycler is not only fully capable of recycling the hazardous waste, but will also properly dispose of any remaining still bottoms, in a manner expressly approved by Mexican authorities.

IV. Conclusion

Mexico's environmental laws and regulations are in a state of rapid evolution. Although the complete picture cannot be determined until additional regulations and Technical Standards are published, the direction of this evolution is evident. Mexico has effectively declared that it will not be a dumping ground for the hazardous wastes of other nations and has adopted strong environmental laws backed by stringent sanctions. While some doubts continue to linger regarding the extent to which Mexican authorities will actively pursue enforcement, there are clear indications that risking non-enforcement could have very serious consequences. The well-advised company doing business in Mexico will not take this risk.

CHAPTER 14

Options for Resolving Commercial Disputes in the NAFTA Era

William E. Mooz, Jr., Esq.
Holland & Hart

Lic. Alejandro Ortega A.
Barrera, Siqueiros y Torres Landa, S.C.

I. Introduction

With the recent passage of the North American Free Trade Agreement ("NAFTA"), commerce between the United States and Mexico appears destined to continue its pattern of rapid expansion. As commerce between businesses in the United States and businesses in Mexico increases, so too will the number of commercial disputes.

NAFTA, unfortunately, provides little assistance in the way of creating a mechanism for the efficient and just resolution of such disputes.[1] Rather, it leaves the parties with the traditional alternatives of

---

[1] NAFTA simply treats these garden variety disputes with the platitude that "[e]ach Party shall . . . encourage and facilitate the use of arbitration . . . for the settlement of international commercial disputes between private parties in the free trade area," Art. 2022(1), and the creation of an Advisory Committee on Private Commercial Disputes (the "Advisory Committee") to report on how well the encouraged process is working, Art. 2022(4). Compare, e.g., NAFTA, Arts. 1115–38 and Annexes 1120.1, 1137.2

litigation, or some form of arbitration. While neither of these alternatives is ideal, each offers certain advantages and disadvantages that need to be weighed. With some attention and foresight at the outset, businesses can ensure that any disputes that arise are handled as efficiently and fairly as possible.

II. Judicial Resolution of U.S.–Mexico Commercial Disputes

For years, the judicial system has been the forum of choice for most parties to a dispute. Many logical reasons underlie this preference. Court systems are publicly supported, making them virtually free of cost to the litigants. As an arm of the sovereign state, the courts benefit from a wealth of enforcement powers and an air of legitimacy and impartiality. Finally, they are familiar institutions, with rules and procedures that most businesses know and understand.

While these benefits should not be underestimated, the judicial resolution of cross-border disputes can suffer from numerous problems that cannot be ignored. In addition to the common problems of delay, expense, adverse publicity, etc. that plague all judicial proceedings, cross-border proceedings pose their own set of unique problems. Some of the more significant problem areas that are likely to arise and methods for dealing with them are discussed below.

A. The Race to the Courthouse

As a general rule, a party will prefer to have its disputes resolved in the jurisdiction within which it resides. The party typically feels comfortable with the procedures that will be followed, has confidence in the system, and will benefit from the convenience of proximity. These factors alone suffice to provoke parties to take extreme actions to have their *domestic* disputes heard in their local forum of choice.

(providing investors who feel wronged by the actions of a signatory country or its state-owned enterprises are given access to a well-defined arbitration proceeding, which largely incorporates the rules and procedures developed by the International Centre for Settlement of Investment Disputes); *id.*, Ch. 19 (providing for resolution of dumping disputes by bi-national panel).

In trans-border disputes, these same incentives for having a case heard locally exist, but in a heightened fashion; indeed, concerns over the inherent fairness of a foreign tribunal can reach almost paranoic levels.[2] In addition to these factors, the court hearing the dispute will conduct the proceeding in the local language, under local procedural rules.[3] The local court also is likely to decide the dispute under the law of the jurisdiction where it is located, which can greatly affect the outcome of the case.

For these reasons, fights over which court should resolve the dispute can become particularly acrimonious (e.g., long and expensive) in multinational litigation.[4] It is far better to avoid such battles by including a forum-selection clause in the initial contract between the parties. As a general rule, both the United States and Mexico will enforce such clauses[5] so long as the forum chosen has some connection with the dispute, and the dispute does not involve a matter of public policy or purely local import (e.g., a labor dispute, a dispute over title to real property, etc.).[6] In making this choice, one should consider not only the obvious factors

---

[2] These feelings have historic origins. The early European and U.S. trading companies often managed to have their disputes with their Latin partners resolved through proceedings presided over by non-Latins who typically ruled in the foreigner's favor. See Note, "The Future of Arbitration in Latin America: A Study of Its Regional Development," 8 *Case W. Res. J. Int'l L.* 480, 483–87 (1976). The distrust engendered by these proceedings was so great that most latin countries adopted "Calvo clauses" that forbid foreigners from resorting to any procedure that is not available to nationals. See *id.*; Art. 27, § 1, Political Constitution of the United Mexican States. Similarly, the expropriations of Allende and Perez have caused foreign investors to lose faith in the latin courts. *Id.*

[3] See, e.g., *Restatement (Second) of Conflicts of Law* § 122 (1971).

[4] See, e.g., *Dow Chemical Co. v. Alfaro,* 786 S.W.2d 674 (Tex. 1990) (in order to avoid local limitations of damages, Costa Rican plaintiffs filed action in four different courts in the U.S.).

[5] The choice of forum clause must withstand scrutiny by two separate bodies: the court that is being asked to hear the dispute, and the court that is being asked to enforce the judgment.

[6] See, e.g., *Código de Procedimientos Civiles Para el Distrito Federal* ("CPCDF"), Arts. 605, 606 (Mexico will not enforce foreign judgments involving real property or matters of *"orden público"*). *Cf. Mitsubishi Motors Corp. v. Soler Chrysler-Plymouth, Inc.,* 473 U.S. 614 (1985) (laws of U.S. must be applied in matters of public policy); *Gulf Oil Corp. v. Gilbert,* 330 U.S. 501, 509 (1947) (choice of law one factor to consider in deciding whether case should be dismissed on grounds of *forum non conveniens*).

of personal convenience, but also the differences in the substantive and procedural laws that are likely to govern.

B. Procedural Law

The procedural laws of Mexico and the United States differ substantially.[7] The two countries' procedures governing civil actions[8] are similar in that the action begins with the filing of a complaint and an answer. After that point, procedures begin to differ appreciably.

In the United States, the initiation of the action is followed by a period of what often seems like unlimited rights of discovery that can result in expensive and time-consuming depositions and document productions.[9]

In Mexico, once the complaint and counterclaims have been answered, the action proceeds to a conciliation hearing that is akin to mediated settlement negotiations. If the conciliation hearing is unsuccessful, the judge opens an "evidentiary term," in which the parties simultaneously list the proof that they each plan to offer, and requires the parties to submit it (if in writing) to the court in proper form.[10] As a practical matter, the only discovery that is available to a party during this

---

[7] The procedural laws of the U.S. appear in the Federal Rules of Civil Procedure and its state counterparts. The procedural laws of Mexico similarly can be found in the CPCDF and its counterparts in the other Mexican States. For a good general overview of how litigation works in Mexico, see generally José Ovalle Favela, *Derecho Procesal Civil* (2d ed. 1985).

[8] Unlike the U.S., Mexico draws a distinction between civil actions and commercial actions. The procedures for prosecuting a commercial action in Mexico are discussed below.

[9] See generally Fed. R. Civ. P. 26(b) (only limit on scope of discovery requests it that they be reasonably calculated to lead to the discovery of admissible evidence). Cf. Arthur Liman, "The Quantum of Discovery vs. the Quality of Justice," 4 *Litigation* 8, 9 (1977) ("Discovery has become a narcotic for members of our profession. Some litigating lawyers consider themselves almost professionally derelict if they do not ask for every document they can think of, formulate every interrogatory that arouses their curiosity in four different forms—even if they already have full knowledge of the answers—and notice the depositions of every possible witness, no matter how trivial or cumulative his role.").

[10] See José Ovalle Favela, *Derecho Procesal Civil* at 109–10.

process is to review the evidence proffered by its opponent.[11] During the evidentiary term, each party may contest the proof offered by the other party. The judge decides what proof will be admitted based upon the governing law and, in order to determine relevance, the allegations of the parties.

The court is not limited to the proof submitted by the parties. At any time during the proceedings, the judge may order the production of any proof that he or she believes relevant to the matters in controversy.[12]

The discovery period in the United States is likely to be accompanied by a motion to dismiss or for summary judgment and followed by a trial on the merits.[13] Not so in Mexico, where the parties will object to the other side's proof and proceed to an evidentiary hearing to "unveil the proof."[14] At this hearing, the parties present their documents (a mere formality), witnesses testify and experts issue their reports.[15] The only limit on the evidence that may be presented is that it be relevant and submitted to the court during the "evidentiary term."[16] This hearing in theory is supposed to occur before a judge, but in practice often is presided over by a court secretary who, although a lawyer, may have a limited command of the applicable law. A somewhat limited right of cross-examination exists,[17] but is rarely exercised.

---

[11] In theory, the parties can submit letters rogatory asking that specific questions be answered yes or no, CPCDF, Arts. 289, 318, 354, 366, and can bring an action to compel the production of documents.

[12] CPCDF, Art. 279 ("The court may, at all times and notwithstanding the nature of the business, order the practice or extension of any proof, provided that it is necessary for ascertaining the truth of the matters in controversy.")

[13] See, e.g., Fed. R. Civ. P. 12, 56.

[14] See CPCDF, Arts. 278–301, 383.

[15] *Id.*, Arts. 385–400.

[16] See José Ovalle Favela, *Derecho Procesal Civil* at 110–11. There is one exception to these limitations: proof in the form of "confessional proof" may be introduced at any time during the proceedings, but it still must be relevant. CPCDF, Art. 308.

[17] See CPCDF, Arts. 392 (cross examination of experts), 360 (right of both parties to examine witnesses), 389 (right of both parties to examine testifying witnesses), 389 (right to examine witnesses giving testimony in confessional proceeding).

The unveiling hearing is followed by a right to make legal arguments,[18] which is often waived. The court will then, after a delay, hold a hearing to issue its ruling.[19] As in the United States, any one of these hearings can be subject to repeated cancellations and reschedulings.

It is important to note that the above procedures govern civil suits in Mexico. A somewhat more favorable set of procedures may apply in Mexico if the dispute is classified as a commercial one. A dispute will be classified as commercial if (1) the subject matter of the dispute is classified as commercial by the Commercial Code or some other Mexican law, or (2) the dispute concerns a matter that is part of the ordinary course of the defendant's business.[20] The rules of procedure applicable to civil disputes generally parallel those applicable to commercial disputes[21] —with one important exception.

Under Mexico's Commercial Code, suits based upon a negotiable instrument (such as a check, guarantee, mortgage, etc.), can proceed on an expedited basis.[22] The most important aspect of this expedited procedure is that the unpaid creditor can attach the debtor's assets prior to resolution of the dispute.[23] This attribute of Mexican law does not exist in U.S. law, and can make the right kind of judicial action quicker and more effective than arbitration. This expedited procedure, however, applies only where a negotiable instrument is at issue, and will not be available for the resolution of such common commercial disputes as contested terminations of distributors, copyright infringements, etc.

C. Substantive Law

No single factor is likely to have as great an impact on the outcome of a judicial proceeding as the choice of the substantive law that will

---

[18] *Id.*, Art. 393.

[19] See José Ovalle Favela, *Derecho Procesal Civil* at 173–78.

[20] See *Código de Comercio* "C.Com."), Arts. 75, 1049–50.

[21] *Compare* CPCDF with C.Com., Book Fifth.

[22] See, e.g., C.Com., Arts. 1391–1414.

[23] C.Com., Art. 1392.

apply.[24] Over time, this may become less of an issue given that the laws of the two countries appear to be headed down a gradual path of harmonization.[25] Today, however, the choice of law may affect such things as the elements of liability, whether a particular legal claim exists, the right to prejudgment interest, the right to equitable relief, etc.[26]

Perhaps the most significant difference between U.S. law and Mexican law has to do with the damages that a plaintiff may recover. Under Mexican law, plaintiffs can only recover damages that are an immediate and direct consequence of the breach.[27] Mexico's courts apply this limitation strictly, and tend to award very low amounts for damages. Accordingly, it is very common for parties to include clauses in their agreements fixing the amount of the penalty for breaching the agreement. These clauses are enforceable under Mexican law,[28] and will be triggered upon proof that the contract was breached. No proof of damages need be submitted. The main limitation on such clauses is that the amount of the penalty cannot exceed the value of the obligation that is the subject of the contract.[29] United States law contains tighter limits on penalty clauses, but has more liberal standards of proof and, in many cases, permits the

---

[24] See, e.g., *M/S Bremen v. Zapata Off-Shore Co.*, 407 U.S. 1, 8 & n.8 (1972) (whether U.S. or English law applied outcome determinative). See generally Francis J. Higgins, William G. Brown & Patrick J. Roach, "Pitfalls in International Commercial Arbitration," 35 *Bus. Law.* 1035, 1038–41 (1980) (hereinafter "Higgins, Brown & Roach") (some countries do not permit the award of liquidated damages); David J. Branson & Richard E. Wallace, Jr., "Choosing the Substantive Law to Apply in International Commercial Arbitration," 27 *Va. J. of Int'l Law* 39, 39–42 (1986) (hereinafter "Branson & Wallace") (giving number of examples of how choice of law can be partially or totally outcome determinative).

[25] For example, Mexico recently adopted several laws that are clearly based upon their U.S. counterparts. See, e.g., Ley Federal de Competencia Económica, *Diario Oficial* (Dec. 24, 1993) (essentially codifying U.S. antitrust law). This process is strongly encouraged by NAFTA. See, e.g., NAFTA, Ch. 17 (requiring minimum standard level of protections, and procedures for protecting intellectual property rights).

[26] See Branson & Wallace, 39–42. See generally Bernardo M. Cremades, "The Impact of International Arbitration on the Development of Business Law," *Practicioners' Notebook* 526, 530 (1983).

[27] See *Código Civil* ("C.Code"), Art. 2110. An important exception to this limitation is the right to recover "moral damages," e.g., damages to reputation, under C.Code, Art. 1916. Obtaining an award of such damages, however, can be a difficult proposition.

[28] See C.Code, Arts. 1840–44.

[29] *Id.*

recovery of punitive damages. The impact of these differences should not be underestimated.[30]

If the parties have not specified a controlling law in their contract, one can generally expect the court where the action is pending to apply the law of that jurisdiction.[31] This is not a given, however, and it may apply the law of another jurisdiction if logic so dictates.[32] Nonetheless, even where the correct choice of law is clear, nothing prevents plaintiffs from forum shopping until they come across a court that will apply the most favorable substantive law.[33]

The best solution to this problem is for the parties to specify in the contract what substantive law will be controlling. The ability to do so is not unlimited. Both Mexico[34] and the United States[35] require that all disputes relating to certain sensitive national issues and public policies be governed by their respective domestic laws. Aside from these areas,

---

[30] See, e.g., *Dow Chemical Co. v. Alfaro* 786 S.W.2d 674 (Tex. 1990) (highlighting impact of different limits on damages).

[31] See Higgins, Brown & Roach at 1041–43. A good example of the substantive impact of the choice of forum can be found in *M/S Bremen v. Zapata Off-Shore Oil Co.*, 407 U.S. 1 (1972). The contract at issue in that case specified that disputes would be heard by the London Court of Justice, but did not specify an applicable substantive law. The Supreme Court's opinion, however, makes clear that the English court would have applied English law which, unlike U.S. law, would have respected the contracts exculpatory clauses and imposed a far lower ceiling on damages. See *id.* at 8 n.8. Thus, for all practical purposes the forum selection clause proved outcome determinative.

[32] See, e.g., *Randall v. Arabian American Oil Co.*, 778 F.2d 1146, 1147–48 (5th Cir. 1985) (ordering district court to decide case under Saudi Arabian law); *Gutierrez v. Collins,* 583 S.W.2d 312, 319–22 (Tex. 1979) (court cannot refuse to hear case simply because Mexican law applies). But see *Piper Aircraft v. Reyno* 455 U.S. 928 (1982) (choice of law is one element of the forum nonconveniens inquiry).

[33] See, e.g., *Dow Chemical Co. v. Alfaro,* 786 S.W.2d 674 (Tex. 1990) (chronicling plaintiffs extensive forum shopping efforts to escape Costa Rica's limits on damages in personal injury cases).

[34] See, e.g., *Código Federal de Procedimientos Civiles*, Art. 568 (establishing that certain issues must be resolved under Mexican law). Cf. C.Com., Art. 13 (establishing rules for determining which substantive law will apply where the parties have not included a choice of law clause in their contract).

[35] See, e.g., *Mitsubishi Motors Corp. v. Soler Chrysler-Plymouth, Inc.*, 473 U.S. 614 (1985) (antitrust disputes affecting the U.S. must be resolved under U.S. law).

courts in both countries generally will respect a choice-of-law clause specifying the application of foreign law to a commercial dispute.[36]

For obvious reasons, the parties should attempt to coordinate their choice-of-law and choice-of-forum clauses. It makes little sense to select a law that is foreign to the selected forum, and such action is bound to result in delay, if not the outright disregard of one of the conflicting clauses.

D. Obtaining Jurisdiction Over All of the Parties

Obtaining personal jurisdiction typically requires that all parties be found and served personally.[37] Furthermore, due process requires that the named party have a certain level of personal contacts with the forum before it may exercise jurisdiction over his or her person.[38] These problems can be minimized by including provisions in the underlying commercial agreement by which each party (1) appoints an established agent for service of process[39] and (2) consents to the jurisdiction of the court designated to resolve the matter.

---

[36] See Branson & Wallace at 46–63.

[37] See, e.g., Fed. R. Civ. P. 4; CPCDF, Art. 602(IV).

[38] See, e.g., *International Shoe Co. v. Washington,* 326 U.S. 310 (1945) (due process requires that defendant have minimum contacts with state for jurisdiction to attach). Mexico's due process requirements, if anything, are even stricter. See, e.g., CPCDF, Art. 606. While other countries may not subscribe to the minimum contacts requirement for jurisdiction, any judgment awarded against a person lacking minimum contacts with that forum may well be unenforceable in the United States as a matter of public policy. See generally Restatement of Foreign Relations Law of the United States § 482(1)(b) & Comment (c) (failure to satisfy procedural due process requirements renders foreign judgment unenforceable in U.S.).

[39] Mexico's requirement of personal service will be satisfied where service is made on an agent who has a power of attorney over lawsuits and collections. Cf. C.Code, Art. 2554, § 1.

E. Enforcing a Judgment

The domestication and enforcement of a judgment obtained in a foreign jurisdiction is at best difficult and problematic in both the United States and Mexico.[40]

In the United States, judgments of foreign countries are not subject to "full faith and credit," and can be enforced only as a matter of comity.[41] This requires that the following conditions be satisfied:

(1) a full and fair trial in the foreign jurisdiction;

(2) before a court of competent jurisdiction;

(3) with "regular" proceedings;

(4) upon effective service or the voluntary appearance of the judgment debtor;

(5) judgment issued by a system of jurisprudence likely to secure an impartial administration of justice between its own citizens and foreigners; and

(6) the absence of a showing of prejudice in the rendering court or its system of laws or fraud in the procuring of the judgment.[42]

The process of domesticating a judgment issued by a United States court in Mexico is equally cumbersome. There, the domestication of

---

[40] See Dale B. Furnish, "Foreign Judgments in Mexico and the United States," 3 *Ariz. J. Int'l and Comp. L.* 173, 174 (1986) ("In practical effect, the judgment debtor whose assets are across the border will not have to pay the judgment unless it is a very large one or unless neither time nor money are limitations on the judgment plaintiff.").

[41] See, e.g., *Multibanco Comermex v. Gonzales,* 630 P.2d 1053 (Ariz. App. 1981); *State ex rel Domico v. Domico,* 172 S.E.2d 805 (W.V. 1970).

[42] See *Restatement (Second) Conflicts of Laws* § 98 (1971); *Hilton v. Guyot,* 159 U.S. 113 (1885).

foreign judgment will not occur unless the court considering domestication finds that:[43]

(1) it does not involve real estate;

(2) the judgment was rendered by a court of competent jurisdiction;

(3) the defendant was served personally with notice of the proceeding;

(4) the judgment is final and not subject to appeal;

(5) the action giving rise to the judgment is not the subject of a pending proceeding in Mexico;

(6) the judgment is not contrary to public policy;

(7) the judgment is properly authenticated; and

(8) the jurisdiction that rendered the judgment recognizes and enforces Mexican judgments on a reciprocal basis.[44]

In order to authenticate the judgment, the proponent must get a U.S. court to issue a letter rogatory to a Mexican judge requesting that the U.S. judgment be enforced.[45] The letter rogatory must be accompanied by

(1) an authentic copy of the judgment;

(2) authentic documents showing that personal notice was given to the defendant and that the court had jurisdiction; and

(3) evidence that the judgment debtor was given notice of the enforcement proceeding.[46]

---

[43] See CPCDF, Art. 606; C.Com., Art. 1347–A.

[44] States that have adopted the Uniform Foreign Money Judgments Recognition Act are likely to have the simplest time satisfying the reciprocity requirement.

[45] CPCDF, Art. 607.

[46] See CPCDF, Art. 607.

All of these documents must be properly legalized and translated into Spanish. In Mexico as in the United States, the domestication of a foreign judgment is appealable by the defendant.[47]

The practical difficulties associated with the enforcement of a foreign judgment in the United States or Mexico create a strong incentive for selecting a forum where the opposing party has significant assets or security,[48] or choosing to arbitrate where the rules of enforcement are easier.[49]

III. Resolution by Arbitration

The United States and Mexico have both subscribed to the New York Convention regarding the enforcement of arbitral awards, and U.S. law[50] and Mexican law[51] each permit virtually any type of commercial dispute to be arbitrated.[52] These actions make arbitration of commercial disputes

---

[47] See CPCDF, Art. 608.

[48] The opposing party is most likely to have assets in the county where it is based. If this forum is an undesirable one, the parties may wish to consider including a mechanism in their contract which will insure that each party will have assets in a particular county. This can be accomplished in a wide variety of ways, including the use of foreign banks to handle the venture's cash flow, letters of credit, etc.

[49] See Part III.G, *infra*, for a discussion of the rules applicable to enforcing an arbitral award.

[50] See, e.g., *Rodriguez de Quijas v. Shearson/American Express,* 490 U.S. 477 (1989) (any claim subject to arbitration unless Congress intended to preclude a waiver of judicial remedies when passing the applicable statute); *Mitsubishi Motors Corp. v. Soler Chrysler-Plymouth, Inc.,* 473 U.S. 614 (1985) (antitrust disputes are arbitrable); *Scherk v. Alberto-Culver Co.,* 417 U.S. 506 (1974) (finding international securities disputes to be arbitrable). *See generally* Comment, "International Commercial Arbitration: The Nonarbitrable Subject Matter Defense," 9 *J. Int'l Law & Pol'y* 119, 123–39 (1985) (U.S. law now permits arbitration of virtually all matters that were not arbitrable prior to 1970).

[51] Commercial arbitration in Mexico is governed by the provision of Book Five, Title Four of Mexico's Commercial Code. The provisons of Book Five, Title Four were amended substantially on July 22, 1993. By these amendments, Mexico adopted virtually all of the UNCITRAL Model Law on International Commercial Arbitration. The purpose of these amendments was to provide a neutral dispute settlement procedure to solve commercial controversies between foreign and national investors.

[52] The arbitrability of claims involving matters of public policy is conditioned by both the U.S. and Mexico on the application of their respective substantive laws. See, e.g., CPCDF, Art. 615 and *Código Federal de Procedimientos Civiles,* Art. 568 (setting out

between their businesses a realistic alternative.[53] Arbitration offers the parties virtually unlimited flexibility to devise whatever dispute resolution mechanism they desire. However, if not approached carefully, arbitration can subject the parties to a parade of horribles comparable in magnitude to that of litigation gone awry.

A. Submitting a Claim to Arbitration

Just because the laws of both countries permit a claim to be submitted to arbitration does not mean that arbitration will result automatically. The arbitral process derives its jurisdiction from the consent of the parties as reflected in the arbitral agreement.[54] Therefore, it is critical that the parties clearly define the scope of the claims that they are consenting to have resolved in this fashion.[55] This portion of the arbitration agreement should be drafted with as much specificity as possible because, at least prior to the recent amendments of Mexico's Commercial Code, a real question existed as to whether a generic reference to "all disputes arising out of this agreement" would suffice to confer jurisdiction under Mexican law.[56] Furthermore, depending upon who will serve as arbitrator(s) and what law will be applied, a party may want to deliberately exclude certain types of claims from the arbitral process.[57]

---

the types of claims and issues that are not subject to resolution by arbitration); *Mitsubishi Motors Corp. v. Soler Chrysler-Plymouth Inc.*, 473 U.S. 614, 629–40 (1985) (public policy requires that claims such as antitrust claims affecting the U.S. economy be resolved under U.S. law); N.Y. Convention, Art. V (permitting county not to enforce arbitral award for reasons of public policy).

[53] Paramount among these laws and treaties are the New York Convention; 9 U.S.C. § 201 et seq.; CPCDF, Arts. 609–36; C.Com., Book V, Title IV, Arts. 1415–63.

[54] While the agreement to arbitrate a dispute typically appears in the underlying contract between the parties, nothing prevents the parties from agreeing to submit a dispute to arbitration once it has arisen. See, e.g., C.Com., Arts. 1416(I), 1423.

[55] See C.Com., Art. 1457 (I) (C) (award may be annulled to the extent that it resolves controversies not provided for in the arbitration agreement).

[56] Prior to the 1993 revisions to the Commercial Code, counterclaims could be resolved as part of the arbitration only if they were expressly covered by the arbitral agreement or for set off. C.Com., old Art. 1417. The revised portions of the Code are more flexible, and appear to resolve this problem. See C.Com., Art. 1416(I).

[57] See Branson & Wallace at 58–63 (listing types of claims that the plaintiff logically might prefer not to have heard by arbitrators from outside of the U.S.).

B. Establishing a Procedure

1. Institutional Versus Ad Hoc

One of the first decisions that a business must make when drafting an arbitration agreement is whether the arbitration will be institutional or ad hoc.[58] Institutional arbitration involves using one of the arbitration organizations, such as the International Chamber of Commerce, as a private court.[59] The organization selected can play an important administrative role through out the process, assist with the selection of qualified arbitrators, and help with enforcement. These organizations all have their own sets of published rules of procedure that they will follow in conducting the arbitration.[60] Unfortunately, the fees charged for these services can be quite high,[61] and the procedural rules that are followed can contain significant gaps.[62]

Alternatively, the parties may elect to conduct the arbitration ad hoc, i.e., without institutional supervision. Ad hoc arbitrations are likely to be significantly cheaper, but require more effort from the parties and sometimes do not proceed as smoothly as institutional arbitrations where

---

[58] See Higgins, Brown & Roach at 1035.

[59] For a guide to the major organizations that offer arbitral services through out the world, see III Hans Smit & Vratislav Pechota, *The World Arbitration Reporter* Part 2 (Transnational Juris Publications, Inc., 1993).

[60] *Id.* (referencing arbitral rules of world's major institutions).

[61] See, e.g., *International Standard Elec. Corp. v. Bridas Sociedad Anónima Petrolera, Industrial y Commercial,* 745 F. Supp. 172 (S.D.N.Y. 1990) (initial deposit of costs required for ICC arbitration was $190,000). Typically, the organization administering the arbitration will not allow the proceedings to begin until it has received a substantial deposit toward the anticipated costs. In theory, each party is supposed to put up one half of the required deposit, with the winner being reimbursed by the loser. In practice, the defendant often refuses to advance any monies, forcing the plaintiff to pay the entire deposit. See, e.g., *id.*; Higgins, Brown & Roach, at 1041–43; See generally David J. Branson & W. Michael Tupman, "Selecting an Arbitral Forum: A Guide to Cost-Effective International Arbitration," 24 *Va. J. Int'l L.* 917, 930–34 (1984) (hereinafter "Branson & Tupman").

[62] See Part III.B.2, 3, *infra.*

the dispute is acrimonious and complex.[63] If the parties elect to proceed ad hoc, they still may wish to retain the services of an institution to assist with the appointment of the arbitrator(s).[64]

2. Choosing a Set of Procedural Rules

The next step is to designate an applicable set of procedural rules. The parties are free (within broad limits) to specify the rules that they wish to have govern the arbitral proceeding.[65] Organizations such as the American Arbitration Association, the International Chamber of Commerce, the Inter-American Commercial Arbitration Commission ("IACAC"), and the UNCITRAL offer a broad panoply of rules of arbitration to choose from.[66] If the parties do not specify any governing rules in their contract, they may agree on a set of rules when the dispute arises. Barring an agreement of some sort, arbitrations conducted in Mexico will be governed by a set of procedures designated in the Commercial Code (which resemble the conduct of a civil action in Mexico's courts) as supplemented by the arbitrators' predilections.[67] Otherwise, the parties will have to ask a court to make the selection for them.[68]

Many of the institutional rules of arbitration provide little to no guidance as to how the arbitration will be conducted once it gets

---

[63] See Donald B. Straus, "Why International Commercial Arbitration is Lagging in Latin America: Problems and Cures," 33 *Arb. J.* 21, 23 (1997).

[64] The UNCITRAL rules, which are geared primarily toward ad hoc arbitrations, even call for the parties to designate an appointing authority to oversee the appointment of the arbitrators and to hear challenges to their qualifications. See Branson & Tupman at 920–21. If the arbitration takes place in Mexico, the judicial system will provide this type of assistance. C.Com., Arts. 1426–27.

[65] See, e.g., C.Com., Art. 1435 (providing parties with wide, but not unlimited, freedom to select their own procedural rules).

[66] NAFTA expresses a tacit preference for the UNCITRAL rules. NAFTA, Art. 1120.

[67] See C.Com., Arts. 1435, 1439, 1440.

[68] Article 3 of the Panama Convention solves this problem by providing that the IACAC Rules apply to any arbitration that it governs unless the parties provide otherwise. Unfortunately, the N.Y. Convention does not contain an analogous provision, and the United States has yet to ratify the Panama Convention. Since Mexico is a party to the Panama Convention, an arbitral panel in Mexico may well opt to apply the IACAC Rules if the parties have not provided otherwise.

underway.[69] Thus, the arbitrator(s) generally determine what procedure will be followed where the arbitral agreement and the selected rules do not provide specific guidance.[70] If a party finds itself in this position, it must act quickly to propose the procedures that it desires and make a record of its objections to the procedures that it considers to be inadequate.[71]

The procedural gaps in the institutional rules leave the parties with several alternatives. They can draft their own rules (which is costly and highly impractical); they can trust to the arbitrator's discretion; or they can include a choice of procedural law in their arbitration clause.[72]

3. Considerations in Selecting and Shaping the Applicable Procedural Rules

Even the most comprehensive institutional rules leave a number of important procedural points for the parties to resolve.[73] How the parties resolve these issues will play a major role in virtually every aspect of the arbitration process, including how much it costs, how fast it proceeds, and the type of award that ultimately results. The most significant of these variables are set forth below.

---

[69] See, e.g., IACAC Rules, Art. 15(1) (subject to the more specific portions of the IACAC Rules, the arbitrators have full discretion over conduct of proceedings). See Higgins, Brown & Roach at 1045–48.

[70] See C.Com., Art. 1435 (where procedure not specified, arbitrators free to establish manner in which arbitration will be conducted so long as it does not conflict with the express provisons of Title Four); Higgins, Brown & Roach at 1045–48. Compare CPCDF, Art. 619 (requiring that civil (as opposed to commercial) arbitration be conducted with all of the formalities of a court proceeding unless the parties specify otherwise).

[71] See Higgins, Brown & Roach at 1045–48.

[72] Unless the parties specifically state that a jurisdiction's procedural rules are to apply the designation of a particular law as controlling generally will be taken to refer only to that jurisdiction's substantive law. See C.Com., Art. 1435; Branson & Wallace at 44–46.

[73] See, e.g., IACAC Rules, Arts. 15–17, 27.

a. Number and Qualifications of Arbitrators

Most institutional rules establish an elaborate mechanism for selecting the arbitrator(s).[74] These provisions get the job done, but they typically permit too broad a range of persons to serve as arbitrators, without regard to the financial or practical consequences of this largess.[75] Consequently, arbitrating parties often are forced to bear the substantial cost of retaining legal and other experts to help the panel understand the nuances of a designated substantive law, or a subject matter with which the Panel is not wholly familiar.[76] Moreover, persons who are not versed in the substantive law designated by the parties may tend to ignore it entirely and base their decision on their own sense of equity.[77] Parties can avoid this inefficiency by agreeing that only persons versed in the designated substantive law and/or the relevant subject matter will be eligible to serve as arbitrators.[78]

The parties also need to consider the number of arbitrators and how they will be selected. Typically, arbitrations are conducted in front of either one or three arbitrators. While a panel of three arbitrators may be more comforting than a panel of one, it also will be substantially more expensive, particularly if some of the arbitrators do not reside in the forum of the arbitration.[79]

In addition, having a panel of three arbitrators poses potential problems of delay. Selecting three arbitrators naturally will be more cumbersome than selecting one.[80] Furthermore, having three arbitrators

---

[74] See, e.g., IACAC Rules, Arts. 5–14; C.Com., Arts. 1426–29.

[75] See *id.*

[76] See, e.g., C.Com., Arts. 1442–43 (unless parties agree otherwise, arbitral panel can appoint experts at the parties' expense); IACAC Rules, Art. 27 (empowering tribunal to retain experts); ICC Rules, Art. 14(2).

[77] See Higgins, Brown & Roach at 1038–41. But see C.Com., Art. 1445 (arbitrators required to base decision on law and not equity unless parties agree otherwise).

[78] See C.Com., Art. 1428 (permitting arbitrator to be challenged for cause "where he does not possess the qualifications agreed upon by the parties").

[79] See Higgins, Brown & Roach at 1043–45. Under Mexico's arbitration law, only one arbitrator will be appointed unless the parties agree otherwise. C.Com., Art. 1426.

[80] See C.Com., Art. 1427.

will give a disgruntled party additional opportunities to bring challenges for cause—a favorite delaying tactic.[81]

Identifying the arbitrators undoubtedly will be of great importance to both parties and the selection process should be carefully spelled out.[82] The possible methods of selection are virtually unlimited, ranging from vesting a person or an institution with complete authority to appoint the panel member(s) to allowing each party to appoint one arbitrator and having the two appoint the third. In deciding upon a method of selection, the parties should not lose sight of the fact that they are likely to be hostile towards each other when the selection is made. Under these circumstances, institutions can provide invaluable assistance even if they have nothing further to do with the arbitration.[83]

b. Choice of Forum and Language

One clear advantage of arbitration is that all proceedings will be held before a single, certain and neutral tribunal.[84] The location of that tribunal will have a substantial impact on both the outcome and the cost of the arbitration. The parties have the right to specify where the forum will

---

[81] See Branson & Tupman at 926–27. Mexico's new arbitration provisions attempt to minimize this delay by providing that the arbitration proceedings can go forward while the challenge is pending. C.Com., Art. 1429.

[82] If the parties do not specify a method of selection and the arbitration occurs in Mexico, a court will appoint the arbiter upon request of either party. See C.Com., Art. 1427.

[83] Institutions also maintain lists of potential arbitrators having expertise in various areas.

[84] See generally Vitek Danilowicz, "The Choice of Applicable Law in International Arbitration," 9 *Hastings Int'l & Comp. L. Rev.* 235, 236 (1986) (listing this as one of arbitration's chief advantages). Persons having multiple, related dealings with various parties would be well advised to draft their arbitration clauses in a manner that creates the powers of consolidation necessary to ensure that all such disputes can be heard together. See Bernardo M. Cremades, "The Impact of International Arbitration on the Development of Business Law," *Practicioner's Notebook*, 526, 530–31 (1983) (discussing arbitral consolidation). See also NAFTA, Art. 1125 (providing for power to consolidate investment disputes).

be,[85] and should think carefully when doing so. If the parties do not designate a principal location for the arbitration, the tribunal will.[86]

Substantive Impact of Choice of Forum

The significance of the location of the arbitration goes beyond mere convenience. Under Mexican law[87] and the New York Convention, a large portion of the defenses to enforcement of an arbitral award require the court to apply ``the law of the country where the arbitration took place."[88] These provisions have been interpreted as requiring that all applications to limit or set aside an award be addressed to a competent authority of the state where the arbitration took place.[89] Thus, the forum chosen for arbitration may prove to be the forum of appeal.

Furthermore, if the parties agree to a forum but do not specifically designate a controlling substantive law, they may be deemed to have selected the law of the forum state, either through implied consent[90] or pure inertia. This provides astute counsel with another opportunity to maneuver: by agreeing to a particular forum and not specifying a particular substantive law he or she may be able to avoid the enforcement of certain provisions of the contract.[91]

Practical Impact of Choice of Forum and Language

The practical impact of the forum and language chosen for the arbitration should not be underestimated. To the extent that arbitrators, parties, witnesses, and evidence are not located within the chosen forum,

---

[85] See, e.g., C.Com., Art. 1436; IACAC Rules, Art. 16, § 1.

[86] E.g., *id.*

[87] See C.Com., Art. 1462(I).

[88] N.Y. Convention; Art. V, §§ 1(a) and (d).

[89] See, e.g., *International Standard Electric Corp. v. Bridas Sociedad Anónima Petrolera, Industrial y Comercial*, 745 F. Supp. 172, 175–80 (S.D.N.Y. 1990).

[90] See *Scherk v. Alberto-Culver Co.,* 417 U.S. 506, 519 n.13. (1974)

[91] See Higgins, Brown & Roach at 1041–43. For a good example of the substantive impact that the choice of forum can have, see *M/S Bremen v. Zapata Off-Shore Oil Co.*, 407 U.S. 1 (1972).

the parties will have to incur substantial travel costs.[92] Costs will also increase if the language chosen differs from that of most of the documents, requiring substantial translations.[93]

The laws of Mexico[94] and the United States[95] grant the parties virtually unfettered discretion to designate the location of the arbitration.[96] The parties also may designate the language of the arbitration. More than one language may be designated.[97] The arbitrators will select the controlling language(s) if the parties do not.[98]

c. Rights of Discovery

Mexico's commercial code and most institutional rules do not provide for discovery by right.[99] The ability to obtain discovery is likely to be very limited if the arbitration is subject to Mexican law.[100] Institutional rules at least empower the panel to order the parties to "produce documents, exhibits or other evidence within such a period of time as the tribunal shall determine."[101] These provisions appear to contemplate a tribunal-supervised discovery process. Nonetheless, to remove any doubt as to what discovery rights will be available, the parties should address

---

92 See, e.g., C.Com., Art. 1436 (absent a contrary agreement by the parties, the arbitral panel may travel to wherever it deems appropriate); IACAC Rules, Art. 16, § 3 (permitting the tribunal to travel as necessary and expedient to review evidence).

93 See, e.g., C.Com., Art. 1438 (arbitral panel may order that documents be translated).

94 See C.Com., Art. 1436.

95 Cf. 9 U.S.C. § 2.

96 C.Com., Art. 1438.

97 *Id.*

98 *Id.*

99 See, e.g., C.Com., Arts. 1439–40; IACAC Rules, Art. 24, § 3.

100 This is not a foregone conclusion. While the ability to obtain discovery in a Mexican court proceeding is quite limited, the provisions governing commercial arbitration in Mexico's Commercial Code provide the arbitral panel with far more flexibility to deviate from the procedures that govern the judicial resolution of disputes.

101 IACAC Rules, Art. 24, § 3. See also *id.*, Art. 15, § 1 (giving panel broad powers to establish procedures for arbitration).

the issue in their arbitration agreement.[102] One possible approach is to provide for the right to reasonable discovery, as determined by the tribunal, after consideration of the parties' competing discovery plans which are to be submitted within 21 days after all statements of claims, defenses and counterclaims have been filed.

The tribunal has the same power to compel discovery that any court has—if the party refuses to cooperate its claims or defenses face dismissal.[103] Compelling discovery from unrelated third parties poses a more difficult problem. This problem, however, is no different than that faced by a court, and the same procedures for petitioning foreign courts for assistance should be available in either case.[104] Thus, while an arbitration agreement cannot solve this problem it does not exacerbate it.

4. Limits on Shaping Procedure

The parties' ability to select their own rules of procedure is broad,[105] but not unlimited. Because the selection is occurring through the contractual process, it must result from a meeting of the minds, be free

---

[102] Theoretically a party might oppose enforcement of an arbitral award in the United States (which allows broad discovery) on the grounds that it violates public policy because that party was not afforded reasonable discovery. The courts, however, are unlikely to be sympathetic to such a claim if that party signed an arbitration contract that did not expressly provide for the type of discovery that it is now defining as reasonable. See generally Note, "International Commercial Arbitration: Domestic Recognition & Enforcement of the Inter-American Convention on International Commercial Arbitration," 10 *Syr. J. Int'l L. & Com.* 169, 199 (1983) (once party consents to arbitration, only the most egregious violations of due process will prevent enforcement of the award). Cf. *Rodriquez de Quijas v. Shearson/American Express., Inc.,* 490 U.S. 477 (1989) (not against public policy to waive procedural safeguards in arbitration agreement).

[103] See, e.g., IACAC Rules, Art. 28, § 3 (tribunal may "make the award on the evidence before it" where party fails to produce requested documents); *id.*, Art. 15, § 1 (giving tribunal broad powers).

[104] See, e.g., Fed. R.Civ.P. 28(b) and 28 U.S.C. §§ 1781–84 (setting forth procedures for obtaining discovery abroad).

[105] See, e.g., C.Com., Art. 1435. Cf. *M/S Bremen v. Zapata Off-Shore Co.,* 407 U.S. 1, 8–19 (1972) (forum selection clauses appearing in multinational contracts are prima facie valid and will be enforced absent clear showing that clause invalid or unreasonable and unjust).

from fraud, etc.[106] Additionally, it cannot be against the public policy of any country that may be called upon to enforce the award.[107]

Courts in the United States generally have held that public policy does not prohibit the parties from agreeing to whatever procedures they want so long as they receive notice of the claims against them and a chance to be heard.[108] Mexican law also requires that the procedure selected be in accordance with its notions of due process,[109] including personal notice.[110] As long as the procedures selected afford all parties the protection of due process, it is unlikely that they will violate public policy.

---

[106] See, e.g., C.Com., Art. 1462 (lack of capacity to enter into agreement is a defense), 9 U.S.C. § 2 (arbitration clause enforceable "save upon such grounds as exist at law or in equity for the revocation of any contract"); *Mitsubishi Motors Corp. v. Soler Chrysler Plymouth, Inc.*, 473 U.S. 614, 624 & n.13, 627 (1985) (arbitration clauses subject to standard principles of contract interpretation and standard contractual defenses such as fraud); Branson & Wallace at 50–57.

[107] See C.Com., Art. 1462 (II); N.Y Convention, Art. V, § 2.

[108] See, e.g., *Rodriguez de Quijas v. Shearson/American Express, Inc.,* 490 U.S. 477 (1989) (not against public policy for arbitration to include less procedural advantages than those found in federal securities laws).

[109] See C.Com., Art. 1434, 1462(I)(b).

[110] It is somewhat unclear whether the requirement under Mexican law that the defendant be served personally with notice of the claims against it can be waived. See CPCDF, Art. 606(iv) (requiring personal notice); C.Com., Art. 1462(I)(b). Several cases have held that this requirement is waived when a party agrees to arbitrate under rules providing for a different type of notice. Under Mexico's civil law system, however, these decisions are not binding and nothing prevents another court from deeming personal service to be an essential procedural formality which must be satisfied if the award against that defendant is to be enforceable. See Frank E. Nattier, "International Commercial Arbitration in Latin America: Enforcement of Arbitral Agreements and Awards," 21 *Tex. Int'l L.J.* 397, 423–24 (1986) (discussing possibility of party's agreeing to arbitrate in accordance with a set of rules that provides for notice by mail and then challenging the notice given as contrary to law).

C. Selecting a Substantive Law

The parties generally are free to designate whether the arbitral panel will act in law or in equity.[111] Allowing the arbitrators to act in equity, without reference to any particular substantive law, will obviate the possible need for the arbitrators to retain and consult a foreign legal expert. Indeed, if the arbitrators are nonlawyers or lawyers who are not familiar with the law selected, they may base their decision on pure equity in any event. Nonetheless, the parties may prefer the certainty associated with the application of an established substantive law.[112]

Where the arbitral panel is to act in law, the parties may designate the law applicable to the arbitral proceeding.[113] If the parties do not make this designation by contract or otherwise, the panel will determine the applicable law by applying the choice of law rules that it deems applicable.[114] Given the importance of the issue, it should not be left to chance.

---

[111] Art. 1445 of the C.Com., like Art. 33 of the IACAC Rules, permits the parties to allow the arbitrators to serve as amicable composturers. This freedom undoubtedly is qualified by the requirement under both U.S. and Mexican law that matters of public policy be decided in accordance with that country's substantive law. See Ns. 34, 35, *supra.*

[112] If the parties elect to require the arbitrator(s) to follow a particular substantive law, they may be well advised to take steps to ensure that the law, and not equities, forms the basis of the panel's decision. These steps could include limiting the eligible arbitrators to lawyers who are familiar with the selected law and requiring the panel to provide a written opinion explaining the basis for its decision. Mexico's law already provides such protections. See C.Com., Arts. 1445, 1448 (absent agreement by parties to the contrary, decision must be based in law and explained in a written opinion).

[113] See C.Com., Art. 1445.

[114] See, e.g., C.Com., Art. 1445 (arbitral pursuit not required to any particular choice of law rules unless parties specifically provide to contrary); IACAC Rules, Art. 33; C.Com., Art. 1426.

D. Obtaining Jurisdiction Over All of the Parties

By entering into the contract containing the arbitration clause, the parties submit to the jurisdiction of the arbitration process automatically.[115] Privity of contract, however, provides a rather narrow jurisdictional hook, being limited as it is to the parties to the contract. Businesses contracting with a variety of parties for related services or products (e.g., upstream and downstream components) would be well advised to include identical arbitration clauses, coupled with a power of consolidation, in all of their agreements to ensure that all possible defendants can be brought into the proceeding.

Most institutional arbitration rules, and Mexico's arbitration law, empower the tribunal to rule on objections to its jurisdiction, which, necessarily, must rest on challenges to the breadth or validity of the contract containing the arbitration clause.[116] The panel is to decide jurisdictional issues promptly,[117] and this decision is subject to review by the authorities called upon to enforce the arbitral award.[118]

E. Obtaining Jurisdiction Over All of the Claims

The types of claims subject to arbitration also rests in the first instance on the breadth of contract's arbitration clause. The parties will want to give careful consideration to the types of claims that they wish to submit to arbitration.[119]

The New York Convention, however, limits the parties' ability to make the arbitration clause all encompassing. The Convention does not require the enforcement of an arbitral award if the subject of the dispute

---

[115] It is well established that personal jurisdiction may be established in the U.S. by consent. See, e.g., *M/S Bremen v. Zapata Off-Shore Co.,* 407 U.S. 1, 10–11 (1972). The same rule appears to be true in Mexico.

[116] See, e.g., IACAC Rules, Art. 21; C.Com., Art. 1432.

[117] *Id.*

[118] See C.Com., Art. 1423; N.Y. Convention, Art. V, § 1.

[119] See Branson & Wallace at 58–63 (listing the types of claims that a U.S. company may prefer not to have decided by foreign arbitrators).

was one that cannot be arbitrated in the state where enforcement is sought.[120] This limitation rarely applies to purely commercial disputes.

F. Cumbersome Procedures and Untold Delays

In theory, arbitration permits the parties to avoid the cumbersome procedures and slow pace that afflict most of the world's courts. The parties may create their own procedure for the arbitration or rely on the flexible plans set out in existing arbitration rules.[121] Most institutional arbitration rules place a premium on speedy results and contain tight deadlines.[122] The parties remain free to provide for even speedier and more extensive deadlines in their arbitration clause (and in their contract with the arbitrators) if they desire.

In fact, multinational arbitration is subject to a number of vagaries that permit a recalcitrant party to create numerous lengthy delays. Common delaying tactics include refusing to pay part of the deposit toward the cost of arbitration,[123] challenging the arbitrators for cause, fighting over the applicable substantive and procedural laws, and running to the courts of the forum state (and others) to seek interim relief to get the arbitration stopped, stayed or delayed.[124] These tactics cannot be eliminated in their totality, but can be blunted by careful drafting at the outset to specify as many of the key factors (such as the applicable law) as possible and to select a forum where the courts generally refuse to interfere with arbitral proceedings.[125]

---

[120] See N.Y. Convention, Art. V, § 2.

[121] See, e.g., IACAC Rules, Art. 1.

[122] See, e.g., IACAC Rules, Art. 23 (setting a 45-day deadline for providing all written statements). Mexico's arbitration law is somewhat less insistent on prompt action. See C.Com., Arts. 1439–40.

[123] Mexico's arbitration law sets a 30-day deadline for payment. Unfortunately, the remedy suggested for nonpayment by either party is suspension or dismissal of the proceeding. C.Com., Art. 1456.

[124] See Branson & Tupman at 925–34 (listing a variety of delaying tactics).

[125] See Higgins, Brown & Roach at 1048–51 (noting the delay and expense that occur when courts get involved in arbitration and suggesting that parties select a forum such as the U.S. where the courts will stay out of the process).

G. Obtaining and Enforcing a Judgment

1. Private Enforcement

One advantage of arbitration is that in many cases it may be possible to create a private method for enforcing the award. This has the advantage of eliminating the expense and delay associated with another level of judicial proceedings.

Whether such a mechanism is possible, and what form it should take, will depend upon the facts of the case involved. Possible mechanisms including cycling the profits of the venture through an offshore account which is subject to attachment by order of the arbitral panel, providing for put or call rights in the event of a joint venturer's failure to adhere to the arbitrator's decision, etc.

2. Judicial Enforcement

Arbitration presents a meaningful method of dispute resolution only if the world's governments will enforce foreign arbitral decrees.[126] Where the dispute arises out of a United States/Mexico commercial transaction, enforcement of the arbitral decree is likely to turn upon application of the United Nations Convention on Recognition and Enforcement of Foreign Arbitral Awards (the "New York Convention").[127]

---

[126] But see Comment, "Int'l Commercial Arbitration: The Nonarbitral Subject Matter Defense," 9 *J. Int'l Law & Pol'y* 119, 120 n.6 (1985) (over 90% of the arbitral awards made by the International Chamber of Commerce are settled promptly and without question).

[127] Some day in the future, parties may also be able to look to the Inter-American Convention on International Commercial Arbitration (the "Panama Convention") for assistance with enforcement. The Panama Convention was promulgated by the Organization of American States in 1975 and has been adopted by eight nations in Latin America, including Mexico. Another eight American countries, including the U.S., have signed the Convention but have yet to ratify it. The substance of the Panama Convention closely parallels the substance of the N.Y. Convention in that both call for the recognition and enforcement of foreign commercial arbitral awards unless the identical limited, enumerated defenses are proven. Compare N.Y. Convention, Art. V with Panama Convention, Art. 5. The potential for the Panama Convention to harmoniously fill the gaps left by the N.Y. Convention's limited membership in Latin America is significant. The Senate twice has acted to ratify the Convention, but the House has yet to act. When

The New York Convention[128] was signed in 1958 and ratified and implemented by the United States in 1970.[129] Mexico ratified and implemented the Convention the following year. The New York Convention recognizes the parties' right to submit their disputes to arbitration, gives the arbitral award the effect of a judicial decree, and mandates its enforcement unless the losing party carries the burden of establishing one of a very limited number of defenses.[130] These defenses are designed primarily to protect sovereignty over economic regulations (the "public policy" exception to enforcement)[131] and to safeguard the

---

drafting NAFTA, the parties appeared to contemplate that satisfaction will occur eventually. See NAFTA, Art. 2022(3).

[128] The New York Convention applies only to disputes of a commercial nature between private parties. See N.Y. Convention, Art. 1. Where a state is involved, the party may wish to look to NAFTA and the provisions of ICSID. See NAFTA, Arts. 1115–38; James C. Baker & Lois J. Yoder, "ICSID & the Calvo Clause a Hinderance to Foreign Direct Investment in LDCs," 5:1 *J. on Dispute Resolution* 75 (1989).

[129] See 9 U.S.C.A. §§ 201 et seq. (1994 Supp.).

[130] The defenses to enforcement of an arbitral award recognized by the New York Convention are as follows:

(1) the agreement to arbitrate fails to meet the requirements for a binding contract;
(2) failure to provide a party with fair notice and/or a reasonable opportunity to present its case;
(3) arbitral award encompasses matters that exceed the scope of what the parties agreed to arbitrate;
(4) composition of the arbitral panel not in accord with the parties' agreement or, if none, the governing law;
(5) arbitral award is set aside or otherwise not binding;
(6) the subject matter of the dispute is not capable of settlement by arbitration under the law of the country called upon to enforce the award; and
(7) recognition of the award would be against the public policy of the country called upon to enforce it.

N.Y. Convention, Art. V.

For a more detailed explanation of the New York Convention and its defenses, see Comment, "The Express Defenses of the N.Y. Convention on Foreign Arbitral Awards," 5 *N.Y.L. Sch. J. Int'l & Comp. L.* 103 (1983). See also *Biotronek Messund Therapiegeraete Gmb H & Co. v. Medford Medical Instrument Co.*, 415 F.Supp. 133, 136 (D.N.J. 1976) (burden of proof on party challenging award).

[131] N.Y. Convention, Art. V(2)(b); Comment, "The Public Policy Defense To Recognition and Enforcement of Foreign Arbitral Awards," 7 *Cal. W. Int'l L.J.* 228 (1977).

parties' inalienable right to a process that comports with notions of fundamental fairness.

The effect of the New York Convention in the United States has been the regular enforcement of arbitral decrees.[132] While somewhat less clear, the Convention appears to have had a similar effect in Mexico.[133] In either case, it is likely to be easier to enforce an arbitral award than a judicial decision.[134]

Enforcement of Arbitral Awards

In general, the United States courts called upon to enforce such awards have been very pro-arbitration,[135] The procedure for enforcing an arbitral award in the United States under the New York Convention is set out in 9 U.S.C. § 207:

> Within three years after the arbitral award falling under the Convention is made, any party to the arbitration may apply to any court having jurisdiction under this chapter for an order confirming the award as against any other party to the arbitration. The court shall confirm the award unless it finds that one of the grounds for refusal

---

[132] See, e.g., *Mitsubishi Motors Corp. v. Soler Chrysler-Plymouth, Inc.,* 473 U.S. 614 (1985), *Scherk v. Alberto-Culver Co.,* 417 U.S. 506 (1974), *International Standard Electric Corp. v. Brides Sociedad Anónima Petrolera, Industrial y Commercial,* 745 F. Supp. 172 (S.D.N.Y. Aug. 24, 1990); *Cooper v. Ateliers de la Motebecane, S.A.,* 456 N.Y.S.2d 728 (N.Y. App. 1982).

[133] The enforcement provisions in Mexico's new arbitration law closely parallel those of the N.Y. Convention. See C.Com., Arts. 1461–63.

[134] See Comment, "The Express Defenses of the N.Y. Convention On Foreign Arbitral Awards," 5 *N.Y.L. Sch. J. Int'l & Comp. L.* 103, 106–07 (1983) ("It is perhaps ironic that a court will accord more deference to awards rendered by arbitrators than to decisions rendered by trial judges. . . .").

[135] See generally *Mitsubishi Motors Corp. v. Soler Chrysler-Plymouth, Inc.,* 473 U.S. 614, 618–19, 625–28 (1986) (discussing pro arbitration policy brought forth by the passage of the U.S. Arbitration Act, 9 U.S.C. §§ 1, et. seq, including the courts' obligations to assist the arbitral process); 9 U.S.C. §§ 3, 4 (directing courts not to interfere with arbitral proceedings). See Comment, "Enforcement of Foreign Awards—The United National Convention on the Recognition and Enforcement of Foreign Arbitral Awards," 14 *Ga. J. Int'l. & Comp. L.* 217 (1984).

or deferral of recognition or enforcement of the award specified in said Convention.

The most commonly asserted defense to enforcement, the public policy defense, has been interpreted quite narrowly by U.S. Courts.[136] Assertions that particular types of claims are not subject to arbitration,[137] also have not been well received.[138] Challenges to the validity of the agreement to arbitrate under the appropriate law or to the capacity of one or more of the parties have proven similarly ineffective.[139]

While the New York Convention limits the potential challenges to an arbitral award, it is important to be aware that selection of the place of arbitration can have an impact on the scope of appellate rights.[140] An appeal in the issuing country which overturns an arbitral award, will prevent its enforcement abroad.[141] An important consideration in the

---

[136] See, e.g., *Parsons v. Whittemore Overseas Co. v. Societe Generale De L'Industrie Du Papier,* 508 F.2d 969, 974 (2d Cir. 1974) ("Enforcement of foreign arbitral awards may be denied on this basis only where enforcement would violate the forum state's most basic notions of morality and justice."); *Fatachome, Inc. v. Copal*, 517 F.2d 515 (2d Cir. 1975) (Bankruptcy Court was without jurisdiction to stay international arbitration in Japan).

[137] See N.Y. Convention, Art. V § 2(a) (fact that claim not subject to arbitration in country where enforcement sought constitutes a defense to enforcement).

[138] See, e.g., *Mitsubishi Motors Corp. v. Soler Chrysler-Plymouth, Inc.,* 473 U.S. 614 (1986) (antitrust claims subject to arbitration); *Scherk v. Alberto-Culver Co.,* 417 U.S. 506 (1974) (securities claims subject to arbitration).

[139] See Note, "The Express Defenses of the N.Y. Convention on Foreign Arbitral Awards," 5 *N.Y.L. Sch. J. Int'l & Corp. L.* 103, 110 (1983); *Prima Paint Co. v. Flood & Conklin Mfg.,* 388 U.S. 395 (1967) (under Federal Arbitration Act, validity defense is itself something for the arbitrator to decide.)

[140] See generally Daniel M. Kolkey, "Attacking Arbitral Awards: Rights of Appeal and Review in International Arbitrations," 22 *Int'l Law.* 693, 701–14 (1988) (right to challenge an international award is most limited in Switzerland, France and Sweden and most liberal in England and Australia; U.S. falls in between, but its scope of review is substantially similar to that allowed in France and Sweden); Jan S. Paulson, "Arbitration Unbound: Award Detached From the Law of Its Country of Origin," 30 *Int'l & Comp. L.Q.* 358 (Apr. 1981) (discussing the need for procedural uniformity of private arbitration recognized by national courts).

[141] See N.Y. Convention, Art. V, § 1(e). See also Albert J. van den Berg, "When is an Arbitral Award Nondomestic Under the New York Convention of 1958?," 6 *Pace L. Rev.* 25, 42 (1985).

drafting of an arbitration clause is whether to expand or exclude the scope of judicial review.[142] The decision cuts both ways: the exclusion of appellate rights can expedite the process, while the expansion of appellate rights can provide for important procedural protections where complicated legal issues are involved. Any agreement to expand appellate rights must be clear and unequivocal.[143]

3. Enforcement of Arbitral Awards in Mexico

Until recently most countries in Latin America have been somewhat reluctant to fully embrace the benefits of international arbitration.[144] Mexico has been less affected by this trend, and its recent changes to the Commercial Code indicate a further willingness to enforce foreign arbitral awards. Indeed, foreign arbitral awards now will be enforced upon the presentation of a certified copy of the award and the arbitration agreement (plus Spanish translations) unless the losing party can establish one of a very limited number of defenses akin to those provided for in the New York Convention.[145]

---

[142] See Kolkey, N. 41, *supra,* at 700.

[143] See *Aerojet General Corporation v. American Arbitration Association,* 478 F.2d 248 (9th Cir. 1973).

[144] See Donald B. Straus, "Why International Commercial Arbitration is Lagging in Latin America," *Arb. J.* 21 (1978); Lionel M. Summers, "Arbitration and Latin America," 3 *Cal. W. Int'l L.J.* 1, 3 (1972) ("At present there seems to be a general unwillingness on the part of Latin American statutes to submit specific controversies to arbitration or adjudication, particularly if the adversary power is the United States"); Henry P. de Vries, "International Commercial Arbitration: A Contractual Substitute for National Courts," 57 *Tul. L. Rev.* 42, 53 (1982) ("In Latin America, except for Chile, commercial arbitration is not generally accepted.").

[145] See C.Com., Arts. 1461–63. Domestic arbitral awards carry the same force and effect as a court judgment. C.Com., Art. 1461.

H. Cost

Unlike the courts, which are basically free,[146] arbitration comes with a price tag. With three arbitrators and panel-appointed experts these costs may run quite high,[147] and much of this money typically must be deposited up front.[148] Thus, the potential exists for arbitration to be much more expensive than litigating in court.

Steps can be taken to keep these costs down.[149] Furthermore, if properly designed, arbitration can generate efficiencies sufficient to offset the cost of what amounts to purchasing court services.

IV. Conclusion

NAFTA has set the stage for a substantial increase in the commercial transactions between the United States and Mexico, but does nothing to provide for the resolution of the most common trade-related disputes. This leaves businesses with the traditional alternatives of the courts and arbitration. Each system has its share of advantages and disadvantages. Careful advance planning can help to ensure that whichever system is selected works as well as possible.

---

[146] See Mex. Const., Art. 17 (prohibiting courts from charging for their services).

[147] See IACAC Rules, Arts. 38–40. See *International Standard Electric Corp. v. Bridas Sociedad Anónima Petrolera, Industrial y Comercial,* 745 F. Supp. 172, 174 (parties required to deposit $190,000 up front to cover costs of arbitration).

[148] See, e.g., C.Com., Arts. 1452–56; IACAC Rules, Art. 41.

[149] The most important factors in keeping costs down are the number and qualifications of the arbitrators, the location of the arbitration and the type of discovery that will be permitted. In addition, Mexico's law permits the parties to curtail the arbitrator from taking steps that cost money. See, e.g., C.Com., Art. 1436.

CHAPTER 15

Mexico's Antitrust Laws*

Lic. Eduardo Siqueiros T.
Barrera, Siqueiros y Torres Landa, S.C.

On June 24, 1993, Mexico's new Federal Law of Economic Competition (the "FLEC" or the "Law") took effect. The adoption of the FLEC marks an important change in Mexico's attitude toward monopolies. Even though Mexico has had laws and regulations pertaining to monopolies for decades,[1] these provisions were applied only sporadically. While the policy for enforcement of the new Law is still uncertain, a number of its provisions virtually guarantee that it will have a marked impact on the country's economic life. If nothing more, these provisions will require investors contemplating certain mergers and acquisitions to provide prior notice to the government. Failure to provide the requisite notice can give rise to administrative penalties and, in certain cases, the nullification of the transaction.

The Law clearly has its origins in legislation and judicial precedents on antitrust in the United States.[2] Nonetheless, in contrast to the United States' antitrust laws, the FLEC does not expressly prohibit certain types of behavior, including predatory or discriminatory pricing. Thus, the

* This chapter was edited by William E. Mooz, Jr., Esq., Holland & Hart.

1 The Monopolies Law (*Ley Reglamentaria del Articulo 28 Constitucional en Materia de Monopolios*) of 1934.

2 For example, the Sherman Act and the Federal Trade Commission Act (for horizontal restraints), the Clayton Act (for conditioned or exclusive sales, as well as concentrations) and the Robinson Patman Act (for discriminatory pricing).

FLEC should prove to be more pro-consumer than the United States' antitrust laws, although possibly less favorable for manufacturers and distributors seeking to prevent what they consider to be unfair competition.

The FLEC grants powers to the Executive to fix maximum prices on goods and services, and addresses three practices that may be illegal: absolute restraints (horizontal agreements among competitors), relative restraints (vertical agreements between a manufacturer and a distributor, or among other economic agents in the chain of sale and distribution of goods and services, and certain unilateral actions) and concentrations (mergers and acquisitions). Violation of the Law's provisions can result in serious administrative penalties, and damages. The enforcement of the FLEC's provisions is delegated to a Federal Competition Commission.

I. Persons Subject to the Law

Generally speaking, the Law applies to all "economic agents," whether individuals or corporate entities, associations or trusts, and regardless of whether they are Mexican or foreign. The FLEC also applies to parastate and decentralized entities, insofar as their activities may be considered as commercial and provided they are not within the strategic activities entrusted to them directly by Mexican law (e.g., oil in the case of Pemex or generation and sale of electricity in the case of the Federal Electricity Commission). Unions and export cooperatives are generally exempted from the Law's provisions.

II. Maximum Prices

Article 7 of the Law confirms the power of the Executive to establish maximum prices for goods and services. In this regard, the FLEC repeals the prior Law on Powers to the Federal Executive on Economic Matters of 1950.

III. Absolute Restraints

Absolute restraints (also known as horizontal restrictions on trade) are agreements between economic agents who are competitors, and have the purpose or effect of:

(1) fixing prices;

(2) allocating markets, whether with regard to suppliers, territories, or periods of time;

(3) assigning production quotas; or

(4) the rigging of public bids.

These agreements are deemed illegal per se. Thus, whether the parties intend to restrain trade or displace competitors is irrelevant if they actually do so. Similarly, the market power of the participants, or the amount of sales involved, is also irrelevant to determining whether the challenged conduct is illegal. Nonetheless, it is somewhat unclear when an activity will be subject to per se condemnation. It is possible that the Regulations to the FLEC will contain clarifying provisions in this respect, or that the enforcement policy of the Commission will be to permit certain joint activities among competitors where true overriding efficiencies exist.

Persons engaging in absolute restraints may be sentenced to fines of up to approximately $5,625,000 new pesos[3] (or approximately $1,800,000 USD), and a term in prison of up to nine years as provided for in the Criminal Code for the Federal District. The Commission also has the discretion to impose an additional fine in serious cases of up to 10 percent of the value of the defendant's assets or 10 percent of the amount of the defendant's sales for the preceding fiscal year. Finally, all agreements between competitors which constitute absolute restraints will be deemed null and void, and produce no legal effect whatsoever.

---

[3] The exact amount of the fine is 375,000 times the minimum wage for the Federal District (MWDF) which means that the applicable fine will go up as the MWDF is increased over time.

IV. Relative Restraints

Relative restraints consist primarily of limitations found in vertical agreements (such as agreements between suppliers and distributors, or between wholesalers and retailers) and, to a lesser extent, certain restrictions that are unilaterally created by an economic agent. A relative restraint will exist only if it has the purpose or effect of imposing restrictions on competition or on free trade in the production, process, distribution, or marketing of goods and services.

The FLEC provides a nonexhaustive list of agreements that may constitute relative restraints, including the following:

(1) exclusive distribution agreements for goods or services that contain geographic, temporal, or product limitations or that require a party to the agreement not to manufacture or supply goods and services;

(2) the imposition of a mandatory resale price or conditions of resale for goods or services (i.e., resale price maintenance);

(3) "tying" arrangements that condition the sale of a good or service on the purchase or sale of a separate good or service, or upon a refusal to deal with third parties;

(4) boycotts (i.e., a refusal to deal with a specific person) whether conducted unilaterally or as part of a group action;

(5) concerted action by a group of actors to pressure a third party to take, or refrain from taking, a certain action.

Unlike absolute restraints that will be declared illegal per se, relative restraints cannot be declared illegal without full consideration of the facts and circumstances surrounding the challenged activity. Thus, many common contractual arrangements such as exclusive distributorships, are likely to continue to be lawful.

Relative restraints will be declared unlawful only if they cause substantial economic displacement or harm. This requires that the actor has *substantial power in the relevant market*, and the restraint occurs in the *relevant market.*

Defining the *relevant market* begins with a focus on the particular good or service at issue and, more particularly, the extent to which substitutes for the good or service exist. In determining whether substitutes exist, the following factors will be considered: technical capabilities, options on substitutes, timeliness of availability within a consumer market, distribution and other costs, and practical and legal restrictions on a consumer's ability to obtain the goods or services from other sources. In other words, the easier it is for the consumer to obtain a substitute at a reasonable price and on reasonable terms, the more likely it is that the relevant market will be a broad one, and the relative restraint a legal one.

In determining whether an actor has *substantial power in the relevant market*, the following factors will be considered: the actor's position in the market, whether the actor has the power to fix prices or restrict output without suffering a strong competitive response, the existence of barriers to entry (e.g., import permits), factors that could alter the barriers to entry, the existence and power of the company's competitors, the access by the company or other competitors to supplies for components for the goods and services (i.e., is there an equality of conditions for both economic agents?), and finally, the recent competitive conduct of the company. Despite the fact that the foregoing elements are intended to be objective, one cannot avoid the fact that they ultimately require a subjective analysis that will allow the Commission to evaluate whether the company has substantial power within the market.

It is uncertain to what extent business justifications for the challenged restraint will be considered in this analysis. There may be multiple justifications for a restraint that should be considered by the Commission. For example, restraints will be involved by definition where the good or service at issue is subject to a trademark or patent. Similarly, restrictions may be indispensable to achieve standards of quality for a product or service. Franchises are yet another clear example where a series of restrictions on the franchisee (as regards territory, suppliers, conduct of services, etc.) will be justified from a business point of view, and should, therefore, not cause a violation of the Law. It is possible that the regulations to the FLEC will address these issues.

Should the Commission find that a relative restraint violates the law, it may impose a fine of up to approximately $3,375,000 new pesos[4] (approximately $1,090,000 USD), and may impose an additional penalty of up to 10 percent of the value of assets or sales of the convicted party for the preceding year in serious cases.

V. Concentrations

The approach taken toward concentrations in the FLEC, and in particular the creation of a Commission to review mergers and acquisitions, represents a significant departure from the prior Monopolies Law.

The FLEC prohibits any concentration, merger, or acquisition of control ("*concentration*") that may have the purpose or effect of restricting competition and free trade of goods and services within the relevant market. Contrary to monopolistic practices, the Law makes no distinctions between horizontal concentrations (among competitors) and vertical concentrations (e.g., suppliers and distributors). Concentrations, like relative restraints, will not be deemed illegal per se; rather, it will be necessary to examine the *relevant market* and to determine the *power* wielded by the entity resulting from the concentration. An important element of this analysis will be the *degree of concentration in the market* if the concentration were allowed to occur.

The FLEC contains a list of indicators that a concentration is illegal, including where the concentration provides the resulting entity with the power to fix prices or to substantially restrict the supply of goods and services in the relevant market (without provoking an effective response by competitors); may unduly displace or impede the access of other agents to the relevant market; or may substantially facilitate monopolistic practices, whether absolute or relative.

---

[4] The exact fine is equal to 225,000 times the MWDF.

In attempt to control concentrations before they become a *fait accompli*, the FLEC requires that the Commission be given prior notice of concentrations that meet any of the following conditions:

(1) The transaction giving rise to the concentration exceeds approximately $180,000,000 new pesos[5] (approximately $58,065,000 USD).

(2) The transaction results in the acquisition of 35 percent or more of the assets or shares of a company which has assets or sales in excess of approximately $180,000,000 new pesos[6] (approximately $58,065,000 USD).

(3) The transaction involves two or more economic agents having combined assets or annual sales in excess of approximately $720,000,000 new pesos[7] (approximately $232,260,000 USD), and involves an accumulation of assets or capital in excess of approximately $72,000,000 new pesos[8] (approximately $23,226,000 USD). This provision is designed to regulate the growth of large business entities, and, thus, to limit increased growth that could give rise to the negative aspects of concentrations discussed above.

The Commission must decide whether to authorize, reject or impose conditions on a proposed concentration within 45 calendar days of the date on which it receives notification of the proposed concentration and any additional information that it has requested. If the Commission fails to act within this time period, the concentration is deemed approved. In evaluating a proposed concentration, the Commission is likely to consider a variety of factors, including the extent to which the market will become more concentrated, the reasons for the proposed transaction, the world conditions of competition, and others.

---

5 The exact threshold is 12,000,000 times the MWDF.

6 The exact threshold is 12,000,000 times the MWDF.

7 The exact threshold is 48,000,000 times the MWDF.

8 The exact threshold is 480,000 times the MWDF.

In addition to imposing strict time limits on the Commission, the Law also has taken steps to provide certainty to investors. Once a concentration is approved by the Commission, it cannot be challenged by any other party. Concentrations that do not require prior notification to the Commission can only be challenged within one year of the date on which they are consummated.

The sanction for failing to notify the Commission of a proposed concentration meeting the requisite thresholds is a fine of up to $1'500,000 new pesos[9] (approximately $483,900 USD); engaging in a prohibited concentration can result in a fine of up to $3,375,000 new pesos[10] (approximately $1,090,000 USD). The Commission also has the power to impose a fine based on the value of assets or annual sales of the company (in serious cases). Where a concentration that violates the Law and meets the notification thresholds is carried out without the prior approval of the Commission, the Commission also can order the partial or total break-up of the resulting entity or entities.

VI. Federal Competition Commission

The Commission will be composed of professionals in areas covered by the Law. Each Commissioner will be appointed for a ten year period. (The first Commissioners appointed will have phased-in periods.) Commissioners cannot be removed except for serious cause that has been duly justified. This provision indicates an intent of the legislature to instill confidence in the members of the Commission, and to provide investors with an assurance of consistency and continuity in the Commission's policies and resolutions, even as presidential administrations change.

The FLEC grants the Commission ample powers so that it may, inter alia, investigate the existence of monopolies and other prohibited practices, resolve cases on concentrations, file criminal complaints before the District Attorney for illegal conduct prohibited under the Criminal Code, and give opinions on related matters.

---

[9] The exact threshold is 100,000 times the MWDF.

[10] The exact threshold is 225,000 times the MWDF.

The Commission may conduct investigations and take any actions that it deems necessary on its own initiative. Nonetheless, *any person* may file a complaint with the Commission challenging an absolute restraint. Where relative or vertical restraints, or concentrations are at issue, only the *affected party* has standing to lodge a complaint with the Commission. Persons with standing to complain before the Commission will be allowed to submit proof of the violation and evidence that the complainant has suffered, or may suffer, damages. The issue of standing is likely to receive considerable attention in the forthcoming Regulations to the Law, since the Commission is unlikely to feel sympathetic to complaints by persons whose real objective is to hinder the ability of their competitors to compete more effectively.

Legal proceedings before the Commission shall be in writing, but verbal legal arguments are also contemplated. The Law anticipates that proceedings before the Commission will be completed within six months from the date the defendant receives notice of the charges. In practice, the mandated schedule may be extended because of delays in the submission of evidence, etc. An administrative appeal of the Commission's ruling may be taken before the Commission itself. The Commission's ruling on appeal may be challenged only through an amparo action.

The FLEC also explicitly provides a vehicle for the collection of damages by injured parties. Persons who demonstrate during a proceeding before the Commission that they have suffered damages as a result of a violation of the Law are entitled to file a civil action to recover such damages from the defendant. In such a proceeding, the civil court may rely upon the Commission's finding of damages.

VII. Sanctions

In addition to the sanctions imposed on entities who participate in a monopolistic practices or prohibited concentrations, the Law establishes a sanction equal to $12,500 new pesos for individuals acting on behalf of companies who are directly involved in such practices or concentrations.

VIII. Conclusion

With the adoption of the FLEC, Mexico has embraced an antitrust policy similar to that prevailing in the United States. Violation of the FLEC carries strong sanctions, and all persons doing business in Mexico, including foreigners, need to be aware of its provisions. The FLEC delegates many important points to forthcoming regulations, and its ultimate scope is further dependent upon the enforcement policies adopted by the newly-created Federal Competition Commission. Accordingly, this is an area of the law that bears continued monitoring.